A very merry Christmas!
to Ike
from

Little Howdy, Howard, and
Mariana

Lerenworth, Kansas
October, 1944

WIND IN THE SAHARA

BY THE SAME AUTHOR

WIND IN THE SAHARA

BY

R. V. C. BODLEY

COWARD-MCCANN, INC.
NEW YORK

MANUFACTURED IN THE UNITED STATES OF AMERICA

Van Rees Press, New York

To S.

ACKNOWLEDGMENT

I take this opportunity to record my thanks to Dr. Philip K. Hitti, of Princeton University, to Mr. Hobart Lewis, and to members of the Arabic advisory staff of the *Reader's Digest,* for their assistance in checking some of the details relative to Islam in this book. To Mr. Barclay Acheson, whose insight into Oriental questions gave me new and rich ideas concerning the Arab problem. To Mr. Henry Morton Robinson for encouraging me to bring to life in book form my days with the nomads of the Sahara.

Also to Miss Mary Phelps for her painstaking revision of my manuscript and for her advice.

Also to Mrs. G. Macculloch Miller who indirectly made it possible for *Wind in the Sahara* to be written, and to Miss Janet Flanner and Countess Eleanor Palffy who unwittingly contributed.

R. V. C. B.

FOREWORD

THE POINT OF VIEW of this book is local. It belongs to the Sahara
tribesmen, who, for centuries, have pastured their flocks on the vast
expanses of French North Africa south of Algiers. Where the
Occidental opinion is unleashed and allowed to prowl among
international affairs affecting the Arabs, it prowls as would the
mind of a nomad who thought about these things.

The book makes no attempt to teach, and certainly none to
preach. Where there is information, it is information which any
clear-thinking desert Arab could give. None of it is library information or hearsay information. The facts recorded were obtained
first hand. Everything took place as told.

Some of the occurrences have been moved around and put in
different settings and at different times. This was necessary for
organization. Apart from these manipulations, all the rest is as
it happened. The people, what they said, what they did, how I
reacted—all is true. What is not true has been omitted.

There is nothing about sheiks as imagined by motion picture
fans. During the years I lived with the Arabs, I never saw such
sheiks. I do not think they exist.

There is nothing about the Foreign Legion because, although
I visited its headquarters at Sidi bel Abbes, members of this famous
corps never go near the Sahara except as tourists. They have no
reason to. The Foreign Legion only goes where there is fighting.
There is no fighting in the Sahara.

There is little about sand. Less than one-sixth of the Sahara is
sand, and the dune country is a long way from the frequented
caravan trails. The sand desert is an unpleasant place which does
no one any good. The Arabs avoid it. I only went there once
because a tourist with a mania for sight-seeing forced me to take
him.

There is a good deal about the contentment and health I found among the desert people. The peace of mind which the Sahara gave me is something which I can never forget.

There are many details of our everyday lives—what we ate, how we slept, what we wore. There are stories of love and of laughter and of hardship.

Parts of this book may shock the conventional. It may cause distress to men and women who still look down imperially on all non-Occidentals. It may have the same effect as a book I wrote on Algeria some years ago had on an ex-colonel of mine. The frontispiece to this work was a picture of myself in Arab robes. For a reason which I forgot, probably because I was going to an official party, my war medals and decorations were pinned on my burnous. The book fell into the hands of the colonel. I feel certain he never got beyond that frontispiece. Taking pen and paper, he wrote:

Dear Bodley,
I have just read your book about Algeria. I would like to draw your attention to paragraph xyz of King's Regulations in which it is stated that officers may not wear decorations in fancy dress.
Yours sincerely,
opq

That was all. No comments on the book. The "fancy dress" had hit the colonel square in the eyes and left him groggy. To his way of thinking, I had smirched my military medals, I had degraded myself—I had "gone native."

I am not sure what constitutes going native. It depends on the conception of the word "native." Have the Americans and Britons who settle in the Pays Basque or on the Riviera and wear the local berets and the fishermen's trousers gone native? Have the same type of people who occupy palazzos in Venice and eat spaghetti and drink Chianti and murder the Italian language gone native? Had the Agha Khan when he wore a morning coat and a grey top hat at Epsom and Longchamps gone native? Neither he nor the "Venetians" nor the "Niçois" nor the "Biarrots" were living or dressing or eating as they did in their own homes. They were observing the customs of the natives of England or Italy or France.

If what they did constitutes going native, then I most certainly was guilty.

I wore the Arab dress because it was the most suitable for desert life. I ate the Arab food because it was all I could get, and also because I liked it. I practiced the Moslem faith and did not drink wine or eat pork because otherwise I would have seemed an outsider, a kind of disguised tourist, watching my Arab companions but not being one of them. But I did not bring my turban or my Arab customs with me to Europe, like the Anglo-Saxons who cannot be separated from their berets, and continue to talk bad French in London and New York. I did not bring them back, any more than the Agha Khan took his grey top hat and his race horses to India.

That I was completely happy with my Arabs in the Sahara desert, I will never deny. I *was* happy. I had a contentment which I have never known before or since. The Arabs proved themselves to be a noble people and showed me the kind of friendship which has no ulterior motives.

Most foreigners do not meet this kind of Arab. All they see are the degenerates in the Mediterranean seaports. These men have lost their finer feelings. They drink, they steal, they do not pray. Some have even lost their faith. When an Arab gives up Islam, he has fallen very low. These loafers have little in common with the desert people, whom nothing has changed throughout the centuries.

It is a pity that the American soldiers who went to North Africa never had an opportunity to see the fine Arabs of the South. Their only contact with "natives" was with the evil-smelling, dirty derelicts who pick up a dishonest living on the quays. The French, whose policy is not to raise Arab prestige abroad, did nothing to counteract these false impressions. I hope this book will do so. The Arabs are as described in these pages.

I have made no attempt to have my characters talk in translated Arabic. It is impossible to do justice to that rich, majestic language in English. Under any circumstances, making people speak in dialect or foreign idiom is unsatisfactory and usually irritating. I have, therefore, done nothing about this.

In their way, these Arabs were no different from unspoiled villagers and farmers in England or the United States. Their problems were, fundamentally, much the same. They spoke like ordinary people about ordinary things. So, I have made them talk in this book in a manner which I hope will give the impression of the normal human beings they were.

With the same idea, I have spelled Arab names in the simplest phonetic approximation. It is impossible to convey Arab sounds in any characters but Arabic. An Arab when he writes rarely uses anything but consonants. These consonants vary according to whether they come at the beginning or middle or end of a word. Furthermore, the sound which they produce, when conveyed from the Arab mind to the Arab tongue, are unlike anything in our language. Some of them are nothing more than coughs and gargles. So, reproducing the nearest equivalent by the most natural English spelling, I have used "Ahmed" instead of the approved "Achmed," and "Kadi" in place of the more correct "Qadhi."

Arab words and expressions are explained on first use or will be clear from the context. However, a glossary (page 223) is provided.

Some information necessary to the reader's journey which would have been cumbersome to include in the story, I have given in the Introduction.

There is no leavetaking of the desert at the end of the book, for that I am not there now is accidental.

Seven years after coming to the Sahara, I left. I had a feeling that there were other things to do, other places to see. I was not convinced about this, but the idea was sufficiently strong to cause me to make a move.

I traveled without fuss like a nomad Arab, lingering in the Dutch Indies and China and Japan and the South Seas, wandering about the United States. In fact, so leisurely was I that I did not reach my home in France until the eve of this war. There, various things delayed me, and by the time I was ready to go back to the Sahara, it was too late. I had to make up my mind to waiting until peace should be declared.

But the waiting will not change anything. Nothing changes out there. Nothing touches those golden wildernesses. Nothing will alter my feelings toward that country. I have seen most of the world. I have met thousands of men and women. But nowhere have I found the same contentment as in the Great Sahara Desert.

R. V. C. Bodley

Goshen, N. Y.
January, 1944.

INTRODUCTION

THE SAHARA about which I have written is the Sahara of North-west Africa. It has nothing to do with Libya or Egypt or Tripoli or the Sudan. It has nothing remotely connected with Arabia, except as that was the birthplace of its Arab inhabitants. It is what the *Encyclopaedia Britannica* refers to as the "Sahara proper": the French Sahara, bounded on the north by Morocco, Algeria, and Tunisia, and on the south by the river Niger. Its western boundaries rest on the Moroccan Atlas, Rio del Oro, and the Atlantic; its eastern, on Libya.

The Sahara of my story is about half the size of the United States and, like the United States, is a country of great contrasts in climate and scenery. In the summer it is very hot, with temperatures up to 150° Fahrenheit and an average of over 100° throughout the twenty-four hours. In the winter, cold winds sweep down from the snowclad Atlas range to the north, and it often freezes at night.

The Sahara is not flat and not low-lying. It has steep mountains and deep valleys. There are areas of brightly colored rock formations, not unlike Arizona's Painted Desert, and rolling pastures where great flocks of sheep are raised. It abounds in game, and there are hundreds of different kinds of birds and animals. When rain falls, flowers and grass appear and turn it into a huge meadow. The sand dunes occupy only one-sixth of its surface.

Coming from the north, the first contact with the Sahara is the pasture land, a scrub country of undulating plains lying from 1000 to 2500 feet above sea level. Moving south, the grass and camel thorn thins out until one comes to a wilderness of rocks and stones. It is the land of thirst and silence, of the great sand desert.

But even in these most desolate parts, there are oases. They are

xii

rarer in the south than in the north, but they are never completely absent. Within their perimeters, anything will grow, from a date palm to a bougainvillia.

In the center of the Sahara is the Ahaggar, the home of the veiled Touaregs. This is a volcanic, precipitous country with peaks running up to 10,000 feet.

The Sahara Desert, therefore, is divided into pastures, oases, sand-rock wildernesses, and volcanic mountains.

This scenery, obviously, does not make the Sahara unique. Some of the North American deserts are just as arid. Several are more colorful. Where it is different from anything else in the world, and outside normal powers of description, is in the sense of vastness which it produces. It is not the actual area in miles which gives this feeling of immensity. It is more the environment, the lack of anything to which the eye or the mind is accustomed.

Supposing one undertakes a journey through a country which is fertile, inhabited, and with good roads: mileage can be underestimated and will never be a cause of anxiety. Consequently, all fear of not reaching one's destination, of distance, of being alone does not enter into calculation.

No one thinks twice about crossing the United States or Canada, but a lot of thought is involved when it comes to embarking on a journey over the desolate wastes of the Sahara. Even when the trip has been carefully planned, the turning of the back on water, on fertility, on human habitations, is accompanied by a frightening sensation of finality.

It is rare to find tourists penetrating into the Sahara. They usually take a peep at it from the foothills which fringe its northern approaches, and quickly step back into the friendly, tree-clad mountains. Even the inhabitants have a deep-rooted, superstitious respect for the desert. It is their home which they love, but they are never sure what it will do to them next. It is the land of djinns, and the realm of the storm gods, the great empire of silence. "If you should visit it," say the Arabs, "tighten your belt. There is no lying down in comfort there; you will not find much food; and if you miss the water hole, you will die."

Yet the Sahara was not always this wilderness. Its present aspect is of comparatively recent date.

When the last great ice sheet covered Europe and the United

States, the Sahara lay in a warm, moist zone. Torrential rains, blown in on clouds from the north, formed a mature system of rivers and lakes, and the Sahara was covered with rich semitropical vegetation. It was during this period that equatorial animals established themselves in North Africa. Hannibal's elephants originally came from Central Africa, and the few panthers and lions still found in the Atlas mountains are descendants of the creatures which wandered up from the Niger during the Quaternary era. Then, just as man was beginning to appear on earth, a monster cataclysm shook the Sahara region. In North Africa two gigantic fissures opened in the earth's crust, and the portion between the fissures (the present Sahara) was pushed up a thousand feet. These violent disturbances caused the rivers and lakes to disappear beneath the surface of the earth. Today those waters still flow *under* the Sahara, and it is their emergence to the surface which forms oases.

This cataclysm cut off the moisture-laden clouds coming from the Mediterranean, by throwing up a string of mountains later to be classified as the Atlas range. Dry, hot winds began to blow across the Sahara and to mold the country as had the earlier rivers. Swirling particles of rock borne by the wind acted like floating belts of emery paper, and in the course of centuries gigantic boulders were polished down to sand. That process is still going on. It accounts for the fantastic rock shapes frequently seen, as well as for the Sahara sand itself.

It does not require a magnifying glass to watch the particles of sand continually flowing from northeast to southwest with the ever-blowing wind. As with water, the only thing which arrests their flow is an obstacle or a depression. One never finds sand dunes in any of the Sahara highlands. They are always in depressed areas or where there are natural barriers.

Practically all the dunes have a kernel of rock. They are nothing more than rocky hillocks covered with sand which the wind has brought. These hillocks rise to altitudes of from 60 to 500 feet. The depth of the sand outside the kernel is about 120 feet.

The moving sand dunes which are supposed to overwhelm oases and camps are rare. They consist of heaps of sand temporarily halted by an obstacle which is not rock. After a while the obstacle gives way and the wind pushes the sand on until it is held for good. What gives the dune country an impression of motion is the superficial sand being blown from dune to dune. But as one layer dances on like spray, it is replaced by another.

Contrasting with these arid wildernesses are the oases, which vary in size from groups of 15,000 to 300,000 date palms; that is, from four to fifty square miles. These desert gardens come into being when a fault in the underlying rock enables the subterranean water of one of the prehistoric rivers to mount to within 150 feet of the surface. This is the extreme length to which the tap root of a palm tree can grow. Whereas outside the perimeter of the oasis there is only scant rain-bred vegetation, inside the effect is more of the South Sea Islands than of a desert. As we have said, it is a country of unexpected contrasts.

The people who live there, too, are varied. They are for the most part Arabs. There are also Jews and Touaregs and the men of the Mzab. But the Arabs predominate. Not, as is generally imagined, because it is their native land. It is not their native land. The Arabs are no more indigenous to North Africa than the Hebrews. They are invaders like all the others who came and conquered, and established empires, and vanished again when the African sun made them indolent. The only true natives of North Africa are the Berbers, whose name is derived from the Roman *barbari*. They have been in this part of the world since the dawn of history. Their origins are obscure and very ancient. A warlike, white people, they have always managed to keep more or less independent. The invasions which have passed by their homes through the ages have reduced their numbers but have not destroyed the race. Today only a few groups are found in remote parts of the mountains and in the desert, but they are as purebred a people as any in the world.

The Arab's appearance in North Africa is of a much later date, actually no earlier than the seventh century of our era. Thousands of years before, the Berbers had been there. Carthage had come and gone as the trade center of the world. The kingdom of Numidia had been civilized and powerful. The Roman Empire had risen and fallen. Hannibal, Scipio, Jugurtha, Genseric had passed into history before the Arab period. The daughter of Antony and Cleopatra had married one of the Numidian kings defeated on the same battleground where the Anglo-American troops fought the Germans and Italians in 1943. There had been war and peace

xv

and changes of rulers over a period of ten centuries before the Arabs first drifted west. They took the same sandy route followed thirteen hundred years later by the British Eighth Army, and rolled up the decadent Byzantine Romans as easily as General Montgomery rolled up Mussolini's legions. Rome's warworn eagle disappeared over the Mediterranean and for twelve centuries made no effort to return. The Berbers, as usual, let the new invaders surge around them and, although they accepted Islam, remained otherwise untouched.

This first Arab invasion was little more than a series of huge raids, without much objective other than raiding. The warriors who came had certainly no idea that they would sweep from Egypt to Morocco until their way was barred by the Atlantic. Neither did they imagine that their desert hordes would drive through Spain and halfway across France. But even with the success of these unpremeditated ventures there was no question yet of permanent settlement divorced from the home tribes in Arabia.

It was not until the twelfth century that the real domination of North Africa by the Arabs began. This time they came in swarms, bringing with them their flocks and their camels and their families, pouring over the land like clouds of hungry locusts. For the next two hundred years Arab rule was absolute.

That a great Moslem empire was not founded at the western end of the Mediterranean was due more to the invaders than to anything else. The original raiders had shown their worth as administrators and architects in Spain and Morocco, but their successors were nomad shepherds with little use for the life of cities. When, therefore, the Spaniards and then the Turkish corsairs of Barbarossa occupied the North African seacoast, the Arabs withdrew into the interior and settled in the desert. Some of them sided with the Turks when the French attacked Algiers at the beginning of the nineteenth century; but, on principle, they remained on their southern pastures, asking only to be left alone.

This the French did. Not from altruism, but as the simplest thing to do. The Sahara was valueless except as a pasture area. Even as a pasture area it required nomad shepherds to produce any results. So the French remained in the background, with local military administration in the oases, and let the Arab chiefs have a free hand in the desert.

The hierarchy among Arab chiefs in North Africa is not complicated. The highest in rank is the bash agha, who is at the head of a confederation of ten or twelve tribes consisting of anything up to ten thousand families or tents. (The actual number of human beings is impossible to estimate as, for all purposes of census, the Arab of the desert counts in this way.) The bash agha has under him two senior aides called aghas. At the head of each tribe is a caid. The caid's tribe is subdivided into four "fractions," each under a sheik. The sheik, about whom so much fantasy has been bred in books and motion pictures, is usually nothing more than a shepherd. He can usually neither speak nor write French, which denotes education among the Sahara Arabs, and he has never thought of an Occidental woman except as something shameless and unprepossessing. He does not wear flowing robes, à la Valentino; his horse is usually ungroomed; and the only home he knows is a kind of camel-hair shelter which he calls a tent. I had many friends who were sheiks, but none who had ever thought of the world except in terms of deserts or had visualized men and women who were not continually on the wander.

And so are all the people of the Sahara. Some of the richer nomads have traveled and take a vague interest in what goes on in the rest of the world, but the majority do not. The chiefs, big and small, the sheep raisers, the shepherds live as they have throughout the centuries, before Columbus discovered America, before printing, before the world was known to be round. Twelve hundred years ago they came to the Sahara wearing the same kind of clothing, living in the same kind of tents, driving the same breed of sheep as today. To them the Occidental is still Roumi (Roman), the first European whom their ancestors encountered in North Africa. Even the airplane and the automobile, which have made their appearance in the Sahara, have done little to alter the habits of the Arabs. They are nomad sheep raisers, and all the buses and planes of America are not going to help them in the pasturing of their flocks. Had I written this book in 1500 or 1800 or 2000 A.D., I would have had the same story to tell. The Arabs, like the desert, have remained untroubled by the social upheavals which have shaken the world. As they lived in the days of coats of mail and bows and arrows, so do they now, and they do not want anything else. The Sahara is their home, the Garden of Allah from which

God has removed all surplus human and animal life so that there may be one place where He can walk in peace. Neither do they consider it unhospitable as many Occidentals do. To them it is not desert or wilderness but a land of which they know every feature, a mother country whose smallest product has use according with their needs. They know how to rejoice in great spaces and how to honor the fall of rain. They are content, and the little they have seen of modern "progress" has not convinced them that they are on the wrong track.

After living among them for many years, I have an idea that they are probably right.

CHAPTER I

A S I LOOK BACK, I see Lawrence of Arabia as the primary cause of what happened.

It was at the time of the Paris Peace Conference. I had been serving there as assistant military attaché ever since it came into being soon after the Armistice, and I was beginning to realize that the ideals for which we had been ready to give our lives were little more than talk. The whole of this glamorous war-waging for which my services had been hired suddenly appeared as the racket it was. I was too junior to comment, but I used to boil as I watched politicians, who had kept safely out of harm's way, laying the road toward another massacre. I thought of my friends who had died in the mud, I thought of their girl widows and of their children who were being raised to take our places in the next bloody fight. I could not protest, but neither could I go on being taken in by this going-to-glory-for-the-flag nonsense.

This sentiment was not unpatriotic. I had started to war enthusiastically. I had believed in the cause. I had fought convinced that I was making the world safe for democracy, or something of the kind. I had lived up to the slogan inscribed on my medal: "The War to End All Wars." I was a typical young officer without complexes. That I now felt differently was due to the peacemakers. It was they who were showing me the futility of all I had been through during four years on the Western Front.... "The War to End All Wars." If they had said, "To intensify the antagonisms of nationalism, to revive the intrigues of secret diplomacy," it would have been nearer the truth. For, as I saw it now, it was to be everyone for himself. Britain for herself, France for herself, Italy for herself. The little countries grabbing what they could, quarreling over frontiers, threatening, pleading. The only person who still seemed to have illusions was President Wilson. But Mr. Wilson was no match for Mr. Lloyd George or M. Clémenceau. He no more understood the European political game or the imperialisms of his colleagues than did Lawrence and Feisal. The emir Feisal understood them better. He knew that if he wanted to save anything from his Arabian territories, he must keep faith with the British. He must forget their promises made in times of peril, broken in times of security. He must sink his pride.

In this Feisal was astute. In this he was also lucky. Among the Britons at the conference was one who wanted to see the Arabs get a square deal. This was Gertrude Bell.

Gertrude Bell had known the desert and the Arabs long before Lawrence had become Arabia-minded. She had undoubtedly done much to influence him at the outset of his Arabian career. After Lawrence she was the biggest factor in influencing mine. For the moment, she was peacemaking. Her creation of Irak and making Feisal its king was one of the few constructive things done at the conference. But then Gertrude was as practical as Lawrence was impractical. She said: "Here am I, a peace delegate! I haven't seen Paris for ages. It may be years before I return. I'm going to make the best of it." This she did, keeping her hand on the pulse of the conference whenever it showed signs of beating for the Arabs.

Lawrence could have done the same, but he had none of Gertrude Bell's worldly experience, and he moped. He moped as he wandered about the gilded halls of the Hotel Majestic in his faded Arab headdress while, out of the corners of their eyes, the Colonel Blimps watched him suspiciously. "There goes that crazy chap, Lawrence," they muttered into their moustaches. "Gone native, you know, actually slept in the same tent as a bedouin. Damned disgrace. What's England coming to!" And Lawrence had no comeback. He had done something which would live through the ages as one of the world's greatest stories of adventure. He did not realize this himself. If he had he would not have mentioned it. He never mentioned anything he had done.

While he brooded, I went to all the parties given by the peace delegates at the expense of their governments. I used official cars for my amusement and wasted taxpayers' money. I took on the philosophy of Gertrude Bell and mocked Lawrence and his gloom. Occasionally, I let myself think. But not often. Thoughts at such a time hurt. For whether I was at a ball given by the British

4

peace delegation or in the rich salons of some French home, I could not forget that, out there to the north, millions of men lay rotting beneath the mud of a great devastated country. Neither was there any consolation in the thought that we were here assembled to remedy this. Without any cynicism, it was obvious that reparations and the future of Europe could not be settled without a great deal of unanimous good will, without a lot of give and take. But few thought as I did, and we danced, as it were, on a floor supported by corpses, but without hearing the crunching of the bones. We had won "The Great War for Civilization"; for was it not graven in letters of brass on our Victory Decorations? The Huns were no more, the Russians were killing each other off, President Wilson was going to turn the world into the gardens beside the waters of Paradise, and if everything did not turn out according to plan, it would all be the same a hundred years hence. So why worry?

But after a while, I *did* worry.

With the Treaty of Versailles signed, the more important delegates began drifting back to their countries: Mr. Lloyd George to a short-lived triumph; President Wilson to disaster and disillusion; the others to explain to puzzled countrymen why Great Britain and her Dominions beyond the seas had got away with most of the loot. Minor delegates were assigned the tiresome duties of finishing off the details. The elegant houses of Paris closed their shutters as their owners made for the country. The lights and the music and the merrymaking faded; and with the fading one came face to face with reality. *I* came face to face with reality. What was I to do with my life? I was young, I was whole, I still had ideals. They had been shaken, but not nearly destroyed. What must I do?

For ten years I had been a soldier. I had served in India. I had played polo. I had explored and hunted in the Himalayas. I had felt the magic of being alone in those mighty mountains. I had been through the storm and mud of war. I had seen my friends maimed and killed. I had now watched the politicians, who had sent these men to death and mutilation, playing with the futures of a new generation as if they were stakes in a poker game. I suddenly felt fiercely against the traditions and discipline in which I had been brought up. The idea of going back to peacetime society and regimental routine frightened me. But what else could I do? I knew no useful trade. I had no money. The army was a safe way to earn a living without too much effort. Could I stand it? Could I stand following the narrow groove which would relentlessly lead me to retirement, to pension and the four walls of a "service" club in which to reminisce or dream about the might-have-beens over highballs which I could not afford? There were, of course, the great mountains which I had glimpsed above Kashmir. There were the jungles of central India. But they would only be interludes in the drudgery of army life.

For the first time, I spent sleepless nights turning and re-turning this problem over in my mind. I prayed for sufficient pluck to break the chains of convention which held me from the life which I knew was beckoning to me through the mists of indecision.

Then Lawrence entered more actively into my life, entered and rushed out again, altering the whole of it: uprooting the foundations on which I had been raised, causing consternation to my family and joy in my heart. It came about this way.

Lawrence liked me and rather despised me. That is, he despised my way of living. He was himself an ascetic and could not understand that a man could lead a gay life, drink, dance, make love, and still have other thoughts. I do not believe that Lawrence had ever had any sexual emotions or felt the gaiety of wine. His ecstasies had been confined to spiritual exaltation while leading his Arabs over the blinking desert. That I should join in the gay round and not let it dominate me, he could not appreciate. Still, he liked me, tolerated my failings, and hoped time would mend them.

One day, when I told him that a suggestion had been made to me by Lloyd George to take up politics, he blew up. He called me a lunatic, a moron, a traitor to my principles. When finally I was able to get in a word, I said:

"It's all very well to talk like that, but what else can I do? With the war over, a uniform's a handicap. You know what civilian employers think of ex-officers of the regular army. With the market jammed with men looking for jobs, what chance do I stand?"

"None," replied Lawrence.

"Well then?"

"Go and live with the Arabs."

I stared, waiting for more. "Go and live with the Arabs." I thought Lawrence had gone crazy. But he was calm now and talking earnestly. He reminded me that what had first made him take an interest in me was my connections with North Africa and my curiosity about desert people. He pointed out that nomad Arabs lived by sheep. A small capital would buy the preliminary flock. The sheep would multiply. The nomad had few needs. In time I might become rich among the Arabs. But even if I did not find material wealth, I would regain my health, I would become young again, I would have peace of mind.

"Go and live with the Arabs!" he cried. "Go and live with the Arabs!" His frail figure was trembling. His blue eyes pierced me. His thin lips were set. His emaciated face shone. Then he was gone.

For a while I stood staring at the door which had closed on the little man. I tried to shrug my shoulders. I tried to laugh, but I knew that Lawrence had planted something in my mind which would have to grow. An idea had come into being which was to lead me onto the strangest route any Occidental ever followed.

I never saw Lawrence again. But I often feel those piercing eyes destining my future. I often hear that voice ordering me away from all that had been given me by birth and upbringing. . . .

Although Lawrence had permanently thrown me off my course; although I knew that military and official life for me were over, I did not make a move at once. I had many things to settle.

It was not so easy for a man with my upbringing just to turn his back on everything. The army had not yet broken my spirit, but it had narrowed my mind. From its point of view, what I contemplated doing would put me outside the caste of officers to which I belonged. For a while I temporized. I fooled around with other escapist professions, but they always brought me back to the same point. *The postwar world had learned nothing from its years of trial.* Society was even more futile than before. Statesmanship had made no progress. The reverse had happened. Instead of remembering the humiliating days of 1914 and '15 and '16; instead of recollecting that, had it not been for the United States, Great Britain's empire might now be no more; instead of thinking out some plan whereby we might enhance our name, we British were

7

drifting back into the Kiplingesque spirit of the Victorians. Arrogantly we stalked into our imperial past—

> For the Lord OUR God most high
> Hath made the sea as dry
> And hath smote for US a path to the ends of all the earth.

This was no place for me. I might have preached a warning. But I knew it would do no good. I remembered how they had failed to honor Gertrude Bell, how they had scoffed at Lawrence. Once more the words of the little man returned. "Go and live with the Arabs!" Yes? But how? When it came to considering the advice practically, it was not as simple as it sounded.

Why on earth should these proud men of the desert wish to have a disillusioned Occidental come and live with them merely because he was tired of his own brand of civilization?

With Lawrence there had been no such problem. He had come inspired with a mission. He had convinced Feisal that he was in a position to make him king of Arabia. He had been able to hand out gold to the more mercenary-minded chiefs. He had shown the tribesmen an easy way to acquire loot. From all points of view, Lawrence looked like a good bet to the Arabs.

In my case, however, there was no inspired mission, no gold, no prospect of loot. I was nobody. I brought nothing which an Arab might understand. I had only one asset, a small one, it is true, but sufficient to have made me choose the Arabs of the Sahara Desert as my future companions rather than the bedouins of Arabia.

In the eighteen sixties my grandfather, who was Gertrude Bell's uncle, had visited Algiers. The French conquest of North Africa was rather recent, and no one had yet thought of settling in this beautiful Mediterranean port. My grandfather decided that it was time someone did. He bought what had been the home of a Barbary corsair on the Mustapha Hill overlooking the Bay of Algiers.

My mother-to-be had spent her girlhood winters in this one-time palace of the Barbary pirate. She had driven the length and breadth of Algeria in a six-horse coach. She had met the desert Arabs. One evening, at a ball given by the governor-general, she danced with a young Englishman called Bodley. They were married in the English church in Algiers. They honeymooned in Constantine. If

8

prenatal influence plays any part in a man's life, it certainly did in mine.

I was not born in North Africa, but I came there at a very early age and continued to do so. Algeria, the fringes of the Sahara, and the Arabs were known to me. Thus, if I was to carry out Lawrence's orders, the place where I stood the greatest chance of success was here. I told some of my more intimate friends of what I had in mind. A few of them thought fit to give me a farewell party. There was a lot of champagne and a lot of kidding. One of the toasts was to a speedy return. Six weeks was set as the limit of time I would last in the Sahara. I did not come back for seven years.

From Algiers to the first real Sahara oasis is not far as the crow flies. By road or rail it is a long, circuitous, upward journey. At least fifteen hours of continuous traveling separates it from the Mediterranean.

At a dismal place called Djelfa the railway comes to an end. It is a relief. There is nothing dirtier, slower, more uncomfortable than a North African train.

Djelfa is the last Occidental town before the desert and has no equal in the world for squalor. There is nothing to redeem it, not even a temperate climate. Two miserable inns face one another on the main street. They are kept by Europeans whose rivalry apparently consists in seeing which can be the most filthy. They are examples of the odd way in which some Occidentals behave when they get away from their normal surroundings. Their squalor has nothing to do with the native inhabitants. No cleaner people exist than the Arabs of the desert. It is a kind of degeneracy which sets in when certain white men lose touch with their home ties. Many nomads' only contact with the Occident is Djelfa. This would be another handicap in my project to live with them.

A motor bus continues the journey south. This Sahara bus service is an amazing institution. From Djelfa to Timbuctoo, nearly two thousand miles away, the trans-Saharan journey can be carried out, almost nonstop, by bus. During the initial stages of the trip the buses are modern affairs comparing favorably with those of the Greyhound lines. With each stage of southward progress, transportation deteriorates. In the same way, tickets at first assure seating accommodation, and there are more or less regular stopping places and time schedules. But once in the real desert world, the buses are piled from running board to roof with men and women and children and baggage. The nomads who wish to travel wait anywhere along the roadside, taking their chances whether the bus will be along in a few minutes or a few days.

When there is a breakdown, there is no commotion. To the Arabs, as to Einstein, time is relative. They are not bothered by the tiresome details which ruin the lives of Occidentals. They carry their clothes on them, and their baggage includes provisions and cooking utensils. When the bus splutters and gives up, they tumble out on the roadside, where they settle peacefully until the driver has made the necessary repairs or another bus has come along. Whether they reach their destination that day or a week later is of no consequence.

Djelfa stands at 6000 feet above sea level. From its windswept plateau the country slopes gradually toward the Sahara. It is the land of alfa, the source of paper for slick magazines. Bare hills with jagged crests, and wide panoramas. The road can be seen like a long white ribbon unrolling itself toward the south. The only signs of human habitation are a few caravanserais. In the days when the Arabs were still "unsubdued," the "diligences" used to spend the night behind their walls. Now they are only used as places to discharge and pick up passengers and to drink coffee. The country becomes more desolate. Grave nomads watch over flocks of sheep within sight of the road. Camels and donkeys replace other means of transport. The bus has begun to look incongruous. There is a feeling of something new. The people of the north have been left behind. With every revolution of the wheels, one seems to be speeding into the past. The flocks, the shepherds are the same as they were twelve hundred years ago. The few buses and trucks which bring the stores have had no effect on them.

The road turns sharply to the left round the flank of a barren ridge like the teeth of a saw. A dark mass breaks up the empty panorama. The mass defines itself more clearly. Palm trees detach themselves, then more palm trees, and more and more and more, thousands of them. Rosy rocks break the horizon. A white column leaps to the sky. It is the minaret of the mosque. It is the first great oasis of the Sahara...

The bus stopping before the Hotel Saharien jolted me into

action. It was as different as possible from the Djelfa inns. Before a gaily painted arcade Arabs and a sprinkling of French officers sat at small tables. A pillared gallery, pink and blue, ran the whole length of the first floor. Onto this opened the bedrooms.

The passengers began climbing out of the bus. Porters handed down packages, bundles, boxes. Arabs greeted friends. Their dignified salutes were mingled with the laughter of a group of black Senegalese soldiers. An officer of the Spahis in his scarlet cloak, who had spoken a few words to me during the trip from Djelfa, saluted and went to find out when the next bus started. His final destination was much farther on. For a moment I stood a little bewildered. I was the only one who had no plan, no one to say hello to.

A wave of discouragement passed over me. It was all very well for Lawrence to order: "Go and live with the Arabs!" But how did one set about it? What had sounded fantastic in Paris was doubly so here on the edge of the desert.

I glanced at the calm faces of the Arabs, who did not seem to be aware that I was there. What would they say if I went up to them and suggested that I wished to live with them? Would they laugh? Or would they merely tell me to go back to where I came from? If they did, I would be getting no more than I deserved. For a moment I thought of leaving my bags in the bus and traveling in it when it left again for Djelfa.

The owner of the inn put an end to this idea. He stood before me, bowing, smiling, showing his white teeth. By his accent and appearance, I judged him a Corsican. But whatever his background, he was so cordial and so eager to make me feel at home that I no longer hesitated, and had my things brought in.

Monsieur Paoli never knew how much he had to do with the reshaping of my life.

CHAPTER II

THERE IS NO SUNLIGHT in the world equal to that of the Sahara. It has a quality which no painter has been able to convey to canvas. Its brilliance baffles photographers. It saturates everything, penetrates shades and shutters, purifies all that comes within its range. That there is no disease in the Sahara is due, I am sure, to its sunshine.

I had gone to bed discouraged. I woke elated. The sun and the fresh, dry air were giving new life to my tired blood. Breakfast, which used to be a formality, became a necessity. My body was straining to be up and about. A month before, sentence of death would not have upset me. Today I would have protested. I wanted to do things.

Monsieur Paoli had fed me with chunks of bread and mugs of chicory-flavored coffee. Now I sat under the arcades of his inn looking into the sun-drenched street. Arabs and camels passed slowly before me like extras creating atmosphere for a movie. Behind them palms rustled in the breeze. In the immediate foreground a boy, so black that he seemed to be carved out of coal, squatted in the dust. His round head was covered with tightly crinkled, woolly hair, on which rested a scarlet skullcap. The clothes which covered his body consisted more of patches than of the original material. His slippers belonged to the Numidian era. He was obviously a descendant of Jugurtha. As I caught his eye, a grin displaying a row of white teeth spread across the polished ebony face. It was so engaging that I grinned, too. For a moment we remained on those terms. Then I asked if His Blackness spoke any French? The grin broadened and was followed by a nod. This was something.

"What is your name?" I inquired.

"Blanchet!" The information was accompanied by that happy

laughter peculiar to colored people. "Would you like to take a walk?"

He did not wait for an answer and, gathering his rags about him, led me through the gateway of the stone wall which surrounded the oasis town, beyond which I found myself in a long arcaded street lined with shops. At one end of this street I could see the entrance to military barracks, at the other a Catholic church. The view ahead of me was obstructed by a rocky ridge crowned by the mosque, the minaret of which I had seen from the bus. Blanchet hesitated as if he expected me to decide which way I wished to go.

"I want to see the Sahara," I said.

Blanchet turned to the left past the church and up a steep, narrow alley. It was a busy quarter, but none of the Arabs took any notice of me. An Occidental in their midst did not seem to interest them. Once more I had the hopeless sensation of the previous night. These were no "damned natives" brought into the world to believe in the superiority of Occidentals. They were people who owed nobody anything and wanted nothing from anybody. I wondered what Lawrence would have done.

Blanchet showed as little interest as the others. He stumped along ahead of me with patches of shiny black skin showing through his tatters. After a while he left the street and began scaling the rocky ridge. He reached the crest first and sat down to put on the remains of shoes which he had taken off for the climb. Then he turned his smiling blackness toward me and pointed in the direction of something I could not see. I quickly joined him and stopped. Blanchet said, "Sahara!" and looked up at me as if he expected some comment. But I could find nothing to say.

The first view of the Sahara is one of the most amazing sights of the world. It has an immensity which creates a greater feeling of awe than the Himalayas or the Grand Canyon or the Arctic Sea. There is nothing to which the mind can compare this vast expanse rolling out until it merges into an infinite horizon. It is frighteningly empty, yet strangely attractive. The blinking wastes of stones and scrub, the rosy rocks, the brilliance of the light overpower one as might a giant. All other parts of the world become tame and without size. The desolate majesty is more inspiring than any of the great oceans. —A great ocean is, perhaps, the best simile. The oasis is a tropical island with its palm trees growing down to the water's edge, and then the "sea," away, away, until the next island.

For a while I let this fantastic panorama soak into me. Then I took a look at the oasis. From where I stood, I could see the town, clustering on either side of the rocky ridge. The mosque was in the center, and to the north and south were gardens and date palms. There seemed to be a great many, and I gauged the circumference of the oasis to be not less than ten miles. I turned to Blanchet, who sat on a boulder scratching himself.

"How big is this oasis?"

"Fifty thousand palm trees," he replied without hesitation.

I accepted this reckoning and from then on adopted the Arab method of calculating the size of oases.

I turned again to my contemplation of the desert. I felt drugged by its silent vastness.

My thoughts were interrupted by feeling someone beside me. A slim youth of about eighteen was watching me. He was poorly dressed, but his clothes were not in tatters like Blanchet's. Had he been in rags, however, they would not have deprived him of his dignified calm. There was something sublime in the peace of his grey eyes. His smile as I faced him was different from Blanchet's. It was not unfriendly, but it was reserved.

"Good morning," he said in French. "You are admiring the Sahara."

I nodded. For a moment he continued to look out at the view. Then he asked, "What is your name?"

I told him.

"Boodli," he repeated; "that is not French?"

I shook my head, "No, it's English."

"Ah, yes, English." He thought for a while. Then he said, "My name is Mohammed ben Tahar."

I repeated the name, pronouncing the "ben" as one might in English. Mohammed corrected me. "B'n," he said, "is not part of the name. It means 'son of.' We are all 'so and so' the son of 'so and so,' or daughter of 'so and so.' The female word is 'b'nt.' "

"The Russians employ the same system," I said.

Mohammed did not seem interested, for all he said was, "You

came in on the bus last night. You have lost no time in seeing the Sahara."

"Yes," I replied; "Blanchet brought me up here."

Mohammed let his eyes rest for a minute on the black boy who had curled up on a rock and gone to sleep. He shrugged his shoulders. "What a savage! He sleeps when he has this to look at!"

"He has probably seen it often," I suggested.

"I have seen it often," said Mohammed.

"And you are never tired of looking at it?"

"Can one ever be tired of what is never the same? Look, even now the Sahara is changing color. It has changed many times since you reached this rock with the savage."

"It's like the sea," I said, "without storms."

Mohammed ben Tahar seated himself on a boulder and stared over the desert. "I have never seen the sea," he said after a while, "but here there are storms. When the sirocco blows, you cannot see three yards before you for the dust. No one dares to go out when the south wind blows. Today the Sahara is kind, but she can be very wicked."

I laughed. "You say 'her' as if she was a woman."

Mohammed nodded. "She *is* like a woman. A capricious woman whose moods are always changing. Some days she is so bad that you swear you will go away and never see her again. But before you have turned your back, she is smiling, and you are once more in her arms." He paused and considered me thoughtfully. "I don't know you, Sidi Boodli, but if you let the Sahara take hold of you, she will never let you go."

He returned to his contemplation. I watched with him as the sun grew stronger and the country began to blink and shimmer.

"Tell me, Mohammed ben Tahar," I asked after a while, "what is beyond that horizon? More desert and more desert, or are there oases?"

"There are both," he replied. "There are oases and desert, and desert and oases. Wherever there is water, wherever the Behar Tahtami comes to within a hundred and fifty feet of the surface of the ground so that it can be reached by the roots of the date palms, there is an oasis. The palms spring up with their feet in the water and their heads in the flames."

"What do you mean by 'Behar Tahtami'?" I asked.

"It is the sea of the underworld," replied Mohammed. "It is what makes oases."

"And how often does the water come to the surface?"

Mohammed shrugged. "It depends." He pointed to the south. "Over there, the nearest oasis is a hundred and twenty-five miles, the next is a hundred and eighty. Over there," he pointed to the east, "it is a hundred and fifty miles to the next oasis. The rising of the water belongs to the history of the rocks. My teacher taught me at school, but I did not understand well. All I know is that there *are* oases, and without oases, I and my family could not live."

"They stretch a long way into the desert?" I suggested.

Mohammed nodded. "It is like an avenue of palms."

"How long is it?"

Mohammed shrugged his shoulders. "A female camel mated at the beginning of the journey would have time to bring forth her young before arriving at the other end."

This did not tell me much, but I liked Mohammed's metaphors and left it at that.

For a while we sat watching the palms swaying and fluttering in the breeze. Cloud shadows had again changed the aspect of the Sahara. That peculiar feeling of living in the past came back, and with it, great peace. I glanced at my companions to see if they felt as I did. There was no question about Mohammed's mind being at rest, and Blanchet's black face was shut tight in sleep. Save for the rustle of the palms there was no sound.

Without turning, Mohammed asked, "Are you staying here for long?"

"I hope so." Now that it came to the point of bringing up my plan, I found it difficult to put it into words. The short conversation I had had with this boy had shown me the gulf which separated us. He had not said much, but he had given me a sensation that he was spiritually above me. Not intentionally or even in his mind. It was more by his sincerity, by his admission that he had never seen the sea and did not understand geology, by his appreciation of the Sahara where he had been born. I thought of myself at the same age. Blasé, boastful, self-satisfied. This boy had a philosophy superior to mine at any time. He had discovered the worth-whiles. He had found peace. He had probably found truth. But would he, or any of the Arabs, be able to share this with me, even if they wanted to? I approached the problem indirectly.

"Have any Occidentals ever settled in the Sahara?"

Mohammed thought for a moment before replying. "Some of the officers of the African regiments live in the oases when they retire."

"But like Occidentals? As they always have?" I suggested.

"Oh, yes. The only difference is the shedding of uniforms."

"None of them go and live in the desert with the nomads?" The idea seemed to amuse Mohammed, for he laughed without replying. "But if they don't change their way of living, why don't they settle in France or in Algiers?" I added.

Mohammed had evidently not considered this, for he did not say anything. His reply when it came, was as logical as the rest of his remarks.

"They stay here, I suppose, because they have become accustomed to the climate and the sunshine. Life is easy, living is cheap, and of course there is the Sahara. That is the most important, the Sahara."

"Then no foreigner has ever become a nomad and lived in a tent?"

Mohammed looked at me with his big grey eyes wide and questioning. "Of course not. How could he?"

"Why not?" I wanted to find out what I was up against.

"Because he couldn't be an Arab."

"But what's to stop anyone, an Englishman, an American, one of these ex-officers, from getting a tent and buying some sheep and going to live out there? Why do you have to be an Arab?"

Mohammed made a circular gesture with his hand. "All that out there is Arab land. All the pastures belong to the Arabs."

"Belong to the Arabs?"

Mohammed nodded.

"And the French?"

"The French only interfere in case of trouble. The desert is the nomads'. Only the nomads know the desert. Only the nomads can live there."

"But supposing I became a nomad?" Unintentionally I had let out my secret.

"If *you* became a nomad? But you only arrived last night." Mohammed stared at me, his calm ruffled for the first time. "But you cannot speak Arabic. You are not a Moslem. You are accustomed to European food, you sleep in a bed, you wear foreign clothes—" He looked at me anxiously, then laughed. "*You* a nomad—" And, before I could say anything, he added, "Even I, who am an Arab of pure descent, could not be a nomad. My parents are oasis people who live in houses. We could not wander. We know nothing of the raising of sheep. My father is a taleb; he teaches the Koran. Soon I will teach, but I could not be a nomad any more than I could be an Englishman or an American."

There was not a loophole in Mohammed's argument. The verdict sounded final. But I took a deep breath of pure Sahara air and made up my mind not to accept defeat—yet.

"Who is the most important chief in these parts?" I inquired.

"Sidi el Hadj Jelloul ben Lahkdar, Bash Agha of the Larba tribes which pasture in this area," replied Mohammed.

"Has he been here always?"

Mohammed nodded. "He and his ancestors have always been here; that is, ever since the Arabs came to North Africa, twelve hundred years ago."

"Does he live all the time out there?" I pointed to the desert.

"Not always. He is old and has a home in the oasis. He only goes to his flocks when they are pasturing near by."

I did not want to give Mohammed any more shocks, but I felt that I must get his theories confirmed. "Could you arrange for me to speak to him?" I asked.

"I can take you to the café where he always goes," replied Mohammed unhesitatingly, "and you can sit with him. *I* am too young to go into the same place where he is, but he knows French well and is interested in foreigners. He knows many."

This sounded practical. After all, the most this paramount chief could do would be to send me about my business. I turned to Mohammed.

"Lead the way, Mohammed ben Tahar," I said. "I will speak with the Bash Agha of all the Larbas."

Mohammed gathered his robes about him and, with a final glance at the desert, began making his way down the cliff. Blanchet roused himself. His eyes twinkled in his ebony head, the grin divided his face in half; and taking off his slippers, he stumped after us.

CHAPTER III

Jelloul ben lahkdar, Bash Agha of the Larbas, had the dignity of an emperor before democracy made royalty commonplace. He was a blond Arab with hazel eyes and a white beard which at one time had been fair. Like most of his race, he was not tall, but he had a majestic way of talking and walking that made up for any lack of stature. During the years I knew him, I never felt his equal. This had nothing to do with anything in the Bash Agha's manner toward me. If he had thought there were moments when I felt inclined to kneel with his tribesmen and kiss his hand, he would have been most embarrassed. He was a kindly, humorous old gentleman; but his personality was overwhelming.

My first glimpse of Jelloul was given me by Mohammed ben Tahar that original morning of my life in the Sahara. He was sitting outside an Arab café at the foot of the mosque opposite another fine old Arab with a long brown beard. Mohammed whispered to me that it was El Hadj Yahia ben Lahkdar, the Bash Agha's brother. At respectful distances stood younger chiefs, among whom Mohammed pointed out the agha Daylis, the Bash Agha's son, and the sheik Marhoun, his grandson. Both these men were fair-haired and blue-eyed. A little outside the circle of chiefs were the retainers: a tremendous Negro and two men in royal blue burnouses. None of them spoke or smoked or sat. They stood like courtiers in the presence of their king.

Occasionally a passer-by came into the café to kiss the Bash Agha's forehead or shoulder. The more humble kissed his hand. The old man took no notice of these salutations and continued to smoke his water pipe and chat with his brother as if no one had been near him. Occasionally he would address one of the chiefs, who would bound forward and listen attentively. It was another picture of the past which had no connection with me or anything

19

to which I belonged. I came to the conclusion that the moment was not opportune to carry out the plan of introducing myself. So I walked on with *my* two retainers, trying to look dignified, or at any rate un-self-conscious.

As a matter of fact, there was nothing to be self-conscious about. The Arab chiefs showed no more interest in me than in black Blanchet in his tatters.

I continued on my way down the arcaded street, which by now was thronged with people walking to and fro as if they had nothing else to do. I noticed that most of them smiled and all of them had contented expressions. They moved without hurry, greeting their friends formally and courteously. Occasionally a group would drift into one of the shops under the arcades. The shopman would spread out his goods on the counter, but I did not see anything bought. The transaction usually resolved itself into a friendly visit, with tea or coffee at the expense of the tradesman. The few women in the street were veiled from head to foot in a shroudlike garment which allowed no more than one eye to peek at the world. Now and then a camel came padding slowly by, looking disdainfully to right and to left through half-closed eyes. There were donkeys, too, and an occasional horseman, but no cars or carriages. There could not have been. It was all too dignified and of another age.

Without thinking about it, *I* ceased to strut and fell into the stately gait of the promenaders; but I wished I wore robes. In a sports coat and flannel trousers I could never achieve the proud bearing of these wanderers of the desert.

My walk was halted by a fantastic little man who came smilingly toward me from the entrance of a shop. He was darker and more Semitic than the chiefs I had seen at the café, but he would not have attracted my attention if it had not been for his clothes. He wore a bright red velvet fez, a European cloth jacket, and dark green, embroidered, baggy trousers. His slippers were orange, and he completed his outfit with a pair of white cotton gloves and huge horn-rimmed spectacles.

"It's Atalla Bouameur," muttered Mohammed. "He keeps the curio shop."

Before he could say more, Atalla was beside me, bowing and smirking in such an engaging manner that I accepted his offer of coffee and followed him into the store. This, also, was an amazing contrast of East and West. Brass trays, hookahs, hair tonics, talcum powder, scimitars, scissors, cigarettes, tapestries, print dresses and I know not what, were strewn everywhere. Atalla pushed his way through the customers who crowded round the counter, and led the way behind. He raised one of the tapestries, disclosing a staircase.

"It will be more comfortable if we take our coffee upstairs," he suggested in educated French. Again he bowed, and addressing an elderly man in orthodox Arab clothes who sat in a corner telling his beads, said a few words in Arabic. Turning to me again, he added, "My father will look after the shop while I am with you. He will sell the wrong things at the wrong prices, but it can't be helped. It is not often that I have an honored guest."

We had now reached the kind of room which Occidentals associate with Arabs and the Orient but rarely see. It had a huge divan heaped with embroidered cushions. The floor was strewn with carpets. On the walls hung tapestries, ivory-stocked guns, scimitars, and daggers. Brass trays, brass coffee pots, brass ablution bowls, tables and chairs inlaid with mother-of-pearl, were littered about. From censers, aromatic smoke curled up toward the dimness of the ceiling.

Atalla clapped his hands, and a Negro in a scarlet jacket and blue embroidered trousers appeared with coffee and almond cakes. I lay back on the divan and felt that I had crossed the threshold of Arab life. Anything might happen now.

On a huge cushion Atalla sat cross-legged, looking owlish in the semiobscurity. The ebony face of Blanchet under the red skull cap, the dignified calm of Mohammed ben Tahar, added to the illusion.

For a while we passed the time of day in leisurely Arab fashion. Atalla did most of the talking, skillfully cross-examining me and finding out who I was and where I came from. Then he casually turned to business, so casually that it seemed to be part of the conversation. Would I not like some small souvenir to take back with me to England? As I said nothing, a bad imitation of a Persian carpet was spread before me. This was followed by a brass tray with "factory made" written all over it. An ablution bowl and a ewer with the same trade-mark came next. Then an inlaid table which no Arab had ever had anything to do with. I began

21

to feel irritated. Although I was no more than a tourist in these parts, I resented being taken for one. I resented being gauged sufficiently gullible to be offered this junk.

Genuine Arab brassware is very rare and very old. The desert people are no craftsmen. The few good modern things come from Morocco. Carpets are made by the women of sedentary Arabs. They are coarse-woven and able to stand much wear. They have nothing of the fine texture of Persian rugs. No Arab uses furniture except when he has guest rooms for Occidentals, and then the tables and chairs and beds come from department stores in Algiers.

I glanced at my two guides, wondering if they would give any indication of knowing what was being put over on their potential benefactor. Blanchet had curled up on a heap of cushions and was out. Mohammed sipped his coffee, but his thoughts were far away. I turned to Atalla. He was coming toward me with an obviously made-to-order scimitar. I did not want to offend him, but I wanted him to realize that I knew something of North Africa, so I said casually,

"Where do these things come from?"

"Where?" Atalla had obviously not had that question before. He hesitated. I gave him no opportunity to get embroiled in a face-saving lie which might make him resent me.

"Yes. Where?" I continued quickly. "What factory? You must have some big place within reach to turn out trays and bowls and carpets by the dozen like this?"

"But—" Atalla was peering at me curiously through his thick-lensed glasses. I still gave him no time to become embarrassed.

"We all know that the old stuff is only found in private homes or in museums, and I've always wondered where the kind of things you sell originate. Other dealers have never told me the truth, but you are obviously not an ordinary dealer and I am sure you will understand my curiosity."

Atalla's grin gave me hope that I had not fared badly in my first attempt at dealing with Arab psychology. He laid the scimitar on a chair and sat beside me. He helped himself to coffee and lit a cigarette.

"Practically everything in here comes from a central factory in Damascus," he said unhesitatingly. "Some of the carpets are woven in Belgium, but they are delivered a little *too* fresh-looking, and I place most of my orders in Syria. The goods are well made and look sufficiently genuine."

"It is the same firm, I suppose, which supplies the pedlars in Port Said and the Algerian tourist centers?" I suggested.

Atalla nodded. "The traveling salesman comes here twice a year on his tour of the southern Mediterranean."

"You have nothing Arab then at all?"

Atalla shrugged. "The Arabs make so little. I have a few good Moorish pieces and some fine carpets from the Djebel Amour, but tourists won't pay the price they are worth. They are better pleased with a Damascene machine-turned tray or a Brussels carpet. As for the scarfs which I import from the Galleries Lafayette for the dancing girls of the reserved quarter, I could sell ten times as many."

I laughed. "And this room," I hinted, "is it also arranged for the benefit of tourists? I'm sure you don't live in the midst of all this stuff?"

Atalla chuckled. "You are a wizard," was all he said.

But as I had guessed, it was all fake. The astute little man had traveled and, unlike most of his kind who went abroad with their eyes shut, had kept his wide open. He had gauged Occidental mentality and realized what visitors expected to see in the Orient. He realized, therefore, that if he gave them the "genuine Arabian nights atmosphere," it would be easier to sell the "genuine article," so he had arranged this room. Here, for an hour, the few Americans and Britons who penetrated so far south could relax on cushions smelling of stale amber. They could breathe the heavy incense which smoldered in the brass censers. They could finger the exotic goods in a state of exotic abandon. Later they could drink coffee which tasted like what they thought Oriental coffee should taste like, instead of being choked by the grounds-filled mixture which the Arabs enjoy. Atalla never told them that he imported the incense from Paris and had learned to make the coffee from a phony Arab on a ship of the French Line.

I was delighted by Atalla's frankness and sense of humor. He seemed to be far removed from the stately life of the oasis and the desert. Actually he was not, but he had the ability to see things from the Occidental as well as from the Oriental angle. I felt, therefore, that he might understand my problem, and I decided to try and approach the Arabs through him.

Without confessing what was at the back of my mind, I suggested that I would like to be on friendly terms with the people of the desert. Mohammed ben Tahar stirred uneasily. I saw a glance pass between him and Atalla. There was a short period of silence. I knew that I had raised an issue which must be faced or evaded. Without speaking, Mohammed and Atalla were flinging the problem to and fro. Atalla spoke first. He said.

"You are not in any way connected with the French government?"

I shook my head.

"You are not connected with any government?"

Again I shook my head. "I am not. Why do you ask?"

"It is not usual for a foreigner to interest himself in desert Arabs."

This was an obstacle I had never thought of. It had caught me off balance, so I said bluntly, "You think I might be an agent sent to spy on them?"

Atalla hesitated a second. "Yes."

"I have no means of proving this," I said, "but one of the reasons I came here was to escape officials and officialdom, to be natural, to be among men who seem to lead sensible lives."

Mohammed spoke. "It is strange to hear a foreigner talk in such a way."

Atalla thought for a moment. Then he said, "I have been to Europe. I spent two weeks in Paris once. I have been lost in the metro and taken the wrong bus. I have heard the noise of a big city. When I first went to France, I had only one thought—how to get away, how to return to the peace of the Sahara. I know what this man feels."

Mohammed said, "You are older and wiser than I, Atalla Bouameur."

Atalla turned to me again. "I do not know how the nomads will take to your idea. They are people with century-old customs which nothing has changed. They are strangers to motorcars and planes and modern inventions. They live in the same way, think the same way, wear the same kind of clothes as their ancestors did twelve hundred years ago. They are Moslems, as we all are, but stricter and

24

more primitive. Before anything else, you will be to them an infidel!"

"I have said all this," interrupted Mohammed.

"Then I say it again," continued Atalla, "because, otherwise, you will be disappointed. I will have you meet the nomad chiefs. They will ask you to dine. They will take you out hunting. They may even lend you their horses, but they will not understand your wish to live among them."

Atalla smiled good-naturedly and clapped his hands for more coffee. The black boy sat up and yawned. Then he grinned. I wished he had been awake and joined in the conversation. His reactions would have interested me. I had spent barely twenty-four hours in the Sahara and had met nothing but opposition and discouragement. The lack of curiosity I aroused among the oasis Arabs; the attitude of Atalla and Mohammed; my own ignorance of desert lore—all of these seemed to be indications that I should turn back. That I did not was due partly to perverseness, but chiefly to the wonderful sensation of well-being which was soaking into my mind and body, which had not known real health for five years. I quickly decided not to give in; at any rate, not before attacking the problem from every side.

With that ability which Arabs have of remaining silent without appearing rude, Atalla and Mohammed and Blanchet said nothing. We sat quietly on the divan in the fake harem room surrounded by Damascene junk and sipped our coffee. I discovered a third reason why I should not turn back:

I instinctively liked these Arabs. I felt at ease in their company.

CHAPTER IV

M<small>Y TRANSFORMATION FROM</small> an Occidental citizen into a
desert wanderer took quite a while. When it came, the
change was unexpected and rapid.

After leaving Atalla's bogus harem, I returned to my hotel with
Blanchet and Mohammed ben Tahar. I gave them a few francs,
and they said goodbye at the door with appropriate thanks. They
made no suggestion to see me again and behaved as if our acquaint-
ance had begun and ended with that walk. I shrugged my shoulders
and went to find Monsieur Paoli and lunch. The Arabs obviously
had no use for me.—This reflection just showed how little I knew
about Orientals and their ways of thinking.

The fact that Blanchet had presented himself to me the moment
I had breakfasted; the fact that Mohammed ben Tahar had
appeared beside me on the rock above the Sahara; the meeting
with Atalla Bouameur, and my invitation to take coffee should
have given me an idea that my arrival in the oasis had been noted.
These should have made me appreciate that the Arabs were giving
me thought. It might be only a thought, but a stranger who was
not French and arrived with several bags could not be ignored.

I should have realized that the chiefs and the big shots were
not going to fling themselves at a newcomer just because he *was*
a newcomer. They were going to find out about him, study him,
and, if he seemed worthy of their attention, and friendly, consider
meeting him. Had I followed the black boy and the son of the
Taleb, I might have seen them converging with the dealer in
"antiques" on the café where the Bash Agha held court. But I
did not follow them, and ate a large lunch instead and drank a
bottle of heavy Algerian wine which made it not difficult to follow
the soothing southern custom of taking a siesta.

When I woke, one of the hotel servants handed me a dirty visit-

26

ing card on which was printed, "Cyprien Couteau," and underneath, *"Commissaire de Police."*

I went out and was greeted by one of my Occidentals gone dirty by expatriation. Cyprien Couteau had on the greasiest, shiniest suit I had ever seen on a European. His shirt was grimy; so was his collar. His tie was frayed and his boots unpolished. He had not shaved for several days, and his fingernails were black. He wore the traditional heavy moustache of a gendarme and the derby hat of a plain-clothes policeman. If anyone looked out of place in this sun-kissed oasis, it was Cyprien Couteau.

We sat down at a table under the arcaded sidewalk. My visitor eyed me fiercely and, before I could speak, reclaimed his card, which he put away in the inside pocket of his coat as if he were afraid I might steal it. For something to say, I proposed a drink. It was refused with a gesture which implied that if I thought that Cyprien Couteau was the kind of ordinary police officer who could be suborned by a vermouth-cassis, I was making a big mistake. This was followed by a pause and evident disappointment that I did not press the invitation. But I played dumb and allowed Cyprien to embark on his routine cross-examination of foreigners before suggesting that if he would not drink, I would.

Cyprien shrugged his shoulders. Well, perhaps he would take a little something. It was a hot day, and—

I called the waiter, who evidently knew the tastes of the Commissary of Police. He returned almost at once with that sickly drink of Algeria, anisette, a kind of bastard absinthe which has all its faults and none of its qualities. This did not seem to worry Cyprien, and in an incredibly short time the "little something" had become the best part of a bottle.

As the milky, nauseous liquor warmed the blood of the police officer, it became obvious that he did not care two hoots what I was doing in a Sahara oasis. All that he wanted was to talk to someone fresh from Europe. I gave him every opportunity. By the time he left me, I had become his dear friend, his *"cher Monsieur et ami"* (with tears in the eyes), to whom he could never be adequately grateful.

Like all Frenchmen of his class, Cyprien Couteau was wretched in this Sahara outpost. For many happy years he had been a contented policeman in a small town on the Somme. He had had little to do and could indulge his favorite sport—*pêche à la ligne*. I could see him sitting under a bridge, his tunic unbuttoned, a box of worms beside him, a pipe in his mouth, his eyes fixed on a bobbing float. And then, suddenly, this metamorphosis, this transplantation from the lush greenery of the Somme valley, with its meadows and streams, to the waterless, blinking wastes of the Sahara. What had brought it about?

"Ambition, Monsieur, foolish ambition! —And a woman!" Cyprien's voice was strained. "I loved, Monsieur. I loved the young lady who kept the baker's shop in the village. She was a widow, good-looking and with a little money. For me she had a certain affection, but she could not marry an ordinary *sergeant de ville*. My case seemed hopeless until, by some devil-sent mischance," Cyprien groaned, "I heard that an examination would be held for a police commissariat in North Africa. I applied. I was selected. I was appointed to this sacred city of perdition. I came here eagerly to make a home for my bride-to-be. But when I wrote and told her that my post was in the desert, she refused to join me." Cyprien swallowed half a tumbler of anisette. "I have heard since that she married the son of the *juge de paix*." The sigh which came from the soup-stained chest of the little man seemed to draw back the curtain on this village drama. The picture was as vivid as Couteau himself. But before I could say anything, he went on. "Monsieur," he said dramatically, "I am a very unhappy man. I have no wife, and I have not even the compensation of the *pêche à la ligne!*"

He tipped his battered derby hat and faded into the sun-drenched street.

But if the *Commissaire de Police* was not professionally interested in me, the French officers in charge of the administration were. Of all the suspicious busybodies I have ever encountered, these were the worst. Without hesitation they made up their minds that I had been sent to the Sahara to spy. Questions of what I could find out about a waterless desert half the size of the United States, or what use any foreign power could make of my information, did not bother them. I was a spy, and that was all there was to it. —It took them several years to convince themselves that I was only mentally deranged!

With the exception of a few old Sahara hands who had got the desert into their blood, the majority of the French officers had the same attitude to this life of exile as Cyprien Couteau. They could not understand how a man like myself who had the choice of the world to live in should choose the Sahara and, having chosen it, add to its numerous inconveniences and discomforts by making his home in an Arab tent. I never spoke to one of these soldiers who was not counting the days when his leave would come round or he could retire and *pêche à la ligne* in some dreary provincial town in France. The vast majesty of the Sahara, the exhilarating desert air, the magnificence of the starlit nights, the rustle of the wind in the palm trees, the scent of the orange blossoms in the oasis made no impression. A café, a local paper, a little money, and plenty of *pêche à la ligne* were worth a million desert nights.

I was standing one evening on my rock above the desert watching one of those orange sunsets which belong to the Sahara. The whole country seemed to be clothed in a mantle of gold dust. The local military doctor, a big-bellied, red-faced, anisette-saturated creature, sat on a boulder near by smoking an evil-smelling French cigar. His being there was spoiling the fairy-land picture at my feet. Nevertheless, it seemed impossible that anyone could remain unimpressed by such beauty. But all the man said, when I suggested that we were looking at loveliness unique in the world was:

"Perhaps? But how much better the view from my window at Dijon."

I saw little of these soldiers. Soon they passed completely out of my life and, in so doing, inadvertently opened me the door to the nomad's home.

As I should have appreciated, every Arab, with perhaps the exception of the Bash Agha, who was above gossip, was intrigued by my arrival. Their interest increased when Mohammed and Atalla repeated what I had said about living in the desert. The first reaction was astonishment; the second, suspicion. The younger Arabs scoffed. The older shook their heads and wagged their beards. I was no Briton, or if I was, not an honest one. I was a spy, an *agent provocateur* sent by the French government to see what the Sahara Arabs were up to. It was as clear as day! —Luckily not clear to me, as, had I known what was passing through the

Arab minds, I might have packed up and gone to the South Sea Islands. But I did not know, and one day when I was walking in the oasis with Mohammed ben Tahar, I complained of the stupidity of the French military. Mohammed become alert and asked for an explanation. I gave it him. Two weeks later, I was asked to dine with the agha Daylis.

Although a nomad by birth, Daylis had a house in a kind of oasis suburb. He had not deserted the Sahara life; but he had married a city girl whose father farmed in the North, and it would have been impossible to break her to the wanderer's existence. Being rich, and rather inclined to comfort himself, Daylis kept a desert and a "city" establishment, and divided his time between the two families. He was a jovial little man with a fair, pointed beard like George V and twinkling blue eyes. He was admirable company, and the lighter side of my Arab life took place with him.

The dinner was a fine one, with all the princely dishes, including the lamb roast whole, reserved for honored guests. And honored I was, for not only was I fed the animal's testicles as a cocktail but, at the moment of serving the lamb, Daylis plunged his hand into the carcass and handed me a steaming kidney. His son, the sheik Marhoun, offered me the animal's bleery eye!

Men only, of course, were present, and after the meal we sat on cushions and drank coffee and passed the time of day. It all seemed quite informal, but I felt that I was being studied, analyzed, judged. This was not done rudely. There was dignity; there was tact and courtesy; there was infinite charm in the way I was treated. I felt the same warm feeling toward these desert men sipping their coffee as I had toward Atalla in his fake harem. I understood all that Lawrence had meant when he used to speak of his affection for the Arab people. The drugging peace of mind which is bred between human beings who think alike was slowly seeping through me. It enveloped me in a kind of magic web. Soon I had the impression that my hosts felt as I did. They had gauged my worth and passed me as worthy to sit with them on a level of equality.

One of the chiefs especially attracted me. He did not wear the party robes which the others had put on in my honor. His burnous was of coarse camel hair. His turban might have been a shepherd's. But his deep blue eyes were noble and looked at me with friendly sincerity. His pink cheeks and flaming red hair and heavy moustache (he had no beard), made him look more like a Scotch gamekeeper than an Arab nomad. I liked him, and I knew he liked me.

While some of my hosts dozed and others played dominoes on the floor, the caid Madani and I talked. His French was excellent, and I learned that he had fought through the war as an officer in a cavalry regiment in France. We discussed sheep raising in the desert, and I told him about the huge flocks in Australia. He was essentially sheep-minded and warmed up as I showed interest in his pet subject. But he was taken aback when I suggested that I would like to take up sheep farming myself in the Sahara.

"But no Roumi has ever tried this!" he exclaimed.

I replied, "All the more reason why one of us should make a start."

"But you are not a nomad," he protested. "How can you take up something about which you know nothing?"

I shrugged. "A man can do anything if he wants to enough."

This platitude seemed to interest Madani. He pushed his turban onto the back of his head and eyed me thoughtfully for a moment. A smile gradually spread over his red face. He held out his hand and said,

"In sha Allah!" (If God wills it!)

In this way our partnership was formed. The word of the Arab chief would be sufficient guarantee; the handclasp had sealed the deal. There was no point in drawing up Occidental contracts which would be no more binding, probably less so. I smiled and felt elated.

But though I had taken a step forward toward my objective, it was only a step: an investment in sheep, made by me, which Madani would look after. That was all. I was no more a nomad than Cyprien Couteau. Still, I must not complain. I had now direct contact with the desert people, which had seemed impossible at first. And with this contact many barriers were lifted. If I was not a nomad, I was a business associate of one.

From being asked to dine formally, I was advanced to being told to drop in when I pleased. Sometimes I was given the place of honor, sometimes I was not. But whether I was sitting with the elders or with the juniors, conversation went on as if I was part of the family. I was lent horses and taken out hunting. I was initiated into the mysteries of falconry and often spent several days in Madani's camp. I was still under observation, and some of the more anti-Occidental chiefs held aloof; but gradually even they admitted that I seemed a friendly sort of fellow who knew how to behave.

As the envelopes of reserve fell apart, I discovered what real men these Arabs were. Their splendid dignity was not put on; it was the breeding of generations. They were proud, but not arrogant. They had a high opinion of Arab culture, but did not despise other races and faiths. They had the manners of great gentlemen. In fact, they *were* great gentlemen, old-fashioned country gentlemen to whom honor and a thoroughbred horse meant more than wealth. But above all, they had infinite kindness and charity. There was none of the business rivalry of Occidentals, where friend tries to outwit friend in the struggle for position or money. Each one worked for a common cause—the tribe, the Arab, Islam. In bad years they helped each other. When times were good, they rejoiced together, sharing the dangers and delights of that wanton creature, the Sahara Desert, courting her, fighting her, subduing her.

Gradually I began to think as they did. I learned to believe in the fatalistic outlook of these wanderers of the south who have always lived face to face with nature, who are born and married and finally buried in the desert; and I wondered how I had ever bothered to wage the uneven battle at home. My new life was never monotonous, and I easily became accustomed to never seeing a newspaper or knowing who governed the land in England or America. It did not seem to matter.

But even with this way of thinking, I was still not a nomad. My intimacy with Madani and the others went to a certain point, and stopped. Three things held me to my Occidental past: my clothes; my language; and my faith, or lack of it.

A man in European dress in the desert looks out of place, and is. From his hat which blows away and gets him a sunstroke, to his boots which he cannot slip off when he goes into a carpeted tent, he is all wrong.

The Arab's outfit, on the other hand, is adapted to desert wear. His jacket, plain or embroidered, has large pockets in which he can carry all the odds and ends which an Occidental puts in a suitcase. Baggy trousers enable the wearer to walk or squat or ride without getting them rumpled or creased. Covering the legs are long soleless boots; in reality, strong leather stockings. On the feet, for riding or walking, thick-soled slippers. The man has thus a combined riding boot and walking shoe, the latter being easy to slip off when he prays or goes into a tent or mosque.

On the head is the turban, which is made up of three separate pieces. The gannoure, a high framework made of felt on which is placed the white linen shesh which covers it, surrounds the face and neck and is tucked away inside the coat. To keep the shesh in place, strands of camel-hair cords are wound around the gannoure. These are called kheite. The kheite serve two practical purposes: the first, to protect the head from the sun, as does the puggree on the sola topee; the second, that of an emergency rope to let a bucket down into a desert well when, as is usually the case, there is no rope available at the water point. The kheite of Arab chiefs in ceremonial dress is often of silk interwoven with strands of silver or gold.

Over the coat and trousers is worn a long white robe made of wool, or sometimes of silk, called a gandoura. The costume is completed by the two burnouses.

These are hooded cloaks worn one on top of the other and reaching from the shoulders to the feet. The under burnous is made of white wool; for city dwellers, of silk. The outer burnous is of woven camel and goat's hair. It is impermeable to rain, and the best possible protection to the winter wind. When the sandstorm rages, the Arab pulls his shesh up over his nose, wraps his burnous around him, draws the hood over his turban, and is completely protected.

Dressy Arabs may have a selection of cloth burnouses stored away in the oasis for when they pay a visit to Algiers. These can be of different shades, light blue, green, black, plum-colored, anything but scarlet. The scarlet burnous embroidered with gold lace is the insignia of chieftainship; it can be worn only by the chiefs and, usually, only on official occasions.

On principle, however, the Arab has only the clothes on his back. He has no encumbering baggage, and what he cannot carry on his horse, he leaves behind. The outfit does not vary in summer or winter. As the weather gets hot, one burnous is discarded and laid across the saddle, then a second. At sunset one or both burnouses are put on again. At night the Arab rolls himself up in them to sleep.

It was not difficult for me to discard my unsuitable European clothes and dress like an Arab. It was comparatively simple for me to learn the desert dialect which the shepherds spoke. The first two steps toward nomadization presented no real obstacle. The third was not so easy.

CHAPTER V

MANY CHRISTIANS HAVE AN IDEA that Moslems are heathens.

An educated New York woman once said to me: "But the Arabs worship Allah!"—as she might have said Baal or Amun Ra. When I pointed out that Allah was the Arabic for God, like Jehovah or Dieu, she showed surprise. I am sure she did not believe me.

An American of standing, speaking at a dinner after a hurricane trip around the world, told of a reception in Baghdad where his Moslem hosts had shown their appreciation of his visit by foregoing their principles about touching liquor. This seemed to please the speaker, and he talked glowingly of progressive Americanism breaking down "age-worn priestcraft," as it might primitive idolatry! Like so many others, he was evidently unaware that the Moslem faith is six hundred years younger than the Christian and is one of the few religions where there are no priests.

During a lecture tour of California, I let myself in to preach in a church.

A minister of a dissenting sect had heard me give a talk on the Arabs and asked me if I would do the same for his flock. I did not like working on Sundays, so I quickly made the excuse that I was a Moslem. The minister replied at once that this did not matter. His congregation would love to hear about Islam. There was nothing I could do, therefore, but give my sermon. This I did with the eloquence of Mohammed on his camel outside Medina.

As I left the pulpit, one of the church officials, a well-to-do small-business executive type, thanked me. In conclusion he said:

"Some guy, that Mohammed!" He smiled. "Who was he any-way?"

I tried to think of a quick explanation, but all I could say was,

"Oh, some guy." And then I thought. "That isn't as silly as it sounds. That's all Mohammed was. A man."—A man like you or me or him, only with more imagination and character and courage. A man who had a message to give his people and preached it so well that within eighty years of his death, his followers had spread over the whole of western Asia as far as Afghanistan, and across North Africa to the Atlantic, and on into Spain. A few more years and they had made their way to China, to Malaya and the Dutch Indies. They had established themselves in equatorial Africa. But though these new adherents to Islam sometimes called themselves Mohammedans, they did not worship Mohammed. They do not do so now. The idea that Moslems regard Mohammed as a god, or in the way that Christians do Jesus, is inexact.

Mohammed never suggested that he was of divine origin, and claimed no relationship to Allah. He was just an Arab with ideas and, when he died, was buried like any other Arab. His bones lie today in their tomb at Medina, and at Gabriel's last trump he will be judged by God like any other poor guys who have died since the world began. According to the standards of some of his puritan descendants, he may even be judged severely. But perhaps he won't. He had so many fine characteristics. As an administrator, general, theologian, lawmaker, he was centuries before his time. It is true that the faith which he devised has caused almost as much trouble in the world as the Christian, but without his being any more responsible than was Jesus for the things done in *His* name. Both men believed in their missions, but with no idea of the repercussions they would cause.

It seems certain that when Mohammed founded the tiny state around Medina in 622 A.D., he had no conception of how his words would spread. He would have scoffed if anyone had told him that, in thirteen hundred years, two hundred and seventy-five million people would be members of the religion named after him. Why, two hundred and seventy-five million people were outside the scope of his imagination! States within the Arabian peninsular and on its borders were about all the world he knew. The principles of Islam reflect this; they were worked out for men and women living in predominantly desert countries.

Take, for example, the removal of shoes, not of the headdress, on going into a mosque or holy place. An Arab turban *cannot* be taken off like a hat, while the slipper without laces comes off easily. The floor of the mosque is sacred ground and must not be dirtied. But whether the ground is sacred or not, the Arab always sheds his slippers on entering his tent or his home. He wishes to protect his carpets on which he sits and sleeps.

Making almsgiving part of the creed would very likely not have occurred to a man living in a town among sedentary people. But it was difficult to levy taxes from wandering tribes which came and went with the seasons. So the payment of a percentage on property, or income, toward the maintenance of the faith became a religious observance. In the same way the wealthy sheep raiser was told to look after the poorer nomad, so that today, among law-abiding Arabs, there is none of the destitution seen in many other communities. That is why begging is tolerated among Moslems. It is the duty of the fortunate to care for the unfortunate.

Mohammed was not, like Jesus, celibate. He was a fine-looking man and liked women as any other normal healthy adult. His first marriage to the wealthy Khadija had been happy, and some years after her death he married again. Realistically he recognized that the average male was not satisfied with one female. But he was against prostitution and the indiscriminate polygamy which was prevalent in Arabia. So he compromised. A Moslem would be restricted to three legal wives and, under certain circumstances, concubines. Respectable Mohammedan homes were the result.

But he did not stop there. He was man of the world enough to know that being married did not necessarily lead to happiness. So he revised the existing laws for divorce and made the grounds not too complicated.

Eating pork was banned because the pig in the Orient is an even fouler feeder than in the Occident. The Arabs did not know how to cure the meat and might not even cook it properly.

"Prohibition" was ordered on account of the weakness of the Arab for a raw spirit made from the fermented sap of the date palm, known in Sahara oases as lagmi. It is extremely potent and especially bad for men who live in hot countries. Had Arabia been a wine country this ban on drinking could not have been imposed.

An Arab with whom I was discussing the origins of the drink question gave me this story as a version:

In the early days of Islam two pagans got hold of a Moslem convert and said they would kill him unless he did one of two things: drink a bottle of the palm liquor, or kill the local holy man. The Moslem accepted what he thought was the lesser of the two evils and drank the liquor; with the result that he also murdered the holy man!

The Moslem prayer is a mild setting-up exercise. The bowing, the bending, the kneeling are not unlike what we should do daily before breakfast. Mohammed suspected that many Arabs were lazy, mentally and physically, so he gave them something to remind them of their religion five times a day. In order to make them get up early, the first prayer was ordained before sunrise. At noon a praying session curtailed a too-long siesta. The last three prayers, midafternoon, sunset, and two hours after sunset, prevented lingering over huge meals or going to sleep on a heavy stomach.

The idolators of Arabia, whom Mohammed converted to Islam, were dirty; so they were told to wash before saying their prayers. As there was not much water in the desert, they were informed that they could perform their ablutions with sand, the next best cleanser.

Mohammed knew that two great religions had preceded him and there could be no question of his ignoring them. He had heard stories from the Old Testament of the Jews and the New Testament of the Christians. He found that the legend of the creation, the tales of Moses' adventures, of the patriarchs and the early kings, made inspiring reading. So did much of the teaching of Jesus. At the same time, there were a good many things which took a lot of accepting, and others which had become the basis of controversy. The last thing Mohammed wanted to do in this new venture was to have issues which were hard to believe or could start arguments. So he began to sift the older scriptures.

One of the first things he appreciated was the bad influence which priestcraft could develop. So he decided to have no Moslem priests.

There are Mohammedan religious teachers and preachers and Mosque officials. There are seminaries where students are trained in Moslem theology. There are men who become saints by holiness.

But there are no priests, in the Protestant or Catholic sense, who are intermediaries between the believer and his God.

A Moslem is in direct relationship with Allah, and his actions are left a good deal to his conscience. For example, there is no obligation for him to set foot in a mosque. Many of my nomad shepherds had never been inside one. Yet they were as good Moslems as those who spent half the day listening to the expounding of the Law.

Mohammed realized that it would be false pride to ignore the holy men who had preached before him. They were too big to belittle, and keeping them in his religion might bring him Jewish and Christian adherents. So Moses and Abraham and Jacob remained as major prophets, and Jesus, called Issa, appeared as a divinely sent redeemer but not as the Son of God.

The idea of the Trinity was discarded as too complex for an Arab to work out. Mohammed, however, admitted the Virgin birth but denounced the possible fatherhood by God as blasphemy. Over the crucifixion and resurrection, he compromised.

He decided that though Issa was not a god, neither was he an ordinary man who could be put to death with criminals. It did not make sense to an Arab way of thinking. He therefore allowed everything to take place up to the moment when Jesus was hoisted on the cross. Then God intervened and removed the man who was ready to die for an idea and took him straight to heaven, leaving a shadow in his place. In this Mohammed seems to have failed in his usual astuteness. His version of the story is less simple than that of the New Testament.

However, the important thing to remember is that Mohammed, far from being a pagan repudiator of Jesus, placed him on a higher spiritual level than himself. In his tomb chamber in the mosque at Medina, he had an extra grave dug for Jesus when he returns to earth to die and be buried. He will thus be able to rise with Mohammed and be judged with him. The only little touch of self-importance was to proclaim himself the last of the great prophets.

According to him, God gave the world three revelations and with each one sent his personal delegate: Moses, Jesus, Mohammed. From Judaism evolved Christianity; from Christianity, Islam, or it should have according to the rules. God also gave the world three books. To the Jews, the Law; to the Christians, the Gospels; to the Moslems, the Koran. This was the final book and different from the others in that it was authored directly by God. For Moslems, Mohammed has not that relationship to the Koran which for Jews the prophets have to the Old Testament and, for Christians, the Gospel writers and Saint Paul have to the New Testament.

Mohammed took several other ideas from these preceding monotheistic faiths and modified them to suit his people; among others, fasting, heaven, and hell.

At death the body again becomes dust, while the soul sinks into a state of unconsciousness until Gabriel sounds the last trump for God's judgment. Then the good will go to Paradise and the wicked to hell. Rather unfairly, among the latter are all those who do not believe in Islam, regardless of how they lived.

I discussed this one day with an Arab, citing a man we knew who was a practicing Moslem but a bad lot, and Père David, Superior of the Order of the White Fathers.

"Which of them will go to hell?" I asked.

"Both, probably," replied the Arab without hesitation.

"But the *père* David has spent the whole of his life doing good, and Belkacem has never been anything but a scoundrel."

"I know, but the *père* David does not believe in Islam, and without Islam you cannot make Paradise."

I shrugged. "And the *père* David says you cannot make it without his brand of Christianity."

"The *père* David is wrong."

And there the argument ended, whether I was talking to the Moslem or the Christian. It seemed a great pity.

Mohammed did not copy his Paradise from the Old or New Testaments. He invented a more pleasing and believable prospect than the rather disembodied Christian conception of heaven: gardens, orchards, fountains, rivers, wines which exhilarate and do not intoxicate, lovely unveiled girls to whom one is spiritually wedded; in fact, all those things which an Arab never found in the desert.

The Moslem fasting is based on the same idea as in all religions and is more irksome. During the lunar month of Ramadan a Moslem may not smoke or eat or drink from two hours before dawn until sunset. When, owing to the varying of the lunar calendar, Ramadan falls in midsummer, this is a great hardship. There is no question of lying in bed. All daily duties are carried out as during other periods of the year, and the suffering from thirst can become almost unbearable.

The pilgrimage to Mecca is part of the creed, but for practical reasons is compulsory without being so. Every good Moslem should go and would like to have the right to the title El Hadj. But not everyone can afford to. Foreseeing, therefore, the problem which would arise if the visit to Mecca were conditional to salvation, Mohammed ordained that only those should travel there who could support themselves during the journey and their families while away. For the faithful in Java or South Africa or Afghanistan this presents quite a problem.

That, sketchily, is the basis of Islam as taught in its early days and still practiced by all orthodox Moslems. Many dissents have crept in, and from the two main sects, Sunnis and Shiahs, seventy-two subsects have come into being. It is much the same story as with the Christian religion. What Jesus and Saint Paul preached has been corrupted into anything from the splendors of the Roman Catholics to the fanaticisms of the Holy Rollers. In fact the Moslem dissenters are less divergent from the orthodox than are Christians of the same categories.

At my period of initiation into Arab lore I did not know all this, and whether I was Sunni or Shiah or Kharedjite was not my problem. What I wanted to find out was whether I could live with the Arabs and be outside their faith? It did not look too easy.

To the majority of Christians religion is centered in a church and a minister. Few people believe Protestants who say that they do their worshiping at home. For the Catholics it is a mortal sin to miss Mass on Sundays or on Holy Days of Obligation. With the Moslems it is just the reverse. No one is forced to go to the mosque, and a great many Mohammedans have never taken part in the general prayer recited under the leadership of the Imam. Islam means a complete surrender to God's will and has its place in every phase of a Moslem's daily life. The prayers five times a day, the abstention from pork flesh and liquor, the fast of Ramadan, the giving of alms, the call of the muezzin—"La ilaha, illa Allah;

41

Mohammed rasul Allah!" (There is but one God and Mohammed is his prophet!)—are all part and parcel of the twenty-four hours. If I went and lived among the Arabs and sat around while they prayed and fasted, or cooked myself a dish of ham and eggs, or did not give part of my earnings to charity, I might just as well share a house with Cyprien Couteau.

It was not a matter, either, of repudiating my religion. I had been raised in the Church of England by parents whose families for generations had ordered their lives by King James's Prayer Book and Hymns Ancient and Modern. That did not, however, prevent me from realizing that the difference between what the Dean of Canterbury and the father of Mohammed ben Tahar thought about God was really only detail. A good Unitarian might be horrified if he were told that his creed and the bash agha Jelloul's were half-brothers. But it would be none the less true. It was not dogma which bothered me. It was more a question of conscience.

As a Christian by tradition and habit I had gone through all the motions which my creed demanded, from baptism to communion. That I believed in very little of what I had been taught did not worry me or make me feel ill at ease among my own people, because most of them thought as I did. But with the Arabs it would be quite different. Ninety-nine per cent believed implicitly in all they had learned from the taleb. Ninety per cent practiced their faith conscientiously. During the fast of Ramadan, when anyone could slip away and eat a date or drink a cup of water without being caught, no one did. A few took liquor when they went to Algiers or Europe, but they were in a minority. For these desert people religion was paramount. I would have to make it seem paramount to me, or try to. It began to look as if I should have to cut out all idea of Islamization or else compromise with myself. Then, without any effort on my part, the solution came unexpectedly.

With a sensation akin to ecstasy, I discovered that it was less difficult to be sincere here than at home. I found I could not be a complete agnostic in the desert. I felt obliged to put my faith in something more reliable than man. In Europe or America there were telephones, radios, something alive within reach which could be summoned. But in the Sahara there was nothing like that. The

Arabs, I know, felt it; and that is one reason, I am sure, why they never omitted their prayers. It gave them a kind of anchor, a sense of security, a sensation of being protected by something real and reliable. I have never been so conscious of religion as during those years in the desert. I have never felt more convinced that human beings were not created by accident and for no purpose.

I do not know what the Arabs thought of my turning toward Islam, or whether they thought anything. It was never mentioned, and I was never initiated. I initiated myself.

I bought a translation of the Koran and read it with delight. I got Mohammed ben Tahar to explain the ins and outs of the faith, and found there were no ins and outs. It was as simple as I have written it in this chapter. I discussed the whole matter with Madani and watched him and the shepherds when they prayed. I think it was this praying, or its effect on the worshipers, which influenced me most.

In the midst of their daily duties these men would turn aside, slip off their shoes, and face the East. Stooping, they touched the ground with the palms of their hands, then passed them over their arms and faces as if they were washing. After a moment to compose themselves, the prayer began. At first standing, then sitting, then dipping their foreheads in the dust. For a while they sat, and once more stood, till finally they sat again. Turning their heads to the right and to the left, they said: "The blessing of God and His mercy be on thee." These words were addressed to the two guardian angels who accompany Mohammedans on earth, the angel to the right noting the good actions, the angel to the left recording the bad. After that, the praying gradually died away and there was silence. The bodies relaxed. The eyes became calm. All worldly thoughts seemed to be forgotten....

In a few minutes they rose and went back to their occupations. There was no self-consciousness of men smugly satisfied at having done their duty, but there was unmistakable serenity. It was almost breathtaking, and I had a sensation coming at me from all directions that there must be something tremendous in this faith to give such peace of mind.

Soon I learned the prayers myself and repeated them with my companions. They were not really prayers such as Christians

43

employ, asking of God benefits for themselves and their kind. They were rather psalms of praise.

The Arab is confident that God knows he is there and will look after him. He believes also that his life is foreordained; so, apart from the impertinence of imagining that God does not know what is best for His people, there is no point in bothering heaven with personal requests.

One night, after the evening prayer, Madani gave me his rosary. I slipped it over my turban and felt the wooden beads against my neck. . . . "Ani M'slim!" I whispered. "I am a Moslem!" . . . That is as near as I got to public profession of faith. Whether I was a Moslem, I never asked. I don't know to this day.

CHAPTER VI

MEANWHILE, MY RELATIONSHIP with the desert people was changing completely. My giving up tweeds and flannels for turbans and burnouses had led to a lot of discussion and good-natured teasing from my new friends. There was no question of my trying to pass for an Arab, or any other fancy scheme. No Occidental has ever passed for an Oriental among Orientals, not even Lawrence. My only idea was to be comfortable.

When it finally came to the actual choosing of my wardrobe, the Arabs behaved like a lot of girls helping a bride buy her trousseau. Madani was set on my getting the roughest ready-made kit. Daylis recommended the best tailor in the oasis. The Bash Agha wanted me to have my clothes woven in the desert. I forget how I managed to please everyone; but one day, there I was in the arcaded street, where I had walked so disconsolately the first day, in full Arab regalia. Turban, camel-hair burnous, wool burnous, gandoura, embroidered riding boots, and an elegant pair of olive green pantaloons made by Daylis' tailor. I felt like something out of the Arabian Nights, and swooped around like a proud peacock.

Mohammed ben Tahar and black Blanchet stared at me with unbelieving wonder. Atalla, in his velvet fez, pranced up and down clapping his cotton-gloved hands. I felt elated, too, but sufficiently self-conscious to appreciate that I must now make my permanent home in the camp. My new outfit was quite unsuited for the anisette-perfumed hotel. Besides, I could not bear the worried expression of Monsieur Paoli the second morning I appeared for lunch in robes, and he realized that I was not dressed like that for fun. And when I assured Cyprien Couteau that my new clothes had nothing to do with Mardi Gras, he looked as pained as when he had bemoaned his banishment from *pêche à la ligne*.

These Frenchmen were baffled. That I, who was free to live where I pleased, should come to the Sahara at all, passed the bounds of human comprehension. That I should actually go and live on its blinking wastes in a burnous and a gandoura was plum crazy.

And I did not care what they or anyone else thought. I felt free, relieved, like Christian when the load fell from his back at the end of his pilgrimage. I was getting away from all the complexes and inhibitions which had torn me to pieces for so long. I was getting away from hypocrisy. I was getting away from my false self.

Ever since I could remember, I had been trying to do this. At Eton, in the army, everywhere I had been, I had wanted to escape from people who only thought of custom and convention. It was like fresh air to find myself on the road which led away from all that nonsense.

But if Paoli and Couteau were grieved, the shepherds were delighted. I had already started to learn their dialect. Now that I wore their clothes and began to say a few words to them, they turned their minds inside out to grasp my meaning. Madani watched without comment; but when he saw that I was really feeling my feet and slipping into this nomads' life without effort, he made preparations to establish me in a camp of my own.

Up to that time the sheep I had bought had run with Madani's flocks under his shepherds. Now they were separated and placed in charge of men who would be responsible to me and paid by me. Madani still supervised, but I was the boss in my own sphere and had an executive's tent. From now on, this tent would be my home, the desert my country.

One of the hardest things for an Occidental to grasp is that the nomad's only home is his tent. Many Americans and Europeans have been on camping expeditions in various degrees of luxury. For days or weeks, sometimes for months, they have lived under canvas. They have experienced that gorgeous sensation of stepping from their beds onto the plain or into the forest. A few have really enjoyed the carefree, healthy existence in the open, but even these have had at the backs of their minds the comforting thought of one day returning to beds and baths and foods served on proper

46

tables. They have put up with insects and heat and damp, feeling that it would make them so much more appreciate the joys of civilization. Even the camps have had many amenities. Servants, camp beds, rubber baths, canned food to supplement the pot, mosquito nets, stoves, electric lamps, plates, knives, forks, mugs, and jugs; and always that thought of the linen and glass and silver at home.

But for the nomad there were none of these luxuries, none of these visions of a higher degree of comfort. The men with whom I now lived had been born on that desert. They had never slept in a bed or sat in a chair or eaten off a plate or used a knife and fork. The only home they knew was their tent, the only food desert food, the only eating implement their fingers, the only resting place the hard Sahara earth. The only service they had experienced was in the cooking of their meals by their women. No one waited on them, were they shepherds or chiefs.

They washed themselves a little when they came to a water hole or when it rained. Otherwise, they cleansed themselves with sand. The only complete baths they ever took were on the rare occasions when they visited oases and could go to the hammam. Yet they never smelled dirty or were, in fact, dirty. Nature kept them clean. The eternal sand-charged wind of the Sahara scoured their skins and kept them as polished as the naked desert rocks.

The tents in which my nomads lived, in which I now lived, have nothing in common with those used by Occidentals, whether soldiers or hunters. They are nothing remotely like the pavilions of motion-picture sheiks. They consist of a kind of very large black-and-tan-striped blanket made of closely woven camel and goat's hair. The blanket is stretched over posts and pegged down on three sides, the fourth left open. It is really a kind of awning. On the floor are thick carpets and hard headrests stuffed tightly with grain. The Arabs call them cushions! For the married, the tent is divided by another blanket. The man occupies one side; the wife, or wives, and the children, the other.

My own camp consisted of eight tents in which fifty men, women, and children made their homes. It was typical of an average community of nomads. The only people responsible to me, and whom I paid, were six shepherds and a head shepherd.

The name of my head shepherd was Ali. He was slender and

47.

of medium height. His hair was straight, his features regular, his nose aquiline. A black beard covered much of his deeply tanned face. In spite of constant hard work his hands were small and beautifully shaped. There is no race which has such consistently beautiful hands as the Arabs. Ali had been born and brought up on the desert. He took his religion even more seriously than most nomads and had, I am sure, never sinned. He dressed much as Madani and I did, but in place of our embroidered riding boots he wore a curious footgear made of camel leather which came halfway up his calf and was soled with rubber from a discarded tire. The soling of nomad's shoes created quite a business, in the desert markets, for old tires.

The other forty-three persons in the camp were the shepherds' families who tagged along with us. Though they were not in my employ, they worked for me and lived on me. The women and the girls cooked for the camp, milked the goats and the ewes, made butter, wove carpets and tents. The youngsters helped look after the sheep and drove the pack animals when the caravan moved. In return for this help they fed at my expense. It was an admirable system and never let me down.

As long as there was enough for our flocks to graze on in the neighborhood, we remained camped in the same place. It might be a day, it might be a week or more. It depended entirely on the weather and the kind of year we were having. In periods of drought we would probably never halt for more than twenty-four to forty-eight hours. But at no time was there ever any question of our remaining in the same area for a year or even a season. We were nomads, following the pastures, following the sun.

When we moved, the tent posts were pulled up and rolled in the blankets, and the bundles placed on the backs of camels or donkeys.

> And the air shall be filled with music,
> And the cares which infest the day
> Will fold their tents like the Arabs
> And silently steal away.

I don't know about the music, but the breaking of camp was smooth and rapid and without fuss. These people had been born on the caravan trails, and each one did his bit instinctively.

The camels also carried the older women and younger children in bassours. The bassour is a kind of palanquin consisting of a framework of wicker hoops covered with drapery. The women and children squat in hammock-like bags which hang on either side of the camel's hump. Occidental women who have used this means of transportation in the desert have told me that the swaying motion often made them seasick.

The Sahara camel is the one-humped dromedary and is used almost exclusively for transport. A young camel in good condition will carry as much as a thousand pounds for an entire day without tiring. To use a camel for riding only, where a horse could serve, would therefore be as wasteful as using a truck in a motorcycle's place. The Mehari, or trotting camel, employed specially for riding, is rarely seen except when one comes across the French Camel Corps, or in the country of the veiled Touaregs.

The camel is not indigenous to North Africa. It did not make its appearance there until after the end of the Roman rule. It came with the Arab invaders. Before this time, oxen and elephants were used for transport. It was the camel that made the invasion by the Arabs possible. Without this creature they could never have crossed the tracts of sand desert separating the Sahara from Arabia.

In some ways the camel has less endurance than the horse and is much more unreliable. He will fill the chambers of the walls of his stomach with water and live on this reserve as long as a week. He will eat sharp-thorned acacias, prickly ground plants, anything he can get, and then, all of a sudden, crack up. When a camel cracks up, there is nothing to be done about it. He just collapses and dies. The expression "the straw that broke the camel's back" does not really refer to the weight of the load. It alludes to this sudden end to endurance.

Nevertheless, the camel *is* enduring. He will do incredibly long marches in terrific heat, he will feed off sticks and date stones, he will go for days without water; but when his own supply runs out and cannot be replenished, he is out. The horse, on the other hand, cannot go as long without water, but he will struggle on and make a great fight before falling by the roadside.

The camel is a treacherous, bad-tempered creature, with affection for no one. He is always waiting to bite the man who looks after him. He is as revengeful as the elephant and will kill anyone who has ill treated him, if he gets the chance. This he does by catching the victim with his hideous teeth, flinging him on the ground, and then battering him to pulp with a kind of pad which grows between his front legs on the breastbone. If a load is badly tied, he will wait till the whole caravan is on the move to throw it. If not watched, he will overeat and give himself such bloat that he is out of commission for days. The Arabs say that when a camel suddenly decides to die on the line of march, he does it from spite.

But, if the camel has these unpleasant characteristics, he serves in many ways which he is powerless to begrudge. When he dies, he is eaten. The flesh is strong-tasting, stringy, and tough, but makes a meal if one has good teeth. Camel's milk is a delicacy, and as a last resource the Arabs will drink the sour fluid secreted in the animal's stomach. On cold mornings they wash their hands and warm them in camel's urine. The women like its aromatic odor and use it to dress their hair. It is also a germicide and death to parasites. The wool of the camel is woven into material for tents and clothes. Its dung provides fuel for fires, and its hide is eventually cut up for water bags, belts, and sandals. The Arabs have a kind of riddle: "What is Allah's greatest gift to man?" The answer is not woman, or Life, or Soul, or Mohammed or the Koran, but the camel! "For," say they, "if there were no camels in the desert, there would be no food, no tents, no nothing. In fact, if there were no camels, there would be no men!"

One day I asked if it was this knowledge which made the camel supercilious?

"Oh, no," replied Madani, "that isn't the reason. It's something much deeper. Allah, you see, has one hundred wonderful names, of which we know ninety-nine. Only the camel knows the hundredth."

The camel is not a noble animal, but he is a useful one. Except for the times when he suddenly decides to die, there is only one occasion when he becomes useless, in spite of himself. When it rains. Then, if he is anywhere near mud, his spongy feet slip and slither and he cannot stand up. Sometimes his long legs splay out to such an extent that he splits open. But under normal desert conditions the camel is equipped for all emergencies, even having eyes and nostrils which he can hermetically seal against the sand-storm.

One feature about the camel always intrigued me, and it was not until I lived with the Arabs that I was given an explanation. Zoologists may challenge it, but I will be surprised if they can put forward a more plausible one.

The genital organ of the camel is small, extremely small, quite out of proportion to the animal's size. It is also the wrong way around. That is to say, it points to the rear, between the animal's hind legs, instead of toward the front as with most creatures.

In zoos and menageries throughout the world this phenomenon had left me baffled. Now that I was surrounded day and night by camels, I could not bear the uncertainty any longer. One evening I called Madani's attention to this freak of nature and asked him point-blank if he knew the reason.

"But of course," he replied, as if I had asked him why animals had legs. "I thought everyone knew that!"

I sat up eagerly and shook my head. The enigma of years was at last going to be solved. Madani looked at me delighted. He loved storytelling, and I was supplying him with a brand new audience for his old pieces.

"You have heard, I suppose, of the Great Deluge and of Noah and his Ark?" he suggested, obviously hoping I had not.

I would have liked to please him by saying no, but that would have made me out too big an ignoramus. It was bad enough not knowing about the camel. So I said: "Yes, as a matter of fact, I *have* heard about the Great Flood."

Madani sighed. Then he shrugged his shoulders and began at the beginning of the story as related in the Old Testament. He did not miss a detail. But the way he told it was so picturesque and so obviously believed literally that it sounded almost new. Finally he came to the part about the camel.

"... When all the animals were assembled to go into the Ark, two of each kind, male and female," he said, "Noah's wife turned to her husband, as she stood beside him watching the parade, and said:

" 'What will happen if these creatures start mating in the Ark and, having mated, then produce young? We haven't any idea of how long this flood is going to last.' Noah scratched his head, but before he could reply, Mrs. Noah went on. 'The Ark which you have built is for two of each kind, not five or six, or even three. If there are any additions to our carrying capacity, we shall surely sink.'

"Noah had certainly never thought of this eventuality, so he again scratched his head without replying. Finally he said: 'You are right, Mother; that possibility had not occurred to me. Have you any suggestions?'

"Mrs. Noah was waiting for this; for, being a well-brought-up woman, she could not advise her man unless he asked her to. 'I think,' she replied, 'that the only thing to do is to remove the genitals of the male animals as they file into the Ark and put them away in the cupboard near the door. You can explain that it is only a precautionary measure, like leaving one's hat or coat, and they'll get their things back when the flood is over.'

"Noah, who thought well of his wife's common sense, wasted no time in putting the proposition before the animals. These, too, were reasonable and agreed to this temporary inconvenience...."

Madani drifted into another picturesque description of the Flood, with intimate sketches of life on board, culminating with the Ark coming to rest on Mount Ararat. The moment had come for the explanation, which so far I had failed to find.

"When Noah was satisfied that the flood was really over," Madani went on, "he took his place with Mrs. Noah at the entrance to the Ark. He bade the animals come out quietly and in the same order in which they had gone in. This was of paramount importance, as there had been no time to write proper labels for the precious appendages he had in the cupboard. Their only identification was by numbers, as in a checkroom. But the animals were docile, and until very near the end everything went according to plan.

"The last animal but one in the outgoing procession was the camel. The last was the donkey. The camel is always a slow mover, and was padding disdainfully toward Noah when the donkey lost patience and slipped past. He was so quick that Noah did not notice the mistake until it was too late. By that time there was nothing to be done but give the camel what was left.

"The camel refused it point-blank. Who did Noah think he was, to accept that snippet? He'd never been so insulted in his life! Noah shrugged. He was extremely sorry, couldn't be more so, but there wasn't anything else left. The camel could see for himself. —The camel closed his nostrils and replied that, in that case, he would go without.

"As the hideous meaning of what the camel had said penetrated Noah's mind, his heart jumped a beat.

" 'But that's impossible,' he cried. 'The breed of camels cannot become extinct just because of a little checkroom error!'

"The camel closed his long-lashed eyes. 'But that is exactly what *will* happen unless you return me my property,' he said coldly. 'When you have it, call me. I must be going now; Mrs. Camel is getting restless. Good day! And thank you for nothing!' So saying, he stalked down the gangplank.

"Mr. Noah stared at Mrs. Noah. Mrs. Noah stared at Mr. Noah. Unless something was done quickly, one of the world's greatest catastrophes was about to take place. A piece of God's handiwork was doomed. It was Mrs. Noah who came to her senses first. Seizing the 'snippet' from her husband's trembling hands, she rushed after the camel and, just as he was disappearing down the slopes of Mount Ararat, stuck it on behind!

"... So you see," said Madani conclusively, "the humble donkey has something quite out of proportion to his size, and the disdainful camel has a tiny snippet stuck on behind. You can perhaps understand now why he is such a disagreeable animal. Under the same circumstances, I think you might be?" ...

Of a horse, now, an Arab would tell in a very different key.

To an Arab, a horse means more than his flocks, his rifle, his tent. In fact, without a horse an Arab is nothing. He is like a centaur without hindquarters.

"He who has a brave horse can undertake anything; he is invulnerable," runs an Arab saying. "A man is never truly courageous except on his horse," says another.

An Arab never walks anywhere. He may stroll in a street or go from one oasis garden to another, but he will make no journey, undertake no hunting except on horseback. The high-backed saddle forms a kind of chair, and on this he will sit and doze during the thirty or forty miles he sometimes covers in a day.

Except when hunting, he does not let his mount break out of a walk.

The horse is looked upon as part of the Arab's family. Although it is heavily bitted, the reins are rarely used. It is controlled by the rider's voice.

When the camp or oasis is reached, the horses are unharnessed and allowed to roam free. They will graze around the place and always come when called. When visitors are present, the Arab chieftain does not introduce his family. Moslem etiquette forbids that; but he summons his horses, and they trot gracefully to the guests for a pat or a lump of sugar.

The Arab horse is stockier and more enduring than his kind in Europe or America. This is probably due to the fact that he is not pampered. He is hardly ever clipped and rarely covered with a rug. He lives naturally like any other animal, and except in bad pasture years his feed is little supplemented by grain. This does not detract from his appearance. There are few creatures whose beauty equals that of the steeds of the desert Arabs.

During my wanderings over the world I have ridden all kinds of horses, from Irish hunters to Mongolian ponies, but I have never found any to equal the Arab stallions of the Sahara.

The most worthy of desert transport animals is the humble donkey. (Though after Madani's story not half as humble as I supposed.) He carries loads twice his size; he eats when he can, drinks when he can, rests when he can. He makes no complaints; and when the caravan is getting to the end of a long, hot march, when men and horses and camels are beginning to droop, the little moke is sure to be there plodding along as hardily as at the beginning of the trek. Perhaps it is the idea that he is part camel which gives him this moral uplift?

The Sahara is, I suppose, the only place in the world where four-legged transport still reigns supreme. Although the airplane and automobile have been there for quite a while, they have done little to alter the century-old habits of the Arabs. All the planes and buses and trucks in the world are not going to help nomadic sheep raisers in the pasturing of their flocks. Some of the chiefs have their own cars, but they use them mainly for pleasure trips to Algiers. There are few macadamized roads over the desert and hardly any gas stations. As far as travel and transportation are concerned, the horse, the camel, and the donkey show no signs of being supplanted.

For my part, I thought of no other way of traveling. In the first place, horses had always been mixed up in my life, and it delighted me to be able to do all my moving around with them. In the second, I wished to make these shepherds of mine understand that I had not taken on this sheep raising as a pastime but as a means of livelihood. I wanted them to look on me as one of them, not as a Roumi friend of their tribal chieftain. It took time; but, like all the rest, the confidence came, and being in camp was taken as a matter of course. Soon they were asking my advice and treating me more as a friend than as a boss. The children were no longer shy when I was around; the sick came to me for medical care. Even the heads of neighboring camps rode over in the evening and discussed their business as if I had never done anything else but raise sheep. In less than a year after landing in North Africa, I had become a full-fledged nomad of the Sahara.

CHAPTER VII

To become a nomad sheep raiser, when one has not been born one, requires a brand new way of thinking. It is no Oriental idyl à la Omar Khayam. It demands attention to all kinds of unusual details, and hard physical work. My day was filled from daylight to darkness, and when the time came, no one went to his bed of carpets more eagerly than I.

At dawn we rose and said our prayers. This was followed by a little coffee or mint tea. One of the hardest things I found to accustom myself to in this new life was the nomad's omission of breakfast and disregard for lunch. Except for an occasional date taken as refreshment in the field, my shepherds ate only one meal, at the end of the day.

After "breakfast" we counted the sheep, and the flocks moved out to pasture. Soon after, the head shepherd and I, and usually Madani, rode onto the desert to look for grazing.

In a country where a really good rainy season consists of ten wet days in spring and ten wet days in autumn, pasture is hardy but scattered. A sheep must roam a long way to fill itself; and when a flock strikes a patch of grass, it is gone in no time. It is thus the business of the head shepherd and the owner of the flocks to look ahead for new pasturage. This job used to take us till around noon. My companions had no watches, but they knew to a second when it was the middle of the day, sun or cloud, and time to pray. With the same preciseness, sun or cloud, they turned directly toward the East. Out of curiosity I checked them with watch and compass, and then gave up carrying either. It was waste of pocket space.

Their powers of observation, their sense of direction and distance were uncanny. We would ride away from the camp over rolling plains which seemed to have no particular landmarks. We would travel north, south, east, and west, perhaps hunt and be on the move for six or seven hours. But on the dot of sunset we were back in that camp which lay in a hollow hidden from view a hundred yards away.

If one asked an Arab how far it was to some obscure well or to an oasis, he would not scratch his head and offer an approximate mileage. The answer would be, unhesitatingly, "So many hours distant," the hours meaning riding hours at a walk. Neither did I ever find such an estimate more than a few minutes out. An illiterate nomad could draw me a clear, accurate map in the sand. He could tell a tribe by the shape of a footprint as easily as an F.B.I. expert can check a fingerprint. As a barometer he was infallible.

Before I became accustomed to desert wandering, I asked Madani what landmarks he saw in this desolate wilderness to show him where he was. He looked about him, tried to point out something which to him looked different, stared doubtfully at me, and finally said:

"I just know." Then, as I did not appear convinced, he added: "Supposing you were dropped from a plane into the middle of London or New York, it would not take you more than a minute to get your bearings, would it?"

I admitted that it wouldn't.

"But it would me," he went on. "I'd be absolutely lost. I wouldn't know east from west; I'd be just as bewildered as a Roumi suddenly dumped on the Sahara. Finding one's way is just a matter of upbringing."

This sounded like a taunt, so I said nothing and began using my eyes. In a week or so I came to the conclusion that I had never used them before. A little over a year in the Sahara, and I had quadrupled my sense of distance, direction, and observation. It was not long before I could find my way almost anywhere on the desert pastures where my flocks roamed. Since then I have never been lost anywhere where I had the lay of the land in my mind. I have still that instinctive feeling that finding or losing my way may be a question of death from thirst or starvation.

By the time we made the noon halt, we might have ridden anything from ten to fifteen miles at a walk. If the Arabs were not going to eat, their horses had to. So they were unharnessed and allowed to graze while we sat around and said nothing, unless there was something to discuss.

The Arabs rarely talk among themselves for the sake of talking. If they have nothing to say, they do not rummage their brains for a subject. They just let their minds relax and keep quiet. The silence is not awkward or strained. On the contrary, it is friendly. Until the Arabs knew me well, they prattled like Occidentals. When I became one of them, they stopped. I, too, fell into their silent habits. I realized how much unnecessary conversation we encourage in our society.

When the Arabs do talk, the topics are always the same: sheep raising, agriculture, and the weather. And it is not the kind of weather we comment on. The sun and the rain mean life or death to the nomads. When it rains at the right time of year, there will be food and clothes and prosperity for millions. When it does not rain, or the sirocco strikes at the wrong moment, there may be famine. One becomes acutely weather-conscious in the Sahara. Watching the sky for clouds in spring and autumn is as tense as waiting for bombers to come over...

During this midday halt I used to eat the dates I had hidden in the hood of my burnous. It was not exactly what I would have ordered from a menu, but there was more nourishment in this sticky fruit than in many full-course meals, and with this hungry, active life I needed nourishment, concentrated.

At about two we were off again. If the pasture question had been settled, we hunted.

There are in the Sahara over a hundred different kinds of birds and nearly fifty different animals. They are not all found in the same area; but except in the thirsty, empty desert there is never complete absence of life. A daily diet of mutton becomes monotonous, even when it is varied by old goat and dead camel, and game makes a welcome change.

If our larder was low in extras, we hunted with sporting guns; if it was well stocked, with falcons. Both sports were on horseback and not remotely like anything of the same kind in Europe or America.

The hunting was never really planned. It kind of happened. My Arabs always carried loaded guns across the bows of their saddles, and when they had got tired of being "inscrutable," they mounted and rode off aimlessly as if they were still looking for pastures. It was rather like taking an umbrella out on a threatening day in the hope that it will keep the rain off. And it usually worked.

Slowly we rode, lolling in our saddles, pretending we were out to take the air. As by a miracle, a hare suddenly appeared in our path. No one showed any sign that he had seen it, but the Arab who was nearest stood up in his stirrups and shot it. If he missed, which was rare, he galloped after it and shot it on the move. There was no interference or shouting of advice. Fate had placed that hare in Ali's path, and it was Ali's job to deal with it.

A little further on we flushed a bustard before it could run. Spreading its great wings, it flapped away. Another Arab was after it at full gallop. Though the bustard is an ungainly bird, he flies fast. It takes a good horse to keep up with him. But these horses were good and sure-footed, and it did not take long for Ali or Madani or Ahmed to maneuver until he was under the bustard, and less time to bring it down. The misses with the first barrel were rare.

I tried several times to shoot a bird from a galloping horse. I never hit one, and I fell off often. I have ridden all my life. I have fox-hunted and played polo, even steeplechased; but there is something about dropping one's reins and aiming at a rapidly flying bird which is unbalancing. As a matter of fact, in comparison to these Arabs, I was no more of a horseman or horsemaster than a baby on a merry-go-round. But they were polite about it and occasionally conceded that I rode better than many Roumis.

Sometimes we sighted a herd of gazelles. Using the folds in the ground, we stalked them until it was no longer possible to keep out of sight and wind. Up would go the heads of the gazelles and away in a mad stampede with us after them. To begin with, they kept their distances, springing up and down the stony hillocks, disappearing into dried-up watercourses. As soon as they showed signs of tiring, the leading hunter made a sign and we formed ourselves into single file. Galloping parallel to the gazelles, we gradually shortened the range. Again the leader gave a signal. The others, minus me, dropped their reins, picked up their guns, and opened fire. An intermittent broadside continued, the horsemen loading and unloading as if they were lying on a rifle range, until the gazelles broke up into terrified groups. Quickly the Arabs rode back to the gazelles they had hit and cut their throats. Even where sport is involved, the Prophet's instructions about the killing of food are observed. Strangers are sometimes taken aback to find Arabs refusing a dish of partridges or hares which they have not seen killed. Unless the throat has been cut, the creature is unclean.

Almost every Arab of standing keeps falcons and falconers. It is like having a Packard or a yacht or an apartment on Park Avenue. The falcons themselves cost nothing. They are snared on the desert when young and trained to hunt for their masters. Their masters are the falconers. It is these who make falconry a luxury. The falcon owner has to pay one or two falconers all the year for the few occasions when he has leisure to hunt. He has to mount them, clothe them, and feed them, the falconer's family included. I never could afford falcons, but I had many friends who could, and with them I always hunted.

Falconry is an ancient sport with all kinds of century-old rites. It belongs to Persia, India, Arabia, Europe in the Middle Ages. It needs setting and dressing. A British falconer on Salisbury Plain or an American in Arizona may pay fervent attention to the ritual and the artistry, but he will not be picturesque. He will merely be eccentric. To the Arabs of the Sahara, falconry is an older tradition than Islam. The humblest shepherd knows all about it, and if, by accident, he cannot have a horse, he will follow the hunt on foot with as much expert interest as the chief.

When we went out with falcons, it was in the same kind of clothes, on the same breed of horses, in the same type of background and with the same rites as before the birth of Christ. There was no book ritual, no deliberate artistry. The picture might have come straight from a Persian print. There were not even elaborate plans or preparations. Sometimes we hunted because we felt in the mood. Sometimes we asked friends to come over from neighboring camps, and made a day of it.

When everyone was ready, we formed a semicircular line. In the center of the line rode the falconers. The birds, hooded with elegant plumed hoods, some of them made of silver or gold, perched on the shoulders and turban of the falconer. The chief gave the signal, and the line of horses slowly advanced. Suddenly, a yell as a hare speeded away through the scrub. The line steadied itself. It is against tradition to hunt the game until the falcon is in the air. This does not take long. In a moment it had been unhooded and was soaring over the hare. A second falcon followed, perhaps a third.

Up they went, their wings twinkling, their eyes watching the hare as he twisted and turned like a ship under a bombing attack. And like a dive bomber, the first falcon made a lightning swoop. The hare dodged just in time. He had escaped the first attack. But hardly had the original hawk swept up into the air again than the second had dropped from the skies. If he missed, there was the third. The teamwork of these wild birds was amazing. They might have been a veteran air force flight.

The most spectacular hunt is between falcon and bustard. In this case only one hawk is used.

The bustard gets up heavily and at first flies low, hoping he will have a chance to land and use his swiftly running legs. When he finds no cover in which to do this, he decides to make for the stratosphere. In so doing, he loses distance, and the hawk, who knows precisely his prey's plans, stoops quickly. With a graceful downward and upward movement at terrific speed, he skims over the bustard's back and turns on himself like a plane looping. There is a shower of grey feathers; the bustard seems to stagger in the air and abruptly spins to earth. The falcon, poised on his pinions, hovers high up marking the place where the prey has fallen.

A few Arabs combine salukis (desert greyhounds) and falcons to hunt gazelles. It is more animated than the straightforward falcon hunt, and the teamwork between dog and bird is interesting. But it has little of the grace or craft of genuine falconry.

Whether we hunted with guns or falcons or salukis, we were back in the camp for that well-earned dinner on the dot of sunset. But before we could restore our bodies, we had to look after our souls. However weak or faint we might feel, the prayer had to be said first. If ever there was a case of the spirit being stronger than the flesh, it was during that first of the evening prayers. But when it was over, with what a feeling of righteousness did we gather at the entrance of my tent! In one group, Madani, the head shepherd, and myself; perhaps a guest or two. In another group, the shepherds, and possibly friends of theirs. This separate grouping, except in cases where a bash agha was dining, was not a matter of caste.

It was merely for convenience. Not more than a certain number of people can dip simultaneously into the same bowl.

As soon as we were settled, one of the shepherd's sons passed around the ablution basin and a ewer from which he poured water over our hands. A second boy placed in our midst a tureen of spiced soup called chorba, in which were several spoons. Each man took his spoon, the only eating implement which an Arab ever handles, and with an eager "Bismillah!" (In the name of God!) began noisily to drink soup.

When we had had enough, the tureen and the spoons were passed to the shepherds. Simultaneously a dish of bourak was placed before us—a kind of sausage roll made of minced mutton, sage and mint, baked in light pastry. After the bourak came leham'lalou, mutton or gazelle or hare or bustard stew seasoned with prunes and sweet almonds. The main and important dish, the dish which no Arab, rich or poor, is without, the famous couscous, came next. Couscous, about which so many inexactitudes have been written, is nothing more than semolina. It is wheat kneaded into tiny round balls and cooked over steam. It comes to the "table" on a wooden platter piled into a huge golden heap. With it is a spicy vegetable sauce called marga, and sometimes legs of partridges or chickens. As with curries in India, there are many kinds of couscous, varying according to localities. But simple or elaborate, it is never omitted from the menu. It takes the same place with the Arab as rice does with the Chinese.

We ate couscous by taking some in our hands and making it into a ball which we shot into our mouths with our thumbs. To do this cleanly requires as much practice as eating properly with chopsticks.

When we were gorged with couscous, cakes made of flour and honey and almond paste and orange water, called heloua, filled up the cracks.

If we had important guests or something in particular to celebrate, there was added to the meal, between the leham'lalou and the couscous, the famous mechoui.

El mechoui, which means "the roasted," is the barbecued three-months-old lamb. It is served whole, head and all, and there is nothing more tender, more succulent, more tasty. According to the Arabs, meat is tender either after being "hung" or immediately after being killed. But it must be *really immediately*. The lamb has to be slaughtered and skinned and spitted so quickly that when the brushwood ember fire starts to cook it, the flesh is still naturally warm. The result certainly makes meat which crumbles in the fingers and melts in the mouth.

If we had killed a gazelle sufficiently near the camp to cook him warm, we had him roasted whole. It tasted even better than the lamb.

When everything had been eaten, we all drew a deep breath and said: "Hamdullah!"—"May God be praised!" or "May God be thanked!" Then the shepherd boy appeared for the final time with the ablution bowl and the tea and coffee.

I never decided which I disliked most, the thick, sweet Arab coffee or the sugary, green tea. Both were sickly.

The coffee is that concoction full of grounds which, before the war, certain restaurants in London and New York had served as an expensive extra by a man in a fez who had probably never been inside an Arab café or touched the stuff himself. It is that throat-tickler which tourists gushed over when they were allowed off cruise ships in the Orient.

The tea has nothing in common with what English people and some Americans drink around five in the afternoon. It is not remotely connected with what the Chinese and Japanese call tea. It is a pure Arab invention. Here is the recipe, copied as I watched the brew being prepared.

In a small teapot place three spoonfuls of rather inferior green tea, two sprigs of fresh mint if you have it, dried mint if you have not, and a quarter of a pound of sugar. More, if you can afford it. Pour boiling water over this and serve in cocktail glasses. The result is very hot, very sweet mint sauce! Not tea! Once or twice I managed to have my mint tea served at the same time as the roast lamb, and it did not taste nearly as bad.

The worst of this tea and coffee business is that the Arabs serve it on the least provocation. It is a gesture of hospitality and impossible to refuse at the risk of giving offense. Some Occidentals remember Arabs only with nausea, and all because of the mint tea!

What is really behind these tea and coffee orgies is the need of a stimulant to replace the forbidden liquor. Some Arabs get so excited by caffeine that they appear to be drunk. The numerous

63

spas in Algeria are jammed with Arabs getting themselves decaffeined, and many chiefs who can afford it go to Vichy. They need to.

The desert Arab's diet and that prescribed by the average Occidental as healthy, differ. An Arab rarely eats fruit or vegetables except when he goes to an oasis. He fills himself with meats and starches. He takes far too much coffee, tea, and candy. Yet he is one hundred per cent healthy. During the seven years I remained in the Sahara in a community of over ten thousand, I do not remember one young or middle-aged man dying except by accident. All the deaths were in infancy or in very old age. This inconsistent good health is due to the pure, dry air; to the living always in the open; to the little smoking and no drinking of liquor; to the continual exercise and regular sleep. Such an existence does not call for vitamins in bottles or for balanced diets. The fresh air makes up for all deficiencies. There was also the spiritual side of the nomad and his mental attitude toward life.

After we had had our coffee or tea, had prayed again, and perhaps listened to some old, old story or to a shepherd playing on a deep-toned reed flute, we slipped onto our carpet under the tent. The long day in the open had tired us physically; the big meal on the hungry stomach had relaxed us. We had no cares which had not been foreordained, so there was nothing to fuss over. There was that majestic silence of the Sahara and the Sahara wind whispering us a lullaby. The only thing to do was to sleep.

Even if we had had intellectual cravings, they could not have been satisfied. The desert Arabs have no books. If they had had them, many could not have read them. But if the Oriental section of the Bodleian had been at our disposal, it would have been no good after sunset. The only artificial light in an Arab camp is the brushwood fire. Our lives were controlled by the rising and the setting of the sun. —Besides, I was too tired to read and somehow forgot about books and newspapers. They no longer entered into my pattern of life. I had escaped from the dreary doings of Park Lane and Park Avenue. I did not care who won the Derby at Epsom or the Derby in Kentucky. Which kings or queens reigned, which presidents were elected, caused me no emotion. I was leading the life I had always longed for. I had peace of mind. When I rolled myself in my burnous and laid my head on the cement-like pillow, I knew I would sleep until daylight when Madani would lead the way onto the desert for our morning prayer. We would do exactly the same thing tomorrow as we had done yesterday and the day before. We would do the same thing six months hence; six years hence. Our routine would be as regular as that of a Westchester commuter. Perhaps more so. And yet how different!

Instead of an indigestible, gulped breakfast—no breakfast.

Instead of a snatched lunch at the counter—no lunch.

Instead of an irritating day in a stuffy office—a peaceful day on horseback in the clear air of the desert.

Instead of a breathtaking swig of gin at sundown—a breath-giving prayer.

Instead of a mob of precocious kids and a plaintive or aggressive or unfaithful wife waiting in the stucco home—a lot of fine men in a camel hair tent ready to eat their dinner without comment.

Our children and our women were there, bless them! They had all helped in the preparing of our meal, but we would neither see them or hear them unless we specially wanted to. If we did want to, the wives would not be plaintive or aggressive, and they had certainly not been unfaithful. Neither would the children be precocious.

There was one thing only I could envy my commuter: his cup of coffee. Yes, I envied him his cup of coffee, and possibly his orange juice.

CHAPTER VIII

Our yearly routine was as regular as our daily and, like it, was controlled by the sun.

During the autumn we pastured not very far from the oasis where I had first met Blanchet and Atalla and Mohammed ben Tahar. If the season was good, we stayed in that area quite a while. The moment it became cold, our migration south began.

Many people associate the Sahara with great heat. It can, indeed, be very hot, but it can also be perishingly cold. Most of the pasture land is over two thousand feet above sea level. When it snows on the Atlas Mountains and the wind blows from that direction, sleeping in an unheated tent is misery.

So, when the first sharp warning of frost made us restless at night, we knew it was time to go. Pasturing as we went, we slowly moved south. Gradually we left the winter behind. We were not so many hundreds of miles away, but we were at a lower level and out of range of the snow wind. The nights were still cold, but the days were hot, very hot sometimes. It was the country of the mirages, the country where the Arabs say the desert speaks.

As darkness blacks out the plain, weird mutterings are mingled with the whispering of the wind. In the middle of the night ghostly grindings and shattering cracks wake one with a start. One listens, tense, but all one can hear is the rolling of a thousand drums announcing an army which never gets any nearer.

Men of science, who have explanations for everything, say that the sudden change of temperature after sunset causes the rocks to be rent apart. The mutterings and the drummings are caused by the ever-blowing Sahara wind, here more charged with sand than in the north. That is as it may be; but the nomads, who know nothing about refrigeration and erosion, attribute the uncanny sounds to djinns.

The mirages on these southern pastures were fantastic. My Arabs were used to them and took no notice when the desert started up its picture making. But I was fascinated.

What we usually saw were expanses of water appearing about a mile away from us. But when I galloped hopefully toward the shimmering lake, it retreated or changed place. Sometimes I would turn around and find myself on an island, with glittering water in all directions. At other times I would catch sight of strange animals with long stiltlike legs which became distorted as I watched. Again I would ride toward them, and they would fly into the air like prehistoric monsters. Occasionally an oasis or a town would come into being, usually beside water. I would call Madani and show him the domes and minarets and palm trees, but before he could comment, they had gone or had changed into something else.

No one could tell me what caused these mirages, but this I learned: With the exception of the water illusion, which is a reflection of the sky, no mirage can appear where there is nothing to reflect. If a town or trees or animals are seen in mirage form, somewhere not far away there *is* a town or trees or animals. This is so true that Arabs traveling over unfamiliar territory check their bearings by a mirage which, on clear mornings, often appears soon after dawn. According to them it gives them a picture of the country beyond the horizon.

The mirage is one of the strangest things in this strange land of purring winds, and no one tells the same tale about it. The encyclopedia's explanation that it is a reflection caused by light rays undergoing refraction does not get one much further!

When it began to get really hot, we turned north again. That is, the flocks turned north. A nomad has really nothing to do with his wandering. He could just as well live in one place as another. It is the flocks which wander in search of grass; the nomads follow the flocks. And it is not the sheep, either, who decide where to roam; it is the goats. Sheep are the stupidest animals in existence. If left to themselves, they would eat the pasture immediately before them and then die of starvation. It would not occur to them that there might be food around the corner. If a lion attacked them, they would unprotestingly submit to being killed. The goats, on the other hand, are as alert as the sheep are dumb. So little exaggerated

67

is this, that my nomads always kept a dozen goats in every flock of two hundred and fifty sheep. These were forever on the lookout for grass and would skip if danger was about. When my shepherds slept, they always had a goat on the end of string attached to their wrists. In this way they were sure of being warned if the sheep were in trouble.

So, when the lengthening of the days made the grazing less fresh, the goats turned north, the sheep turned north, and we, made conscious by the goats of the increasing strength of the sun, turned north too. By midspring we were back in our pastures around the oasis.

There was always great excitement when the tribes came back from their winter or summer pastures. Life in the oasis was never thrilling, and it was quite dead without its nomads. Our arrival was rather like the return from wars of the armies in *Faust* or *Aïda*, and no less picturesque.

The day after pitching our camp in a gully where there was pasture enough for three or four days, Madani and Ali and I rode into the oasis. Our primary objects were to have baths and to find out how the sheep market stood. During the time we had been away, our washing had been a formality, and we had used more sand than water. We had only sold sheep to other breeders. But in the oasis was a fine Turkish bath and a market of importance where we could probably dispose of all our last autumn's lambs.

News of our coming had traveled, and we found Blanchet and Mohammed ben Tahar at the entrance of the oasis. The affection those two boys had for me was touching. I had hardly ever given them a present, but I seemed to mean more to them than a camel load of gold. Blanchet's devotion was primitive and animal. Mohammed's was affectionate and admiring. He regarded my breaking down the barrier between the Roumi and the nomads as nothing less than miraculous. He was also puzzled.

Being a sedentary oasis dweller, he had little notion of how a nomad lived. The idea of roaming for hundreds of miles, regardless of weather and with no real home to come back to, he could not understand. He could not make out how I could satisfy my mind with such stupid people. Mohammed ben Tahar's contempt for nomadic mentality was amusing. It was also justified.

The average nomad knows nothing about anything which does not immediately concern him. If you start talking about something he cannot picture, you have no way of making him see it. If you are new to desert life, you may try to explain that you come from a country beyond the sea where there are rivers and forests and miles of grassy meadowland. The nomad will listen politely, but as he has never seen the sea or meadows or rivers, he will treat your story as one of his Arabian Nights favorites. Your words will throw no light into his boundless ignorance.

Boundless ignorance! Incredible, but true. The nomads have no education and do not want any. They are blissfully content with what they have. They expect nothing of the world but enough to eat and a few clothes to cover their bodies. I often envied them. They seemed to have proved that the less you know, the happier you are.

Storybooks and motion pictures have created a legend about the inscrutable faces and meditative silences of the desert Arabs, supposed to conceal wells of wisdom. They conceal nothing but minds as arid as the Sahara. Even with the educated Arab this Oriental inscrutability is a fantasy. The Oriental is no more inscrutable than a Texan or Scotsman. The unemotional expression, the meditative silence conceal, for the most part, an ability to make the mind a blank. That, in itself, is a feat; probably more of one than generating complicated thoughts. But that is all there is to it. Whenever an Asiatic does not wish to meet a controversial issue, he becomes "inscrutable" and remains so until the argument is over.

Mohammed ben Tahar had a mind above the average Arab. He read and listened. He reasoned, too, and when I talked to him of things which he did not understand, he questioned me intelligently. He was not like one of those little Arab boys I heard in history class in a French school, saying obliviously: "Our ancestors, the Gauls—" Mohammed, without having ever seen anything, thought a good deal more than many people who had.

Atalla, toward whose shop we now rode, with Blanchet and Mohammed hanging on to our stirrups, had also a good mind. He did not know as much as Mohammed, but he thought as quickly as a New Yorker. They were, however, neither of them inscrutable, except when it suited their purposes to be so.

Our going to Atalla's was to pick up news and gossip, and get into touch with the other chiefs, whom we had not seen for several months. It also meant the beginning of one of those tea and coffee sessions. My spirits sank when Madani told me that we would sit in Atalla's fake harem, where our friends would be sure to come sooner or later. I did not want to be sick before going to the Turkish bath. However, there was nothing to be done about it; my suggestion that it would be more practical to go and look for the others was ignored. My only hope was that Atalla would serve me the same "French Line" brand of coffee he had given me when I was a tourist. But I was out of luck. The sticky, grounds-filled cup was handed to me, with the sugary almond cakes and the teapot of boiling mint sauce within easy reaching distance.

I do not know who told that we were in Atalla's reception room, but within a few minutes of our arrival the agha Daylis, his blue eyes twinkling and his beard as trim as a naval officer's, had joined us. Following on his heels was a crowd of caids and sheiks. For a few minutes we hugged one another, inquiring and reinquiring and inquiring again as to the states of our respective healths, praising God that we were well, and asking once more to make sure there had been no misunderstanding or that someone was not hiding a hideous disease.

Arabs always behave in this way when they meet after short or long partings. It is obvious from everyone's appearance that no one could be better, but it does not damp the eager inquiry and the no less sincere reply.

When everyone was satisfied that no one was in imminent danger of falling ill, and more nauseous pots of tea and coffee had been brought, Madani and Daylis and the other chiefs began to talk shop. Sheep, weather; weather, sheep. Blanchet curled up like a dog and went to sleep, Atalla played host, Mohammed allowed himself to become inscrutable and looked blank. I watched, finding it difficult to follow these fireworks of conversation on this not brilliant subject. I was sufficiently out of the picture, however, to dump my drinks and cakes into a large Damascene bowl at my elbow. Soon I became restless and was just wondering how I could get away from this businessmen's conference, and pay a call on Messrs. Paoli and Couteau, when there was an interruption. The curtain across the door was brusquely drawn back, and a *cavalier* in a royal blue burnous appeared dramatically on the threshold.

The Arabs all looked up, then jumped up, as the bash agha Jelloul came majestically into the room. I felt inclined to laugh. It was like a scene in grand opera where all the characters are engineered onto the stage without explanation of why or how they got there so opportunely. The Bash Agha accepted the health inquiries from his subordinates without reassuring them. He nodded acknowledgment to Madani's respectful kiss on the shoulder. Then he asked:

"Where's Boodli?"

I came out of my recess and stood undecided. I did not quite know what to do. Was I still an Occidental who should shake hands and forget about the old man's rank, or was I a nomad of no standing who could only kiss the hand of the paramount chief? The Bash Agha solved the problem by taking me in his arms and kissing me on both cheeks. Then he held me at arm's length and examined me. Then he laughed approvingly. For a few moments he bombarded me with questions about how I was doing as a nomad, chuckling as I told him. Finally he embraced me again and warned me that he expected me to dinner at six. Then he called Madani, and the conversation returned to pastures in the South and the health of the sheep. (Many of the Bash Agha's flocks were running with ours.) Madani sat on a cushion beside the old man. The other chiefs stood at a respectful distance, as I had glimpsed them that first morning when I walked in the town with Mohammed ben Tahar. Everyone was engrossed or asleep, so I slipped behind the curtain and into the street.

It is unbelievable how Oriental-minded one becomes after living for months with Arabs in the desert. When I first saw Monsieur Paoli and Cyprien Couteau, I found myself inquiring ecstatically about their healths and I was unprepared for the proffered chair and the traditional invitation to drink.

I accepted the chair and refused the drink, but not entirely from Moslem principles. I felt so much better without liquor.

It was nevertheless, for a moment, relaxing to talk to these two men in their uncomfortable business suits sitting on hideous chairs in their incongruous Franco-Arab homes. But only for a moment. After the first surprise at meeting and all the questions answered, there was a strained pause.

Monsieur Paoli was solicitous and friendly, but lacking in the spontaneous humor of my shepherds. He knew all about the sea and what the *Fôret de Fontainebleau* looked like, but he did not know anything about life. To him the ambition of any self-respecting mortal exiled from his native land was to make as much money as possible, as quickly as possible, and get back there as quickly as possible to vegetate or meditate. Monsieur Paoli had all the elements necessary for inscrutability! His own personal ambition was to own a hairdressing establishment. He had earned his first wages as a *garçon coiffeur* and had made up his mind, then, to become a *patron*. I felt sorry for Monsieur Paoli; not half as sorry, though, as he felt for me.

With Cyprien Couteau there was not even the hairdressing ambition. His outlook was desperate. As far as he could gauge, he could never afford to be anything but a Saharan *commissaire de police*. *Pêche à la ligne* seemed to be out for keeps. When I suggested that he might find himself involved in the solution of some sensational crime, he flung his arms in the air. Never in his life had he lived among such a law-abiding crowd as these "sacred" Arabs. They never stole, they never murdered, they never even got drunk. Why, in his village on the Somme, he had averaged at least one arrest a week!

I left Cyprien Couteau, sorry for him, too, but in a different way. About me I do not think the *Commissaire* had any feelings. I was not a fisherman; I could not be and live in the Sahara, so I could not understand. We came from different worlds.

Satisfied that my first experiences of desert life had created no yearnings for Europe, I walked peacefully to the Turkish bath.

The words Turkish bath suggest either an athletic club or something out of the Arabian Nights. Neither will be found in the hammams of Sahara oases. They are usually secreted in some alleyway, with nothing outside to indicate what is inside. The rich and the poor use them to bathe in, to pray in, to drink coffee, to discuss business. These haunts of steam and strange odors are the favorite meeting places of the older generation of oasis dwellers who have not elegant reception rooms like Atalla Bouameur's.

I had told Blanchet to warn the owner of the bathhouse that I was coming, so the masseur was waiting for me. He was the thinnest man I have ever seen outside of a circus. I suppose it was the result of spending most of his life in that steaming atmosphere. As soon as I was undressed, a towel was placed about my body and one about my head. My outfit was completed with a pair of wooden clogs the shape of a sole, with a strap to go across the foot. Walking in these things is a nightmare. They seem set against forward progress. They want to go to right or to left, or in both directions at once. Anywhere but to the front. It took perseverance and a good deal of support from the skeleton to get me along the dim slippery passage, which reminded me of the way to the dungeons under the Doges' Palace in Venice. But we made it; and heaving back a heavy door, my supporter pushed me into a stone-vaulted chamber suffocatingly filled with steam. I groped my way to a large stone slab and was deprived of my towels and clogs.

As my eyes became accustomed to the light given by a flickering candle in a lantern, I saw other nebulous figures washing in the corners of the room. The heat was intense; steam swirled about the ceiling, the bathers grunted and groaned. I was no longer in the dungeons of the Doges but in those dim places of torture of Dante's Inferno as pictured by Gustave Doré. However, before I could decide whether I would prefer to be tortured under the auspices of the republic of Venice or the monarchy of Pluto, the skeleton was beside me again. He did not speak but gently pushed me off the slab and onto the floor. He then leaped on me and began to unjoint me. I was too taken aback to resist, and resignedly awaited the rack.

But there was no rack. From the banks of the Grand Canal or the river Styx, I was suddenly transported to the shores of the waters of Paradise. It was delirious. It was unbelievable. Of all the masseurs who have ever "massed" me, I have found none to equal the Arabs of the Sahara. With no training, no knowledge of anatomy, these men, by instinct and heredity, understand the wants of the human body; and as I lay in the soothing steam, I felt all pains and poisons being magically pressed out of me. And when the man put on a coarse mitten and kneaded me like a lump of dough, I hoped he would never stop. But he did stop, and plied me with soap and warm water until he had polished me as the wind in the Sahara polishes rocks. Then he gave me an icy douche and sent me to the drying room walking on air, in spite of the clogs.

The owner of the bath wanted to spoil my feeling of well-being with mint tea. I let him bring the stuff, but I gave it to the masseur's small son, who was rubbing me with towels. When I was rested and my clothes had been brought back from being laundered, it was time to go to the Bash Agha's. I found Madani there and Ali. Both had obviously been bathing, too, but with that admirable Arab habit of minding one's own business, we asked each other no questions.

The dinner was dull. There was no one of high enough rank to sit with the Bash Agha, so I, who had no rank, dined with him alone while my friends sat in another circle a little way off. There was not much conversation, and as soon as we could, Madani and I slipped away. Ali was waiting outside with the horses. We mounted and rode out of the oasis into the black, starry night. The rustling of the ever-blowing Sahara wind was the only sound. The majestic silence of the desert enveloped us as we traveled. Suddenly, Madani began to sing. His song was one of those deep-throated, mournful melodies which one sometimes hears in Spanish music. His voice rose and fell, trailing away into a whisper at the end of each verse. There was a sensual beauty in the singing which belied my partner's rather rough, sheep-minded exterior. I felt carried away by the beauty of the melody. I was in an enchanted world. Anything that had happened before, did not exist. As at the Turkish bath that afternoon, I wished it would go on for ever. But it stopped abruptly: on account of fifty camp dogs which came out in a wild chorus to tell the others that we were back from our jaunt in the "city."

Madani said: "We have a lot to do. The Bash Agha tells me he is going to make an early move to the North this year. We must sell our lambs, sheer, and dip before we go."

Rather taken aback by the sudden change of tempo, I said: "Yes, Madani." And thought, how strange must be the mentality of this man, who sings with such emotion but has always his business in his thoughts! But then, Madani *was* the strangest character. I never discovered exactly how much he knew or did not know in comparison to an Occidental of his birth and wealth. He rarely took refuge behind inscrutability, and when it came to the sheep trade, he was equal to any European or Jewish dealer. So I knew that everything would be done in time, and I was not wrong. The Bash Agha, it turned out, had forgotten all about his idea to get away before the first summer heat, and no one dared to remind him. So we had to sit around and wait till he was ready. However, no one cared. When I began to show impatience, Madani said:

"What does it matter when we start? We'll be doing the same thing there as we are doing here. What's a day or a week or a month in our lives, and anyway, getting excited won't help. It'll only make you hot." He turned to Ali and added, "What a nuisance he is, always asking questions, always trying to get somewhere. He's like a Roumi going to catch a train."

But I was not the only one to become restless. As the days grew longer and sultrier, the goats again turned toward the north. But the summer migration was not as simple as the winter move. Our waiting for the Bash Agha was not just another polite gesture; it was a necessity.

As long as we were in our southern territories, we were in Arab-run country with room for everyone. On the slopes immediately north of the Sahara we would still have room, but we would be encroaching on the great tribe of the Ouled Nail. Beyond them we would be on land not normally occupied by nomads: the alfa country, the grain country. Into this territory we could only penetrate with the permission of the property owners, sedentary Arabs who had taken up farming. These did not like uncontrolled invasions by nomads. The only way, therefore, that we could get there was under the leadership of the Bash Agha.

Finally the old man decided to go and set a date. On that day the whole of the confederation of the Larba tribes gathered at sunrise on the plains outside the oasis. —Ten thousand men, ten thousand women and children, two thousand camels, three thousand horses and as many donkeys and dogs. Each tribe with its chief riding at its head, his tribal banner carried by a retainer in a royal blue burnous. Each bassour decked in tribal colors. Way out in front, the Bash Agha in his scarlet and gold, imperial on his white stallion. Beside him, the retainers with his banner; behind him, the aghas and their retainers. Somewhere in the rear, a grey thoroughbred mounted by an Englishman in burnous and turban, with no retainers, but prouder of his little band of tattered nomads than of any crack regiment.

Our move to the hills was a noble sight, never to be forgotten. Its dignity, its majesty, its vastness impressed me more than Durbar or Coronation, than any parade I had ever seen. There were no words to describe its simple magnificence. Because, in spite of the splendid array and the colors and the prancing horses and the bassours, its tone was simplicity. The Arabs taking part were no more impressed by the sight that so amazed me than by a mirage. This spectacle of another age, this spectacle of the thousand and one nights, this something which belonged to a world of the past, which no one who came upon it unexpectedly would believe was not a super motion picture, was to them part of their life. Their naturalness became part of my wonder.

I have taken many journeys since then by all manner of means and in all sorts of countries, but I have never known anything to equal the march of the Larba tribes from the Sahara to the Atlas.

CHAPTER IX

MADANI'S REBUKE WHEN I SHOWED impatience at the delay in our move north had given me a glimpse of one of the most interesting sides of Islam: the fatalistic.

Most Moslems are fatalists. All of mine were. They believed that there was nothing in their lives which was not foreordained. They said: "When God created the world, He took a handful of dust in either hand and cast one to the right and one to the left. The dust to the right was destined to become people who would always be happy. The dust to the left would become people who would only know unhappiness." And in the thirty-seventh chapter of the Koran it is written: "God created you and all your actions."

That is one reason why Arabs take life so calmly and never hurry or get into unnecessary tempers when things go wrong. They know that what is ordained is ordained, and no one but God can alter anything.

If our sheep died or did not produce lambs, or the sirocco withered the pastures, or locusts ravaged an oasis, we all said: "Mektoub!"—"It is written!"

If someone asked us to dine, we replied: "In sha Allah"—"If God wills it." And if God disarranged our plans between the invitation and the dinner hour, we did not go. Or if God thrust friends in our path on our way to dine, we took them along. In neither case did we advise the host. In neither case was the host put out. He knew that it was foolish of him to tempt providence by planning a dinner ahead of time. If no one—or half a dozen extra guests—showed up, he had only himself to blame.

This philosophy, which was as sincere as the other Arab beliefs, did more to settle my nerves than a hundred sedatives. It was such a relief to feel that one could work hard, plan hard, wish hard and, if things went wrong, put the blame on Fate. It was comforting to know that Madani and I and Daylis, the rich, the poor, had everything worked out for us by Someone whose authority we could not question. Our destinies had been settled long before we appeared in the Sahara. Today I still maintain that happy resignation to the inevitable.

This does not mean that I or my Arab friends sat back and let the world go by. It would never have occurred to us to abandon sheep raising because we had a couple of bad drought years and lost most of our flocks. We would have set to work again, hoping for better luck next time.

People who have not gone into the matter scoff at fatalism. But is it a scoffing matter? Is it any more unlikely than many of the other strange things which science, so far, has failed to explain? How often do we see men and women who lead blameless lives, only thinking good, only doing good, yet having relentless bad luck, having everything go wrong! If we go into their cases, we find, too, that there is no reason why they should have been so unfortunate. It is just something without meaning which pursues them and buffets them and trips them up, whatever they try to do. —The Arabs say it's Fate.

Have we not, also, come across people who have not a grain of moral sense and get away with murder or its equivalent? Men toward whom all the world's fortune seems to flow without their doing anything creditable to attract it? "Crime doesn't pay!" say the preachers. But it does for those whose lives are foreordained to be lucky.

These are extreme cases, but it is worth while to watch the fortunes of individuals in our own circles and see the curious tricks which fate plays them. Since living with the Arabs, I have done this and been astonished at the proof I have found of something which nullifies our most earnest intentions.

We need not even investigate the lives of others. We have only to examine our own. How many of us have not had a minute in our existences when something outside our control has changed everything?

It was an accidental meeting twenty-five years ago which guided me into the extraordinary existence I have led. The Paris Peace Conference, Lawrence, the Sahara, the Dutch Indies, China, Japan, Korea, Manchuria, the South Sea Islands, screenplay writing in

Hollywood, adventures in this war, the publishing of this book are due to my speaking to someone at three minutes past noon on an August day of 1918. If I had not spoken to that person, *or had done so at any other time than at three minutes past noon on that particular day,* I would have followed a completely different road which would certainly have never taken me near the Sahara.

I could point to many other seconds in my life when my route was unexpectedly altered without my having much to do with it. To say that these occasions were *used* by me to make the changes is inexact. In many of the cases the things which happened appeared to be disasters. Later they usually turned out for the good; but at the time, I would have done anything to avoid them. I was pushed out of my groove each time by something stronger than myself. The Arabs call it mektoub, kismet, the will of Allah. I don't know what I call it. All I know is that it does mighty strange things to the lives of men and women.

While this fatalism dominates the Sahara people's lives, they contradictorily believe in spells and witchcraft and djinns. They hang themselves and their children with amulets to ward off evils which, if preordained, no one should be able to escape! The Koran is always placed in the cradle of the newly born; and for those who cannot afford one, there are people who rent pages of the Holy Book.

One of the most peculiar and inexplicable of these "side shows" to Islam in the Sahara is the casting of spells. It is impossible to dismiss it as a superstition. Witchcraft, for lack of a better name, not only is practiced among these desert people but produces results. I have seen it. I can give a first-hand example which is not hearsay.

An oasis man I knew, called Sliman, got bored with his wife and wanted to marry a second. But the wife—her name was Aïcha— unlike most Moslem women happened to be content alone with her husband and did not want a companion Mrs. Sliman. Sliman, however, was set on having the other girl, who was a catch with a big dowry. So he divorced Aïcha.

Aïcha, having put herself in the wrong by refusing to permit what was a perfectly normal and legal thing for a Moslem to do, had no redress. But she made up her mind that she was not going to give up her man without a struggle. When she saw that the divorce was going through, she went to an old witch called Messaouda. I knew this crone; and if ever there was a creepy fourth-dimensional creature, it was this wrinkled hag with glittering eyes like a snake's. Messaouda took on the case and started weaving spells. On the night of Sliman's second wedding, she ordered Aïcha to prepare a feast and invite all her girl friends. "At midnight," she added, "your husband will return to you."

Aïcha did as she was told. It was a gay party, with buckets of mint tea and trays of almond cakes and everyone having a good time. Aïcha enjoyed herself, too, and had almost forgotten about the witchcraft business when, at midnight, there was a banging at the door. A maid opened it and found Sliman in a dazed condition begging to be let in. Acting on Messaouda's instructions, Aïcha refused to receive her husband until he had three times implored her forgiveness.

Sliman was not a nomad, but I was on nodding terms with him, so I cornered him one day and asked him what it was all about. He shrugged his shoulders and assured me he had no idea. All he knew was that just as he was going to see his new bride for the first time, he felt impelled toward Aïcha. He struggled against the impulse, but in vain. Before he knew what was happening, he was running as fast as he could back to his wife's home. That was all he could tell me. Neither can I add anything except that as long as I lived in those parts, Aïcha never had to bother about her husband wanting another wife. I wish I could have met Aïcha. It might have explained a lot. But of course that was out of the question.

When I tackled Madani on the subject, he muttered something about witchcraft and had one of his rare attacks of inscrutability.

Mohammed ben Tahar assured me that it was all perfectly straightforward weaving of spells. He cited me several cases where discord had started in households although the persons who wanted to make mischief, it was proved, had said nothing to anyone concerned.

Atalla Bouameur laughed. But all he said was: "When we understand the minds of women, there won't be any mysteries left for us in the world."

Cyprien Couteau said: "*Les Arabes sont des* ———," a word I cannot print. "If I catch them trying any witchcraft on me, I'll lock them all up. It'll give me something to do."

To which I replied: "You might get Messaouda to wish you back to the Somme valley and weave a spell over the son of the *juge de paix* who took your girl." But Cyprien Couteau was not amused. We came from "different social levels." The *pêche à la ligne* and the *non pêche à la ligne*.

I did not consult the Bash Agha. I am sure his view would have been the same as Mohammed ben Tahar's.

However, one point was clear. Neither the skeptical nor the believing nor the evasive could explain the strange story of Sliman and his wife Aïcha.

Some of the chief dispensers of magic and spells in North Africa are the marabouts.

Marabouts are holy men who claim descent from Mohammed. There are also a few who have become marabouts by virtue of saintliness. They have no official position and have nothing to do with the mufti and the imam and the muezzin, who run the mosque. Aside from their self-made or inherited sanctity, they have the same position in regard to religion as any Moslem.

In some cases, marabouts are men of merit and have a great deal of good influence over the Arabs. However, as practically all the male children of marabouts inherit the title, there are many who do not count at all. Of these a great number are unscrupulous racketeers who trade on this holy reputation to exploit believers. There are few poor marabouts, good or bad. They are landowners, sheep farmers, date cultivators. The land and the sheep and the date palms are offerings from their followers in return for blessings and prayers and charms and spells. They have few expenses, as the Arabs are so afraid of getting in bad with these men, who hawk maledictions and absolutions like peanuts, that they work for them for nothing.

One marabout I knew did simple conjuring tricks which sent his people into states of gibbering astonishment. He was a scamp, and one day I confounded him by explaining the trick. He was very annoyed and, I am sure, cast all kinds of spells on me. But his dupes were not affected. Their faith in this imposter was implicit, and my exposure was discredited.

I also knew a female maraboute who was said to be on intimate terms with a djinn! When I asked for evidence, I was told that someone had peeped through the keyhole of the saintly lady's home and seen her with a naked creature of the male sex!

The only marabout I was on close terms with was Sidi el Hadj Mohktar. He lived in a small town in the foothills above the Sahara, called Chellala.

Nomads and marabouts have little in common, and the reason this one came into my life was that Madani looked after his flocks. He did not do this through fear of spells or to find salvation. Madani was too hardheaded a businessman to give his services and his territory and his shepherds for saintliness. He did it because the Marabout, who knew Madani's abilities as a sheep breeder, made it worth his while.

As a matter of fact, Sidi el Hadj Mohktar was in many ways a saint. He was sixty or over, though like most Arabs of his generation he did not know his age except by his beard and moustache, which were turning white, and which he dyed. He had piercing black eyes and a grand sense of humor. He spoke good French. Although he had twice made the pilgrimage to Mecca, he did not refuse a glass of wine when it was offered him. He probably felt holy enough to take the risk.

One night, soon after our migration north, I found myself in Chellala. The Arab grapevine brought Sidi Mohktar the news that I was around, so he came over to the inn where I had dined, to find out where his flocks were. The Arabs are the most sincerely courteous people in the world. It would never have occurred to Sidi Mohktar to send a retainer or have me come to him. He was a powerful marabout, but I was a guest in his home town.

For a while we talked about the sheep and the pastures. I gave him a good account of a good year, which pleased him, and he got up from the uncomfortable French chair and asked me if I would like to go to more convivial surroundings. I accepted, expecting to be taken to a gathering of wise muftis. The old man, however, had other ideas, for he led the way to that part of the town set aside for the dancing girls. Without announcing ourselves, we walked into one of the houses. The young women trooped into the reception room in their gaudy clothes without recognizing their guest. For a moment they stood around, coy and giggling. Then one of them started and looked more closely at the white robed figure. She gasped, hesitated, seemed about to flee, glanced nervously about her, and, taking courage, reverently kissed the Marabout's turban. The others, seeing who stood there without speaking, wiped their grins off their faces and half closed their eyes. One by one, they demurely followed the first girl and did homage. Then they all rushed away and all rushed back with cushions and carpets and rugs, with which they made a throne for the holy man. A stool was placed for me at the foot of the throne. This was followed by a platter of almond cakes and the inevitable mint tea. To my relief the Marabout waved it away.

"Bring beer!" he commanded.

Beer was brought, and we solemnly clinked glasses. Dancing girls from neighboring houses came shyly into the improvised shrine and kissed the white turban. A few men breezed in inadvertently and, seeing who was there, withdrew.

The Marabout took little notice of this homage. He drank his beer thoughtfully, and eventually, turning to me, asked: "In your country do you have dancing girls, as here?"

I shook my head.

"Neither did we until the French came," he said. "The French have brought a lot of changes to our people. They have brought a *lot* of changes. They have brought many modern inventions, some of which have done good. But they have done much harm, too."

"What kind of harm?"

The Marabout made a sweeping gesture with his hand. "This kind of harm. They have led our men into sin and deserting their homes. They have taught them to forget their prayers. They have taught them to drink. The French would have done well to stay away."

I felt inclined to suggest that the Marabout was not giving a very good example by coming here and drinking beer, but all I said was: "You don't approve of the French?"

"I approve of no strong country taking possession of a weaker one and exploiting it."

"But who would have ruled here if the French had not come?"

"Why, the Arabs!" The Marabout stared at me in surprise.

"But *which* Arab?"

The old man considered me. As I expected, he had no ready reply. I was asking him the great conundrum in relationship to

83

anything to do with Arab autonomy. Who would rule? There was no big chief here or in any other Arab territory who would admit that another big chief was bigger than he. Until that attitude was overcome, a program for Arab self-government would be hard to draw up. After a while the Marabout said:

"The bash agha Jelloul is a fine man. He comes from one of the oldest families, and he is wise."

"But so, I believe, is the bash agha of the Ouled Nail and the bash agha of the Ziban tribes?" I suggested.

"Yes," agreed the Marabout, "and so is the bash agha of the Chamba confederation." He paused again and drank some beer. "That is indeed a problem," he continued, "and until it is settled, we cannot get rid of the French." He eyed me for a moment and added, "You are very young, but you have the wisdom of a great marabout."

He closed his eyes and sat fingering his coral rosary from Mecca. The room was suddenly heavy with silence. Except for the flickering candles which sent fantastic shadows roving over the ceiling, it was as still as a picture. The dark blue and red of the carpets. The snow-white robes of the Marabout. The Damascene tray and the bottles of French beer. The flaming colors of the girls' dresses as they sat in a semicircle before us. The glitter of their anklets and bracelets. And above all, the detachment from all material thought. For one had only to look at the girls' faces to realize that any idea of business for that night had been forgotten. For as long as he cared to stay there, they were the spiritual brides of Sidi el Hadj Mohktar.

The old man slowly opened his eyes and motioned to one of the girls to pour more beer. Then he turned to me again.

"You have a wise doctor called Voronoff, have you not?"

Nothing could catch me off balance now, so I replied casually: "He's not a countryman of mine, but he's European."

"I have studied his teaching," went on the Marabout. "Can he really rejuvenate the old?"

"For a short time, I believe," I said, "but I haven't gone into the matter much. I don't see what one gains by living longer than one is supposed to."

The Marabout smiled. "You are wise," he said, "but you are young. When you feel years weighing on you, you will wish

84

you had again your vitality and your virility." He hesitated, and raised and let fall his hand. "And yet our deaths are destined, so what can a human doctor do? Mektoub!" He bowed his head for a moment, clutching his beads. "Youth fades rapidly and old age lasts long," he said, glancing at the girls, whose eyes never left his. "Come, these young women have other things to do than to stare at a wrinkled old man." He smiled again and, getting up, led the way to the door.

Outside, the warm breeze fanned our faces. The stars looked huge in the black skies. From somewhere down the street we could hear the deep notes of an Arab flute and the rhythmic beat of a tamtam.

"They play a melody of the far South," said Sidi Mohktar. "It is very beautiful. It is very sad. The heart of the Arab under foreign rule is sad. —I will leave you now. May Allah bless you and keep you long. Tomorrow we will visit my flocks. In sha Allah."

He held out his hand, pressed mine, raised his fingers to his lips and then placed them over his heart. He flung the fold of the white burnous over his shoulder and disappeared into the darkness. The note of the flute drifted up on the wind, a jackal yapped on the alfa plain, the world seemed empty of people. I suddenly felt confounded by something which these Arabs had and I lacked. . . . It was a strange sensation, but I knew then that however long I lived with these men, I could never entirely absorb their philosophy or quite find their unbroken peace of mind.

CHAPTER X

As SIDI EL HADJ MOHKTAR had said, it was the French who introduced official prostitution into North Africa.

The French are businesslike about this aspect of sex. There is not a small town in France which has not its red light quarter, and one of the first things the French authorities think of when occupying a new territory is a good brothel.

During the First World War, I met a Frenchman who had a traveling establishment, complete with a "madame," which followed the French armies in Syria and the Lebanon. He confided to me that he was angling for the Legion of Honor. "For," said he in all seriousness, "you cannot deny that what I furnish the troops has contributed a great deal to their morale and fighting capacities, and therefore to victory."

Well, that is a point of view, and explains what pained the Marabout of Chellala.

Although there were Arab prostitutes before the French, they were less in evidence than in monogamous communities. A man with several legitimate wives is not going hunting for loose women except out of perverseness. But as in all matters Mohammedan, there is a paradox.

One great tribe, the Ouled Nail, admits, and has always admitted, prostitution as a legitimate way for a girl to procure herself a dowry. Whereas in other Arab tribes a mother will guard her daughter jealously and never let her out unveiled once she has attained womanhood, an Ouled Nail mother will do the reverse. She will encourage her daughter to prostitute herself as early as possible and as often as possible so as to make enough money to find a husband quickly. The oddest part is that the Ouled Nail men do not mind and have no squeamishness about marrying a girl who has lived this way. But when the ex-prostitute is finally wed, she is locked up tighter than any of her sisters of other tribal groups.

With France's introduction of the special quarter, such as the one I visited with the Marabout, the Ouled Nail young ladies know exactly where to go, and the raising of the dowry is much simpler. These special, or reserved, quarters are unique and amusing places. They are usually surrounded by a high wall and entered by a single gate guarded by a sentry. This guarding has a threefold purpose.

The first is to stop fights between jealous soldiers or crazy nomads.

The second is to prevent girls slipping out to do business on their own. The reserved quarters are under strict medical supervision.

The third is to protect the vast quantities of gold which are hidden behind the walls.

In the old days the girls collected gold pieces in payment for their services. These they strung around their necks and about their ankles and arms. This not only was ornamental but gave evidence of capital. Now that gold is no longer current, the girls convert the paper money into bits of gold which they have beaten into bracelets and earrings and tiaras. A dancing girl looks like a glittering Christmas tree, and as all the glitter really is gold, she has to be watched over.

Inside the walls of the reserved quarter is a self-supporting little city: shops, cafés, miniature streets, and squares where the dancing takes place in the summer. There is also a woman's hammam and a tiny hospital. The girls have small apartments where, in addition to what you might expect, they receive their friends and give dinner parties. Some have their babies with them, others live with their mothers. As Arabs know nothing about contraception, it is astonishing that there are not more babies. I asked Mohammed ben Tahar about this, and he answered without hesitation:

"Spells, of course. Spells! The old women cast spells on the young ones and they can't conceive. When they leave the quarter to marry, the spells are removed."

Well, that is as it may be. It is as good an explanation as any other.

Quite a few girls "go steady" with one man, usually an Arab soldier of the garrison, if he makes it worth their while. But if he loses his money or does not keep up the regular scale of gifts, he is dropped. There is no woman so mercenary as a lady of the Ouled Nail.

But it is all very homely and gay, with some sort of music going most of the day and night. The coffee, too, is better than outside, but the tea is worse. With all that gold, they can afford unlimited sugar and beds of mint. I used to be a regular visitor when I came into the oasis. Here, in contrast with the same kind of quarter in France, one's call is not necessarily for the obvious reasons. Half the men go to listen to the music, to watch the dancing, to drink coffee and relax after the day's work.

That is one aspect of Moslem women, and it is a very small one. The real aspect, that of the harem, is outside the ken of a nomad, and more than outside mine—or ought to have been.

I should have never been allowed inside a harem. I should never have seen a respectable woman unveiled. I should not even have talked to one veiled. That I did, was due to the connivance of someone about whom I will tell later. However, though I did penetrate into this strictly guarded side of an Arab's existence, it was only briefly; I never lived a harem life. But I saw a good deal and I heard a good deal, and I think I know a good deal about how Moslem women live.

Atalla's fake harem, in which he served the nauseous tea and sold Damascene junk, was as far removed from the genuine thing as Ingres' pictures of the ladies of the seraglio lying in various degrees of nudity around a tiled swimming pool. The swimming pool itself is silly; Arab women cannot swim. Neither do Orientals expose their bodies as do Occidentals, except in the steaming dimness of a Turkish bath. If the women did such a thing in broad daylight, they would not look like the ladies around the Ingres swimming pool.

Although Arab men are handsome, their women, with rare exceptions, are not beautiful. They have pretty hands and arms, but their legs and ankles and necks are thick. Most of them have fine eyes, but their bodies are heavy. This is due to eating too much and taking no exercise. To an Arab this does not matter. He prefers his dumpy, homely girl to any streamlined Occidental beauty. He would no more think of carrying off a blonde on the bow of his saddle, as suggested in movies and novels, than omit his prayers. He is shocked by bare arms and dresses which leave nothing to the imagination. His idea of elegance and seduction is someone in a brightly colored, embroidered velvet dress, tied around the middle with a sash, under which are several cotton petticoats, black woolen stockings and leather slippers. The hair is heavy with oil which has nothing about it suggestive of the perfumes that we associate with Araby. The face is daubed with mascara and rouge and powder.

A true harem, which is pronounced "hareem" and not "harum," has nothing in common with our ideas of Haroun al Raschid and Scheherazade. The scents of Araby are as absent from it as from its occupants. There are no gorgeous furnishings or sumptuous divans. No splendid eunuchs or seductive odalisques guard the door. It consists of nothing more than a plain room or rooms, the size of the place varying according to the means of the owner. Maid-servants also are on a par with the master's pocketbook. A poor man has to share the harem with his wife. In this case it is partitioned off by a curtain. A husband and wife, whatever their station in life, never sleep or eat in the same room together.

However, whether the harem is large or small, it is never luxurious. There is no furniture, and the walls are usually bare. The floor is strewn with carpets, more or less rich, and cushions, more or less gaudy. Clothes are kept in gaily painted boxes like old-fashioned traveling trunks. Meals are eaten at low tables which are brought in and placed before the diners, who sit cross-legged on the ground and pick the food from a common dish with their fingers. The night is spent on cushions on the floor. There are usually a number of clocks, all showing different times. This does not matter. Arabs are vague about punctuality and run their lives by the sun. The clocks are there because of that passion of unmechanical people for things mechanical.

In an average harem the wife or wives occupy the main living room. The children have separate quarters, and there is a kitchen and servant accommodation. The eunuch guardians are becoming rare. Except in very rich households there are no bathrooms. Bodily washing is carried out on certain days when the hammam is set aside for women. It is a great place for gossip, and the rare love intrigues of a Moslem community are hatched in the steaming twilight of the Turkish bath.

The husband has his own quarters, to which he summons a wife when he wants to be alone with her.

This gesture does not provoke ill feeling or envy among the other wives. All marriages are arranged by the parents, and without the brides or grooms seeing each other before the wedding day. Consequently there is no love involved. Consequently no jealousy. Except in a case like Aïcha's, polygamy is more the wish of the wives than of the husbands, who find it an expensive luxury. In the monogamous marriage it is the wife who has to be alone all day while her husband is at work. Aside from weaving, a fairly well-to-do woman has nothing to relieve her solitude. She cannot even fall back on her imagination.

Arab women are not educated. They can neither read nor write. They have no idea of what is going on in the world. They are not interested. An American girl I knew was once staying in the agha Daylis' harem. After a while she got deadly bored herself, so to pass away the time, she thought she would teach her hostesses to play bridge. But she encountered an unsurmountable obstacle. None of the women knew how to count.

There was an old matriarch in our oasis who was wealthy in her own right. Every so often her brother would hand her the proceeds of sales of sheep and dates in one-thousand-franc bills. What was written on these bills conveyed nothing to the old lady, and quantity impressed her more than size. She had a grandson, her favorite, a charmer but a rascal. As soon as his grandmother received her dividends, he used to visit her. When no one was looking, she would slip several of the thousand-franc bills into the young man's hands. These he changed into five-franc bills and pocketed half. Granny never worried. She did not realize. All that mattered to her was that she had a fat wad of bills under her cushion instead of a thin one.

I once asked Atalla why women were kept illiterate.

After a moment he replied: "If they could read or write, they could communicate with lovers."

It was an ingenuous thought, and no more true about Arabs than about women of any race. An intention to have a lover is not going to be stopped by a small matter of illiteracy. As the Arabs themselves say:

"It takes less time for a man and a woman to commit the sin than for a slave to cook a dish of eggs."

But affairs are rare, chiefly because men and women are content in their homes and are not tempted to risk their lives to be with someone they barely know and have hardly seen. From the moment the girl has reached womanhood, she disappears from circulation, and any potential lover can only have seen her unveiled when she was in her early teens. When infidelity does occur, it is this Moslem veiling, intended to preserve chastity, which defeats its end.

The veil of the oasis people (nomad women do not veil) is not the traditional yashmak of old Turkey, which covers half the woman's face and often makes her intriguing. The true veil is a cotton shroud, blue or white, which covers the woman from top to toe. Nothing is left showing, not even her hands or feet. One eye peeping through a slit in the shroud is all that enables the wearer to see her way about. So complete is the disguise that one cannot tell whether a young beauty or an old hag is brushing by. In fact, no one can tell *what* is under the blue and white envelope.

If a man has remained sufficiently interested in a childhood girl friend to risk ostracism, and possibly his neck, to see her again; if a woman is ready to take the same risk; if she has a servant she can trust to the extent of placing her honor and her life in her hands—then the veil becomes an aid to the violation of the harem. It is the disguise situation of old-fashioned grand opera, but more foolproof.

All that the lover has to do is to shroud himself and go to the home of his beloved. No one will take any notice of this veiled "woman," and the "confidential maid" will admit him without singing an aria about it. The rest is a matter between the man and the girl.

Should the husband return unexpectedly, after the manner of opera, and wish to see his wife, the maid will stop him. —Mrs. Ali is calling on Mrs. Ahmed, and until Mrs. Ali has veiled herself, Mr. Ahmed cannot go into the harem. —Mr. Ahmed knows this, and the maid slips into the women's quarters and warns the lovers. "Mrs. Ali" quickly veils "herself" and leaves with chaste dignity. Should Mr. Ahmed suspect that Mrs. Ali is *not* Mrs. Ali and burst into the harem or tear off the protecting veil, and it really is

Mrs. Ali, there will be the dickens to pay. It will probably end by Mr. Ali's killing Mr. Ahmed.

Yes, the veil can be an effective means of defeating its object, but the enterprise is seldom thought worth the risk. In matters connected with the honor of the home an Arab has powers of life and death over all those concerned. Besides, most Moslem women are too lazy to complicate their existences, dull though they may be.

The conditions under which the wives of poorer Arabs live are less monotonous than those of their wealthier sisters.

The wives of men like the Bash Agha or Atalla never saw anything outside the interiors of their harems and gardens. As their husbands had summer and winter residences, they actually knew two harems and two gardens. That was all. They did not even know the routes between their two homes. The yearly moves were made at night in cars with drawn shades. Occasionally they saw their mothers or their sisters or their fathers; but paying calls was not encouraged. In fact, such Moslem women of the upper classes were completely ignorant of the outside world except by hearsay.

The wife of a poor man, like Mohammed's mother, had a much gayer time. She had no servants and was obliged to do her own shopping. Shopping took her into the streets; and although bundled up in her shroud, she had that one eye peeping out. Needless to say, it missed nothing—Arab chiefs in their scarlet cloaks, French officers, tourists, automobiles, people and happenings which Mesdames Jelloul and Atalla had hardly dreamed of. She could gossip with other women and with the shopmen from whom she bought. An airplane, which was part of a fairy tale to the real harem women, was as ordinary to unprivileged Mrs. Tahar as her pots and pans.

Birth and position give certain material advantages, but they involve a prisoner's existence from which there is no release except through widowhood or divorce. Oddly enough, Moslem divorce laws do not specially favor men.

An Arab woman has absolute control over her personal property, whether it be money or goods. In cases of divorce the marriage settlement must provide enough for her to live on as she has been accustomed. Her grounds for divorce are more trivial than in most European countries. For example, a woman can divorce her husband for neglect, which would be out of the question in France and difficult in England.

An oasis man I knew was a member of an amateur orchestra which kept him up late at night. He was doing nothing which he should not, but the musical parties which his wife could not attend often sent him home in the small hours. His wife warned him that if he continued to neglect her, she would "go back to mother." The man took no notice. One morning he returned to find his wife gone. The next day he was called before the kadi and divorced. He had no recourse, and it cost him the equivalent of a quarter.

Although Arabs know of their brilliant background in pre-Islamic times, they attribute all their customs to Mohammed. When I told them that he was not the inventor of the harem, they were incredulous. Yet that is so. The seclusion of women belongs to the remote past. There were harems in Babylon and Nineveh, in India and in Palestine. From time immemorial Orientals have insisted on female chastity, on maintenance of a pure strain, on noninterference with the home by outsiders. An enormous majority still believe in the system and do not wish to see it changed.

Mustapha Kemal's reforms in Turkey between 1923 and 1924 shocked Moslems all over the world, but the repercussions were comparatively local. Today more than two hundred and seventy-five million Moslems still observe the laws concerning women which Mohammed gathered into his teaching thirteen hundred years ago.

One of the main reasons for this is the wish of the women themselves. They do not want to be emancipated. They would be unhappy if their husbands decided to imitate Western ways and took them out of their seclusion. Their indolent existences without education please them. They like to feel cared for and protected by their husbands. They have no wish to share in civic responsibilities like their Occidental sisters. They have always known the harem, and what was good enough for their grandmothers is good enough for them. In other words, they have peace of mind.

The only Arab woman I ever knew to give up the veil and leave her harem did so at the suggestion of her husband. He was a chief of the Ziban confederation which pastures near Biskra and had served for several years as an officer in a cavalry regiment in France. The relationship of his French colleagues and their wives appealed to him, and he decided to make an experiment with his own wife.

Unlike many of her kind, this woman could speak French, and in due course she was brought from her oasis in the Sahara to Paris.

The experiment lasted six months. At the end of that time the lady implored her husband to have her taken back to her harem. There I saw her. The things that girl told me were revelations of how irksome modern life can be to someone who has not been brought up in it. The changing of clothes for morning or afternoon or evening occupations. The complicated way of eating with different kinds of spoons and forks instead of fingers. The meaningless conversations. The casual manner in which women uncovered as much of their bodies as propriety permitted. The way men looked at women and the liberties they took with them, even with their husbands in the room. —The catalogue was endless.

The girl assured me that after six months of living Occidental-wise in Paris, she had no longer any fears of hell. If heaven was no more than the peaceful routine of her harem, she would have no complaints.

The fact is that the average Arab household is happy. The men are kind to their wives and devoted to their children. They look after their homes conscientiously. They give their families a feeling of security; and as in most communities, this is what a woman chiefly looks for in marriage. Being confined to a harem and not allowed to see unrelated men is no hardship if it is the custom of the society in which one has been brought up. An Arab wife waiting for her lord may seem a rather grotesque, a rather sad figure to an Occidental. All her finery, all her make-up, which have taken hours to put on, are for the benefit of one man who may be too preoccupied to even notice her when he gets home. But she will not mind. She knows that she is safe. Her husband may be spasmodic in his attentions, but he has his wife in mind, and the welfare and the honor of his home count for him before all.

Well-meaning reformers who would free Moslem women might do well to ask themselves whether the homes they have left in America are as well looked after and as happy as those of the Arabs.

CHAPTER XI

My KNOWLEDGE OF HAREMS and harem women was
superficial, but it was a good deal more comprehensive
than that of my nomads. They had practically no
experience of that side of Moslem life. It was almost as remote from
theirs as from a Christian's. Occasionally a chief from one of the
hill communities married the daughter of a rich tribesman, but
this happened rarely and was discouraged. A girl born and reared
in the desert could never be really "house broken." None of her
instincts and traditions were in keeping with the restrictions of the
veil and the harem. Her way of living was quite different.

Owing to the amount of physical work they had to do, owing
to the constant moving and bustle and unexpectedness of camp
life, our women were never veiled. This does not mean that they
walked around immodestly like Occidentals or Ouled Nails. In
point of fact, one hardly ever saw them. They had the most
extraordinary ability to keep out of the way of their own men and
turn their backs on strangers. Even in the partitioned-off section
of the tents, which corresponded to the harem, one hardly heard
them. This was a pity, as they were much better looking than
their cousins of the oases. The sun and the wind had given their
skins a rich tan, and their active lives had got rid of all the flabby
fat of the town girls. Some had stunning figures. Their clothes, too,
were more becoming than the velvets and taffetas of the house-bred
Arab wives. The colors were more somber, and there were no
flopping petticoats, usually no stockings. Serviceable sandals took
the place of the unpractical high-heeled shoes. Their hair was plaited
and hung in two strands over their shoulders. There was no
make-up except about the eyes. Many wore finely wrought silver
ornaments studded with turquoises, not unlike the Navajo Indian
jewelry. Atalla would have given anything to have some in his

shop as it was the genuine article and had none of the tawdry glitter of the stuff the Ouled Nails decked themselves with.

These nomad women were extremely gay and their babies were gayer. One never heard that aggravating wail of the spoiled child. The few bleats were the normal cries of hunger. Whatever happened, the girls always laughed, and when things really did go wrong, they never complained. At the end of a long march they were as smiling as at the beginning, and set about putting up the tents and getting ready the dinner as if they had been making the move in chauffeur-driven limousines. Often I thought of women with whom I had traveled in Europe and remembered their grumblings if their rooms were not just right or the water was tepid or that dinner they expected was not waiting. And I knew why they had been so tiresome. Their systems were poisoned by overindulgence. If those women had walked our trips; if, at the end of the day, they had had to get dinner and considered themselves lucky if they camped near water, they would not have had time to complain. Besides, they would have felt so well that moods would have been out of the question. Incompatibility and nerves and brain fag and all those things which make townspeople behave like maniacs are unthinkable when the body is well exercised and the lungs are full of clean air. I have never seen women so unneurotic and so hardy as these ladies of the black tents.

When they had babies, no one paid much attention. Sometimes it came up in the conversation that Farradji or Yahia was the father of a new son or daughter, but there was no more celebration than when a lamb was born. It was probably because the babies *were* born rather like lambs. I never actually saw a woman bring forth a child on the caravan trail; but I have seen a far-gone pregnant woman helping to load the camels in the morning, and on the same evening, twenty miles further on, I have seen her suckling an infant.

Good humor gave harmony to the nomad's home life, and there were few divorces. Apart from the fact that everyone was too busy for fault-finding, the camp was a kind of family concern. The chiefs and the shepherds had been raised together, and the majority of the marriages were in the camp circle. It was almost unheard of for a man to marry outside his own tribe.

Added to these co-operative incentives to keeping the home

going, there was no convenient kadi to dissolve marriages for twenty-five cents. Wedding rites on the desert were performed by three witnesses. Only the same three witnesses could divorce the couples they married. If one of the witnesses died or disappeared, it was impossible for husbands and wives to be legally freed.

But they did not want to be freed. The nomads, like most Arabs, were kind husbands; thoughtful, too. A shepherd never went to an oasis or village market without buying some trinket or piece of finery for his wife. There was always a bag of candy for the kids. A little something for his mother. And what appreciation for the humble gifts when the shepherd got back to camp! It made one warm all through to see the smiles and hear the laughter. I do not know who were the happiest, the givers or the receivers.

And the joy of that nomad laughter! It was the gayest, the most sincere sound I have ever known. Sometimes when I am so low that there seems to be no way out, I think of that twittering, waterfall laughing of the girls in our camp. I try to remember the smiles of Ahmed and Ali and Yahia. They had an honest-to-God genuineness rarely found in humans, anywhere, ever.

Madani's wife did not live in the camp. He had reversed the procedure and married a town girl. It was a monogamous marriage, and although I could never see Mrs. Madani, I heard that she was a beauty. I am glad that I could not see her. An Arab's version of good looks was not mine, and I would have wished my partner a fiery, ravishing Scheherazade to match his own red hair.

Mrs. Madani lived in the oasis, and Madani only saw her when he went to "town." Unlike most Arabs, he was ready to talk about women, Moslems as well as others.

He was inclined to be cynical on the whole female question. He declared that all men's troubles came from women; that men were contented creatures with simple tastes and only had them complicated by their womenfolk. He believed that most women acted from material motives. He assured me that any woman who had the instincts of her sex properly developed would torment any man who gave in to her. The only way to handle women was to be indifferent to them. He did not believe that women were any more chaste by nature than men. Hence Mohammed's adoption of the harem system.

"But," he added, "when a woman does love, there is nothing

to equal it. It surpasses anything a man can feel. It is the most perfect and complete emotion which exists." He shrugged his shoulders. "We'd be better off without them, but as we cannot do without them, it's no good arguing about it."

During the early days of my living in the Sahara, these appraisals of womanhood by an Arab surprised me. Much that Madani said was true in relation to Occidental women. But these were free, and the hunting and "tormenting" of men was a legitimate and recognized privilege. How could a Moslem woman, though, have any such traits? I still do not know. Yet there are few women in the world who understand more about the business of being women than Arabs. They have every handicap. No means of holding their husbands by jealousy. Not a grain of intelligence with which to interest them. Usually no fortunes. But with all their docility and slavelike existence, they get more out of their men than many free and lovely Occidentals. It may be that, having nothing else to do, they concentrate on being feminine?

I once asked Madani point-blank if he was genuinely in favor of the harem system. He replied without hesitation that he was. We had been visiting a well which was rumored to be drying up and were driving back to the oasis in a ramshackle old Ford of his. I insisted, and asked if he had any practical reasons for saying this. He said:

"Yes, several."

I asked for some.

Madani chuckled. He loved telling me his stories. No one before me had shown so much interest in what he had to say.

"When I was an officer in the French cavalry," he started off. All Madani's tales about Europe began like that. It gave a kind of ring of authenticity. "When I was an officer in the French cavalry serving in France," he repeated, "we used to go out on maneuvers in the summer. It was all good fun and a fine healthy life like here. Everyone felt fit, and there were no quarrels or misunderstandings the whole time were were out in camp. But!" Madani shook his head. "But, the morning after we returned to barracks, Major X was cutting Captain C, and Lieutenant Z was not talking to Captain W." Madani paused dramatically and, turning toward me, asked: "And *why*, do you suppose?" I shrugged my shoulders. I knew better than to spoil the climaxes of Madani's yarns. The few times I had done so, he had started the whole thing from the beginning again. Satisfied that I was mystified, he nodded his head meaningly and concluded: "Because, my friend, because, during our absence, Mrs. X had quarreled with Mrs. C, and Mrs. W had insulted Mrs. Z. And Mrs. H and J and K had all said something which the other did not like. The *only* person who was on exactly the same terms as before was myself! Why? Because *my* wife was safely locked away and unable to get herself mixed up in these female complications."

Madani gave a triumphant snort and glanced at me as if daring me to suggest that his reasoning was at fault. And I had no wish to challenge him. I remembered the years when I was soldiering in India and the dread with which I made the weekly round of the quarters of the wives of the N.C.O.'s and the men of my company. I remembered how difficult it was for a young and pretty wife to live down her looks with the senior officers' ladies. Madani's story made perfect sense to me. So I said nothing and stared out into the night which had fallen over the desert as Madani talked.

Driving along, we came to a bend in the road near the entrance to the oasis. Our headlights left the track and illuminated a kind of depression to our left. It was not much of a depression and not the kind of place where one would expect to make a startling discovery. For it was startling to see a Citroen coupé parked on the desert. It was even more startling to observe inside the coupé a young French officer of the Spahis and, in the arms of the young French officer, the wife of another French officer of the Spahis. Our headlights had hit them so unexpectedly that they had had no time to move. As we passed on and the depression returned to its normal darkness, Madani chuckled again.

"You see? I don't know where Major O. *thinks* his wife is, but I *know* where mine is."

I thought, for a moment, of asking him if it was not conceivable that the lover-and-the-veil trick might be practiced on him? But I held back. I felt sure that any woman who was lucky enough to have such a fine fellow as Madani for a husband would not cheat. . . .

That Ford of Madani's was a wonderful contraption. He was madly proud of it, though, as with all Arabs, his knowledge of machinery was zero and his ability to control a machine about the same. The first time he tried it out was with me in Chellala, the home of Sidi Mohktar, the marabout.

The sheik Marhoun, the son of the agha Daylis and grandson of the bash agha Jelloul, was going to be married. As he looked after his grandfather's properties in the North, he led a sedentary life and was to marry a girl of the same kind. Madani thought it would be a great idea to produce the car for this festive occasion. What could be more impressive than for the bridegroom to make his appearance at the wedding in a Ford!

Marhoun and I, therefore, and the inevitable Ali, prepared to make a triumphant start from the village square. Madani, resplendent in his scarlet burnous, was at the wheel. Behind us, on the sidewalk outside the inn, Frenchmen and a sprinkling of Arabs sat drinking and smoking. To right and to left had gathered Madani's and Marhoun's retainers to witness the departure of the bridegroom.

After a few false alarms Madani got the motor started and began to fiddle with the gears (it was one of those old Fords with everything on the steering wheel), and, nodding to Marhoun and me on the back seat, glanced ahead of him to see that the way was clear. He then let in the clutch—

I have no idea of what happened exactly, but the car seemed to take a flying leap—backwards—and the next thing I knew, we were all sitting on the bar inside the hotel!

After that, Madani drove only when he was in the desert. It was by order of the Bash Agha. The damage done to the Chellala inn, to the gentlemen and their aperitifs, and to nomadic prestige was incalculable.

An Arab wedding, other than the simple ceremony of the nomads, is a fantastic and paradoxical performance.

The selection of the two to be mated is made by the parents. If the young man is particular, he can have his sisters report on his future wife; but on principle he knows nothing about her. The girl knows still less. Even the marriage contract is drawn up without either of the interested parties being consulted. The kadi does this with the parents, and it usually calls for the bridegroom to furnish his wife with a comfortable home and the means of living to which she has been accustomed. He may even pay a sum down to the girl's father. The bride brings her trousseau, her jewelry, pots and pans and other household goods.

100

In the case of Marhoun it was all much more elaborate. He was a big catch as heir presumptive once removed to the bash-aghaship, and the girl was the daughter of an important landowner of the lower Atlas. The marriage, therefore, joined a desert fortune and a hill fortune, as well as two powerful families. As Madani knowingly said to me:

"With this little setup, we can bring our sheep here to pasture in the summer without asking permission."

The weddings last seven days and seven nights and are conducted at the home of the girl and at the home of the man. For a week the bride's mother entertains the bridegroom's mother and her friends and her daughter's friends. The groom, in the meanwhile, is entertaining all the men connected with the two families.

There is, of course, no drinking of liquor, but a great deal of music and eating, and nauseating quantities of mint tea. On the seventh night of the feast the bride is brought in her bridal finery to the home of the groom. She says goodbye to her mother and her attendants. She is then admitted to the honeymoon chamber, in which, for some reason, her husband is hiding under the bed or in a cupboard. —No one could explain to me this strange procedure. I gathered it was just a custom like orange blossoms and rice. —Anyway, as soon as the door is closed, the bridegroom gives a whoop and leaps from his hiding place. With the same enthusiasm he seizes the bride and flings her on the bed, where he quickly joins her.

After an appreciable time an old woman, whose duty it is, goes into the bridal chamber and makes an examination of the bride. She then comes out and announces that the marriage has been consummated. At this, every kind of old blunderbuss and flintlock, crammed with powder, is let off, and for the next half-hour nothing can be seen for smoke.

But this is not all, and here is the paradoxical element in Arab weddings. If after three days the bride or the bridegroom finds that one or both cannot bear the sight of the other, they may part. Each takes back what was agreed to in the contract; the contract is torn up, and both go their ways free to have another trial marriage. This kind of rupture happens rarely, but it does happen and can always happen, according to law and tradition.

It was one of those subjects about which I could never get a sensible answer out of Madani: one of those topics which sent him into a state of inscrutability.

"Madani," I would say, "for the love of Mike, wouldn't it save endless trouble and vast quantities of mint tea if the boy and girl were allowed to see each other before all these feasts were prepared and all these contracts signed?"

But Madani would only reply: "It is a custom!" and turn his face into a frozen blankness.

On the morning when the nomadic Ford had been landed so neatly against the bar of the Chellala hotel, it was the seventh day of feasting for the Marhoun wedding. Marhoun was liverish from too much coffee and mechoui, and was also nervous at the thought of the ordeal before him that night. —This was his first marriage. —The unexpected journey backwards into the inn put the final touch to his temper, and he did a thing rare for an Arab. He flew into a fiery rage and called Madani all the names under the sun. When he saw that I was laughing, he turned on me and flayed me as the one responsible for the buying of this fiendish machine. He then flounced off to the wedding on foot.

Marhoun was a strange man and a very good-looking one. He was small, but the proportions were perfect. His hands and features were carved from ivory. His eyes were like grey jade and very large. He was the only Arab chief I saw who would not have disappointed sheik fans. If he had been dark, he might have passed for Rudolph Valentino. His temperament was sheikish too. Arabs are courteous people, they are calm people, they do not fuss. Marhoun could fly into a tantrum and be as insolent as any Occidental. Today he looked less like a placid nomad than I did. As he stalked away, I thought: "That lad has the makings of something more than a tribal chief. If he'll keep that temper in check, perhaps *he* is the Arab who one day will be able to rule the others."

However, the rage was short-lived, and the upset of the uncontrolled Ford did not upset the wedding. The next time I saw Marhoun, he was all smiles and saturated me with mint tea. The marriage, too, was consummated successfully. After the three days' trial Marhoun declared himself delighted with the bride, the bride made no complaints, and everyone was pleased.

I was pleased, too. Not so much about Marhoun as by the fact that I could lay off from this eating which had been going on for a week. Whereas in the desert we fed ourselves but once a day and after much exercise, during this feast there had hardly been a moment when we were not gorging, and we hardly walked a yard. The Bash Agha must have slaughtered a flock of lambs to feed the men who turned up claiming kinship with the bridegroom. There were the musicians, too, the dancers, male and female, and a platoon of Negro performers, all with healthy appetites.

These Negroes, descendants of the Numidians of Jugurtha, were as savage and primitive as the Arabs were cultured and civilized. Once they were released from the routine of their occupations and were allowed to dance, every vestige of Moslem refinement left them. Nothing stopped them except physical collapse. They required no music and did their dancing to a low, moaning chant and to the clashing of small cymbals which they carried. It was a barbaric performance which had nothing remotely to do with Islam or North Africa of the twentieth century.

One evening they got themselves so worked up that nothing would make them rest. On and on they went, moaning and stamping and clashing their cymbals. After a while the Bash Agha signaled that he was satisfied, but the Negroes took no more notice than if a fly had settled on their perspiring heads. The Bash Agha ordered one of his retainers to tell the blackamoors to have done. They did not even listen. The dance grew wilder. One of the Negresses began tearing off her clothes. The men followed her example. The Bash Agha became annoyed and commanded that the dancers be thrown out. This was done without effect on the dancing or the chanting. Into the street they went, their cymbals clashing, their bodies rhythmically swaying.

The Bash Agha looked relieved. The party returned to normal, with soothing flutes and singing and guitaring until it came to a dignified close sometime after midnight.

As I was walking back to the Kadi's house, where I was staying for the wedding, I suddenly came upon the black people. They were still dancing. Some of them had fallen out from exhaustion, but eight still moaned their terrible chant as they pranced and swayed and clashed their cymbals. They did not notice me, they did not pause, their bodies no longer belonged to them. Until they fell fainting in the gutter, nothing could arrest their savage rite.

I was violently disturbed. I had again that sensation which I had had with Sidi Mohktar the last time I had been here. There was something in all this which I did not understand, something out of my mental grasp. It was like being on a mountain in a mist. Every now and then, the wind clears the damp shroud away and one finds one's self in daylight, in sunlight. One wonders why one ever lost the way. Then, down comes the mist again and one has no idea which is east or west or north or south.

It was the same with the Arabs. I was happy with them. I was well. I had peace of mind. There were moments when I really felt that I belonged to this nomadic way of living. I could see before me a broad, sunlit path leading onward to happiness. I almost felt that the contentment which every man seeks was within my grasp. And then, suddenly, down would come the mist, blotting everything out. I no longer had any notion of where I was or whither I was going. The Arabs became shadowy, their minds became as impenetrable as the fog. I had no idea what they thought of me or if they thought at all. There was something either in the country or the people or both which eluded me.

I slept fitfully that night. It was probably the result of the seventh or eighth mechoui and the five-hundredth cup of tea. Whenever I woke, I could hear those black people as if they were in my room. Dismally and relentlessly they chanted and clashed. As long as it was dark, their hideous dance continued. If I had had a gun, I would have gone out and killed them all. They seemed to be mocking me. They seemed to be taunting the stranger who had tried to lift the veil which chastely shrouded the Sahara, who had tried to defile its mystery. They seemed to be triumphing over his confusion.

Next day I saw one of these fanatics. She was placidly laundering sheets in the public washing place of Chellala. One of her partners was prodding a small donkey laden with the city garbage.

I turned my back, wondering if I should ever understand.

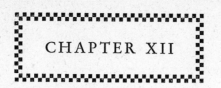

CHAPTER XII

UNTIL THAT NIGHT of the savage dancing I had rather taken the Sahara for granted. It was another place like the Grand Canyon or the Mojave or the Great Lakes. But as I journeyed south from the wedding and came nearer to those vast expanses which rolled out into the horizon, I began to think differently.

I remembered a passage I had read somewhere:

"There is much we think we know, but more that we do not know, about the Great Sahara Desert."

I remembered Pierre Benoît's *Atlantide,* and how I had puzzled whether to accept the story of this strange woman literally or symbolically. Now, either way, it was not nearly so fantastic as when I had first read the book. In that unexplored, wild mountain place in the center of the Sahara called the Ahaggar, among those prehistoric, volcanic peaks, the home of the veiled Touaregs, anything might be. There was no reason why the devastatingly lovely Antinea should not have lived there and made men die of love for her. Why not? No one could tell except the veiled men—and they *never* told.

Or, it might just be the Sahara in the symbolic form of a gorgeous woman? Men were certainly drawn back to die in her cruel embrace. The bones of many explorers and officers whitened on those glittering wastes. No one could say why, any more than they could explain the Antinea legend.

I remembered how Herodotus and Pliny and Strabo and other writers, throughout the ages, had tried to describe the Sahara, had tried to interpret it, and had failed.

I remembered also men like Fromentin and Maupassant speaking of the Sahara as if they knew it intimately merely because they had traveled a few hundred miles inland from Algiers to the fringe of the desert.

Until today I had been a Fromentin or a Maupassant. I had talked familiarly about these desolate plains, where I had made my home, without any qualification to do so.

Because the country charmed me, I thought I knew it. So did Capitaine de St. Avit and the others who fell into the hands of Antinea think they knew about women. Those men had died by their infatuations. —Suddenly I was a little afraid. I did not understand. It was all too big, too bright. That ever-blowing wind which sometimes soothed, sometimes maddened, was not natural. Why did it always blow, this wind in the Sahara? Why was it never quite calm as in other countries, or as at sea sometimes? Who were these Arabs, these Numidians, these other strange races which lived here; the Touaregs?

As if answering my question, or to add to my confusion, Madani, who sat beside me in the bus, said:

"Tomorrow I have to go to the Mzab on business. Would you like to come too?"

"What is the Mzab? Where is it?" I asked as anxiously as if Madani had suggested going to defy Antinea.

"It is about a hundred and fifty miles to the southeast of the oasis," he replied. "But what it is, I do not know. Perhaps, with your foreign learning, you will be able to find out."

He did not say this sarcastically or teasingly, but I suddenly felt like Doctor Faust. I seemed to have sold my soul to something which held me by something which I could not see or grasp. Madani was not Mephistopheles, but in a way he embodied the Sahara and all its baffling mysteries. Until I had solved them, I could never be free. So I accepted Madani's suggestion about going to the Mzab.

We continued the journey to the south next day by bus. This was not exactly Faustlike, but neither was it by any means a banal bus ride to Atlantic City. The kind of conveyance one might see in Europe and America had been left behind at the oasis. So had the majority of normal-looking passengers. The vehicle which now rattled and clanked over the bumpy track was filled with Alice-Through-the-Looking-Glass people. Senegalese soldiers, Arab nomads, Jewish merchants, men of the Mzab, a couple of Ouled

Nail girls going to seek their fortunes in some distant oasis. The driver was another of Jugurtha's descendants. I hoped that no one would suggest dancing before we reached our destination.

The first part of the journey took us over our pasture areas, but after a while the road turned southeast. The country became cruelly desolate. The scrub disappeared. Soon we were in a wilderness of flints and pebbles which glittered and glared. Madani was not interested in the change of scenery. Even when we came to a kind of chasm in the desert in the midst of which a strange city piled itself into a cone, like a giant ant heap, he took no notice. When he was not telling his beads, he was making notes in a dirty little book which he always carried around with him. I did not know what business took him to the Mzab, and I did not ask. As soon as we arrived and he had established me in a kind of caravanserai inn, he disappeared and left me practically to myself for four days. I had plenty of time, therefore, to explore the principal towns of this extraordinary country—or state. The whole area was no bigger than Long Island.

But if not big in area, how tremendous in history and tradition! The Mzabites are now and have always been one of mankind's greatest enigmas, a baffling puzzle for all those who have tried to solve it. Their way of living dates back to traditions which are lost in the mists of fable. Their past is of incredible antiquity. When they were not, no one knows. They existed as a people when the fleets of Carthage roamed the Mediterranean, when Athens was still a center of culture, when the Roman eagles ruled in Britain. The empires of the Aztecs and the Incas are of but yesterday when compared with the Mzabite commonwealth. And the Aztecs and the Incas are gone, and the Mzabites remain. The Mzabites remain, not decadent or disintegrated, but as united and vigorous as when they appeared in the Sahara one thousand years ago to found their desert cities. Their customs and their costumes have in no way changed since those far-off days, and there is no indication that they ever will. There is no indication, either, that the Mzabite will ever be anything but a mystery; for who they are or where they came from originally has never been satisfactorily explained. The Mzabites themselves have little idea or, if they have, will not communicate the information. As a result the reconstruction of their misty background takes the form of conjecture.

One of these conjectures is that they are that lost tribe of Israel which has never been satisfactorily accounted for. They are of Semitic appearance; they have many characteristics of the ancient Hebrews and, while not practicing the Jewish faith, have nothing in common with the Arabs.

Names found in old archives might give them a Canaanite or Philistine background, and from this comes a suggestion that they are the descendants of the Phoenicians who escaped the Roman vengeance when Scipio sacked Carthage in 146 B.C.

There are certainly evidences in the Mzab of Carthaginian traditions. The triangular decorations of the houses; the pictures of fish, of the crescent moon, of the sun and the stars; the phallic door knockers are not Moslem or Jewish. The cemeteries are considered holy ground and are sanctuaries for criminals. On the tombs are placed offerings for the dead. When foundation stones are laid, and at the time of planting and harvesting, camels and goats are sacrificed. None of these things are orthodox Mohammedan or Jewish.

A third suggestion is that the Mzabites are Berbers. It is the more popular idea, and the one which seemed to me to have the least foundation.

The Berbers were the original inhabitants of North Africa and are still found in isolated groups in various parts of the country, ranging from the Ahaggar to the Atlas. But the Berber, be he Touareg or Riff, is a fighting man, which the Mzabite is not. Quite the reverse.

When the French began pushing their conquest into southern Algeria in the middle of the nineteenth century, the Mzabites made peace long before the invaders got anywhere near their territory. To this day they have a separate treaty with France and are exempt from all kinds of obligations to which the Arabs are subject. One clause in the treaty absolves the Mzabite from being conscripted to serve in the French army. All he has to do is to hire an Arab to take his place. During World War I, not one Mzabite fought, but many Arabs accepted a thousand francs to defend the honor of the Mzab.

No Berber would dream of hiring another man to fight for him. At the least excuse he makes war himself.

The Berber is a farmer; the Mzabite belongs to the town. He

never goes near the land unless he is so poor that he cannot hire an Arab or a Negro to work for him. The Mzabite is a prosperous merchant; the Berber thinks himself lucky if he gets enough to eat and wear. During the great famine of 1921, when Berbers and Arabs died of starvation all over North Africa and the Jews and the French were in not-too-good shape, the Mzabites wanted for nothing. On a gold basis they imported grain from the United States.

Another Phoenician characteristic is the way the Mzabite expatriates himself for the sake of trade. In all important cities of North Africa, and occasionally in the Mediterranean ports of Europe, these squat, ivory-faced little men in their snow-white robes are found selling everything from wheat to calico. When it comes to business, they can run races around the Arabs, and there are few Jews who are their equals behind the counter. Their only ambition is to make money so that they can retire and end their days in the desolation of the Mzab. This they have to do. A Mzabite law forbids any woman to leave the Mzab, and as no Mzabite may marry an Arab or a Jewess and vice versa, he is obliged to go home to continue his family. But aside from this, he *wants* to go back. He has seen the world and he prefers the Mzab! —This is as great a mystery as the Mzabite origins.

The part of the Sahara where the Mzab is situated is frighteningly dreary. There is no water gushing naturally as in an oasis. It is on no trade route. There is nothing to suggest why any human being should wish to settle there unless in an act of desperation. And this may be the true reason for the existence of the Mzab.

Like the Jews, this small colony of prospering tradesmen was persecuted. The Arab invaders of the seventh century had converted them to Islam, but they soon dissented from the orthodox and joined the puritan Abhadite sect which was despised by the Sunni nomads. They could drive always a better bargain than any Arab and make a living where he could not. This the Arabs resented and never missed an opportunity to plunder a Mzabite settlement. Persecution did not cause the Mzabites to scatter like the Jews: they moved in a body. But whenever they got themselves established somewhere, the Arabs came after them. Finally, in despair, they decided to make themselves a home where no one would *want* to molest them. So they chose this miserable, sun-scorched, rainless gully in the Sahara. —The few accessible records show this to have been at the beginning of the eleventh century.

But however desperate the need to escape, these people had to live; and to live, the first thing they must have was water. There was none on the surface, and the lack of the lowest form of vegetation indicated that it never rained in this hideous wilderness. But the gully or valley suggested an underground river. These enterprising fanatics went after it. With primitive tools and relentless labor they found it. The first battle had been won. Within a century the victory was complete. The most stubborn natural obstacles had been brushed aside. The desert had been defeated. Where before there had been nothing but wind-polished rocks, six fine cities had sprung up. Six luxuriant oases, all artificially watered, supplied food for the men and animals of the Mzab.

Today there are 43,000 permanent inhabitants, 166,000 palms, and 3300 wells.

The capital of the Mzab, outside the walls of which was my "inn," is Ghardaia. Like its sisters, Beni Sgen, Bou Noura, Melika, Guerrara el Ateuf, and Beriane, it is different from any other town in the world.

The houses are square and made of mud. They are piled one above the other into a colossal pyramid. At the apex of the pyramid is the mosque. The mosque is surmounted by a minaret like an obelisk a hundred feet high, also made of mud. Everything in the Mzab is made of mud. It is heat-resisting, and as rain does not fall more than once in ten or fifteen years, the mud walls last for centuries.

Like all else in the Mzab, the mosque at Ghardaia is unusual. It has no ornamentation and is almost dark. The architecture has no connection with any style, Occidental or Oriental. In the lobby is a kind of checkroom where those going to pray can leave their slippers. On one side of the "checkroom" is a skin full of water, the greatest token of charity in this country where water is more valuable than gold. On the other side is a kind of cage of wire netting in which one might expect to find chickens. It is the lost property office of Ghardaia.

There is a gloomy austerity about this mosque, and in the sunbaked street there is no relief. The silence is oppressive. The children are shy. At the approach of strangers they vanish into the houses. One never sees a woman, and the men pass without greeting. Conversation, which was normal when one began to climb toward the mosque, has dropped to a whisper by the time one has reached the top of the street. The Mzabites are afraid to exclude Arabs and other foreigners from their cities, but their welcome is so frigid that no one stays long. The only people they will not tolerate among them are the Jews. These live in a ghetto to the west of the town. They have their own shops and wear a special costume. Every street of their quarter which leads toward the mosque is blocked by a high wall.

Unlike the Arab oases which surround the cities, those in the Mzab are some distance away. The Mzabites do not regard their oases merely as places in which to grow dates and vegetables. They consider them rather as country estates where they have their summer residences. In addition to the thousands of palms, there are as many fruit trees, grape vines, and flowers. The effect is luxuriant and tropical, more suggestive of the South Sea Islands than of the Sahara. It is unbelievable when one thinks that a little way off is the most desolate desert in the world and no rain for years at a stretch. It is still more unbelievable when one remembers that no water bubbles from the ground and every drop has to be brought to the surface artificially from the wells which the Mzabites have sunk. To have done this today with modern engineering equipment would have been a feat. To have carried it out a thousand years ago with primitive tools is nothing less than a miracle.

There are wells everywhere, over three thousand of them. Some are 180 feet deep, some 500, a few comparatively shallow. Every one of them was burrowed out of the desert by men who had nothing to help them but their fanatical determination to turn this glittering wilderness into a garden. Even when they had found water, their troubles were not over. They had to bring it to the surface, and when they had brought it to the surface, they had to distribute it to the gardens and the cities. It was an engineering problem which required thought and ingenuity. But to men who had succeeded so far, this was a comparatively minor problem.

After the well had been sunk, a stone reservoir was built beside it. From the reservoir, mud channels with sluice gates were splayed out to the areas where water was required. An inclined path was then constructed leading away from the well, and equal in length to its depth. Down this path a camel was made to walk pulling a rope at the other end of which was a huge skin bucket. When the camel reached the end of the path, the bucket had automatically come to the surface, where, by an ingenious contrivance, it emptied itself into the tank. The camel then walked back to the mouth of the well and the bucket returned to the water level. The procedure then recommenced. It can be seen working today, as it could have before the Norman had set foot on Britain, before America had been thought of. The Mzabites have found nothing modern to improve on this irrigation system. It is more economical and reliable than any mechanical device and will no doubt continue until the water gives out in the Mzab.

Every town I visited in this lost country was interesting, but Beni Sgen, the holy city, beats any place in the world for originality. Unlike its sisters, it is enclosed by a huge *stone* wall pierced by three gates at the entrance of which hang the skins with their free drinks of precious water. Within the walls no Arab or Gentile or Jew may remain after sunset. No smoking is permitted in the houses or streets. No music or singing is ever heard. There may be women, but no one has ever seen them. The men are dressed in robes of snowy white and move around in stately silence. From their girdles hang what, paradoxically, appear to be murderous-looking clubs. They are actually their house keys, the fathers of the latchkeys one day to be patented by Linus Yale. If one catches a Beni Sgenite in a friendly mood, these keys are worth looking at. They consist of a flat piece of wood about a foot long at the end of which is arranged a pattern of large nails. To get into the house, the piece of wood is pushed into a deep slot running from the doorpost horizontally toward the center of the door. Here it comes into contact with a bar or bolt on which is a corresponding pattern of nails. The nails on the key and on the bolt coincide. A slight pull unlocks the bolt and lets the owner into his house. No two pieces of wood have the same pattern of nails, so as long as the householder has his "key" hanging from his belt, he can feel his home is safe.

Although the nature of the desert around the Mzab made it impossible for the Mzabites to raise flocks of sheep, they manage to keep a few goats on the scrub which grows on the edge of their artificial oases. At Beni Sgen these animals are looked after by a municipal shepherd paid for out of taxes. Every morning this man collects his charges at the main city gate and drives them off to "pasture." In the evening he brings them back to the gate, where his responsibilities end. The goats know this. Up till now they have been one of a flock. At this point they become individuals. Without confusion, they separate and go independently up the narrow streets to their respective homes. The streets are numerous and intricate, and look identical. The houses seem to be all the same. But this does not baffle the goats. They find their own doors and butt them until they are let in. In the morning their owners release them, and they return to the gate.

The most curious custom in Beni Sgen, probably unique in the world, is the method of doing business. There are no shops in this city. Everything, from a pair of pants to a ton of coal, is sold by auction.

Daily, two hours before sunset, the inhabitants of Beni Sgen assemble in the market place. The buyers and the curious squat under the arcades which fringe the square. The sellers stand in the middle holding shirts, carpets, cans of preserved fruit, lumps of coal, dates, baskets of wheat. A few lead camels or donkeys. On a kind of dais at one end sit the head man and the city elders. Without any apparent signal the auction begins.

The sellers start to tour the market place carrying samples of the goods they want to dispose of. If it is camels or donkeys, they ride them. The bids are made in whispers and can only be raised a franc. No one may name a fancy price, and the merchandise can only go to the man who has made the highest bid. If at sunset the price set by the seller has not been reached, the commodity is withdrawn and reappears on the market the following day at the figure of the last bid. It sometimes takes days to buy a pair of shoes, and there is nothing one can do to get around this custom which, in Beni Sgen, is law.

I tried to get an elegant black burnous, but before the seller's price had been reached, I was on my way back to the camp!

Occasionally, a man wishes to sell his house. In other cities of the Mzab he does this by sitting on the roof while the buyers make bids from the street below. But in Beni Sgen he has to do it at the auction market. In this case the auctioneer announces the building for sale and glides around the market listening to the whispered bids which will only rise by a franc.

Why this market, no one knows. There is no historical tradition for such a custom anywhere else, ever. It belongs to another world: not to the Arab world; hardly to the world of near-by Ghardaia: the calm, the snowy clothing, the aloofness carry one back through the mists of history to a so remote past. The Crusaders, the Reformation, the voyages of Columbus, the Napoleonic Wars, our wars came and went, but the auction market continues.

As I stood watching these ivory-faced men making their gestureless bids, I felt that they were separated from me by an immeasurable gulf. There was no point of contact. Who were they? Could there be anything in the lost tribe theory? Could there? Or was it all fake? Had this been got up for my benefit? When my back was turned, would shops not open and these disdainful, white-robed people become everyday human beings? —No! I knew they would not. It was genuine all right, like everything else in the Mzab. As soon as the head man had left the dais, everyone would follow him to the mosque. The prayer would be said in unison. Thence home to a silent simple meal followed by bed.

The Mzabite is not gay. He takes his life seriously and is not good company like the Arab. He does not want to be good company. All he asks is to be allowed to trade in peace and keep his life undisturbed by modern complications. He travels into parts of the Mediterranean far from the Mzab to make money, as did his ancestors. He rubs shoulders with Occidentals. He learns their languages and lives as they do. But he does not let their ideas touch him. He is always waiting for the day when he can go back to the glittering desert, to the creaking sound of the pulleys as the camels draw the water from the prehistoric underground rivers of the Sahara to water the centuries-old oases. For him the Mzab remains a pleasure garden, a citadel, a costly whim to which he can return and die unmolested by uncouth Arabs and unmoral Occidentals.

As far as I am concerned, he can keep it. Although everything I saw interested me, I found nothing attractive. Most of the time I was baffled. I was more than ever the man on the misty mountain, only here the mist hardly ever lifted. When it did, I did not recognize anything. I was delighted when Madani announced that we could return to the camp. As the bus climbed out of the rocky, rainless gully, that passage came back to me again:

"There is much we think we know, but more that we do not know about the Great Sahara Desert."

CHAPTER XIII

THE AUTUMN OF THAT YEAR came rainless. September passed, October passed without even a cloud. The nomads said little, but their expressions were worried. Morning and night they turned from their prayers and watched the northern horizon. But the sun set in a glory of gold and rose dazzlingly white.

To begin with, there was little to show that anything was amiss. The grass grew scantily, but there was plenty of scrub, and the wells were normally full. The sheep looked all right. I began to think that these fatalist Arabs were for once letting their nerves get the better of their convictions. But the Sahara was unpredictable and still an enigma to me, so I said nothing. When the sirocco hit us, I was glad that I had kept my mouth shut.

I woke at dawn with the sensation that the hair was being scorched off my head. I sat up and saw that Madani had already left. I scrambled quickly out of the tent myself. The nomads, men and women, were working like feverish ants hammering in tent pegs, tightening ropes. The sheep and the camels and the donkeys huddled together, heads down, their backs to the wind which came in suffocating gusts. I looked up at the sky and found none. A pall of yellow dust obliterated everything. As the daylight increased, so did the heat. My throat felt parched, my eyes smarted. It was like standing in front of a furnace in a glass factory. The wind had ceased to be gusty. It came in a steady roaring rush.

Madani and Ali came across the open space between the tents. The shepherds followed. I looked questioningly at Madani. He only shrugged. Turning toward the East, he kicked off his slippers. We all kicked off our slippers. With the wind licking about us like angry flames, we recited the morning prayer. When it was over, Madani led the way back into the tent. He told one of the shepherds to send along some tea.

"I was afraid of this," he said as he squatted on his carpet. "We might have managed the drought, In sha Allah, but combined with the sirocco, it's hopeless.

"What are you going to do?"

"As soon as this is finished, slaughter all the lambs. They couldn't survive, anyway, with nothing to eat, and it may save the ewes."

"And then?"

"Make for the South."

"Will there be more pasture there?"

"In sha Allah."

Madani took out his dirty notebook and began to make calculations. He had his tea poured, and sipped it. Ali watched him and said nothing. I noticed that he had drawn up his shesh so that it covered his mouth and nose. I did likewise. The dust was penetrating everywhere. Already my teeth were full of grit and my eyes clogged with sand.

"How long does this last?" I asked.

Madani looked up. "What, the sirocco?"

I nodded.

"Three days, six days, or nine days," he replied without hesitation. "It never lasts less than three days."

It seemed impossible to believe. How could wind keep up this roaring ferocity for so long? —I have no idea, but it does. It never lets up, it never lulls; it goes on, and on, and on, until one is as near crazy as it is possible for a sane man to be.

Night and day, day and night ... wind. There is nothing but wind. One wonders if there was ever a time when there was no wind. The sun is completely shrouded. The dawn is jaundiced, the sunset dark yellow. One can hardly breathe. It is difficult to stand erect in a gale so strong that sand is often carried across the Mediterranean and sprinkled over the Rhone valley! And all the time, this frightful, infernal heat. It was like being in the engine room of an old-time coal-burning ship with no ventilation.

The animals suffered terribly. We had enough skins of water to have an occasional drink. Food was heavily seasoned with sand, but it was available. The animals could neither eat nor drink. They were too afraid to move, and if they had, there would have been nothing for them. When, on the third evening, the wind died down and stopped as suddenly as it had begun, I saw that every sprig of vegetation had been burned as if there had been a prairie fire. The air was still filled with dust, and it was days before we saw blue sky. It was a relief, though, to sleep without that nerve-wearing scream of the wind.

Madani was magnificent. During the storm he had made no comment. He had said none of those reassuring things which one knows are not true. The sirocco was blowing, and there was nothing to be done about it until it stopped. He prayed at the hours appointed for prayer. He ate when food was brought. He slept, or pretended to, when it was dark. He showed no sign of panic. I firmly believe that he firmly believed in his Fate against which he could do nothing, for that moment. But when the storm was over, he sprang into action.

He sent horsemen to round up all the nomads and flocks of his tribe. Their orders were to make for a water point to the immediate south of where we were now camped. Before moving, all lambs were to be slaughtered. It was a drastic step to take, but I believe it saved many of the tribesmen from ruin.

As the weather cleared, the great migration began. It had none of the splendor of the move to the hills, but it was just as impressive. Men, camels, sheep, horses, donkeys overflowed the desert. The only nourishment for the beasts were small shriveled herbs. These were eaten by the strongest. Those unequal to the struggle died in their tracks.

The discipline at the well was a lesson. The tribal chiefs never lost control of their men. There was no stampeding. Everyone had his share of water. As soon as one group of flocks had drunk, it moved on. Soon we were all streaming across the desert toward the South. In a little while vegetation began to appear. Madani got out his dirty notebook and once more started to make calculations. Including the lambs we had slaughtered, we had lost sixty per cent of our stock, dead by the roadside.

"Not too bad," he said. "We might have lost everything. Now, at least, we have forty per cent with which to make a fresh start."

"Hamdullah!" was all I could say. Madani's philosophy, or was it courage, had something which I lacked. In any case, I was being shown the Sahara under an even stranger aspect. The mist on the mountainside seemed to be less thick? Perhaps, from now on, I would see my way more clearly? Perhaps the ordeal of the sirocco had initiated me into this country's innermost secrets. Perhaps, in future, I could say that I did know a lot about the Great Sahara Desert?

I laugh when I think of my fatuity.

It was soon after the turn of the year. Madani and I had been on a hunting expedition. With our thinned flocks, we had to depend almost entirely on game for meat. The bag today had been good, and we had sent Ali back to the camp with two gazelles and some bustards. Madani wanted to try our luck a bit longer. He had become obsessed with the idea that this was the country for what he called partridges—in reality a kind of fast-flying sand grouse. We had not seen *one*, but Madani was obstinate and continued to search until night began to fall. As the world tipped up and hid the sun, Madani shrugged his shoulders and, dismounting, kicked off his slippers. By the time we had finished praying, it was nearly dark. We mounted without speaking and rode back in the direction from which we had come. After a while Madani said:

"I don't know where we are." Just like that. It was a terrifying admission for a nomad and jerked me bolt upright in my saddle. "I've never been in this part of the Sahara before," he added by way of explanation.

I maintained the Arab's calm and casually asked: "What are you going to do?"

"If I don't spot a landmark soon, we'll just have to sleep out," replied Madani with equal casualness. "In daylight it won't be so difficult."

We rode on in silence. The night was dark and quiet. The Sahara wind barely whispered through the scrub. I began to feel very hungry. In a little while a glow showed on the horizon. A great golden moon crept over the edge of the world and turned the desert into a fairy lake of silver. Madani looked about him and shook his head. Then he glanced at the ground. With an exclamation, he dismounted. For a moment he studied something at his feet. He nodded and remarked:

"We aren't far from a camp."

"How do you know?"

"Come and take a look."

I dismounted and joined him.

"What's that?" he asked, pointing to the ground.

I peered at what his finger indicated in the dust, but I could not see much. "It's something like the print of a man's foot," I ventured, "but I'm not sure."

Madani smiled. Though perfectly sincere, I was playing up beautifully. "It is the print of a young girl, probably unmarried, of the Chamba tribe," he said.

I stared again at the dull outline. "But why? How?" I asked.

"Without two prints before me, I cannot show you the difference between the footprint of a young girl and an older woman," he said, "but I know."

"Still, that doesn't tell you if the camp is near or far," I insisted.

"Oh, yes, it does," he answered. "There's sand always being blown about in these parts. A mark like that would be gone two hours after it was made."

"And how about the tribe?" This time I thought I really would get him.

But he went on like a prize schoolboy who never had his lesson wrong. "There's a date stone beside the footprint," he indicated, "and that kind of date stone comes from a date which grows only in the oases of the Chamba people." He picked up the date stone and examined it. "If you want any more proof as to how far we are from that camp, look for yourself. The date belonging to the stone wasn't eaten more than an hour ago. Come! Let's go! We'll dine and sleep in comfort after all."

Madani handed me the date stone and I saw that, as he had said, it was fresh. With an unconscious gesture I put it in my pocket. I do not know why, but I had an odd feeling that that date stone was in some way mixed up with my life. The thought passed as quickly as it came. Madani had already mounted and was riding in the direction toward which the footprint pointed. I quickly followed him. In about an hour, tents loomed up before us in the moonlight. A pack of fierce dogs leapt out of the gloom and rushed at us barking. A man appeared from one of the tents. Madani said:

"Ask who they are."

I hailed the man, announcing Madani and myself and the name of our tribe. Then I asked the man his.

"Chamba!" he called back.

Madani chuckled triumphantly and let the man take his horse. I did likewise, wondering whether Conan Doyle had ever lived with desert Arabs and how Madani would make out in the secret service. The dogs, hearing our voices, quieted, and Madani walked over to the biggest tent. A fine old nomad got up from the entrance and greeted us. He seemed to be an intimate friend of Madani and did not appear to think it peculiar for us to pay him a visit unannounced and long after sunset. As a matter of fact, even if Madani had known no one in the camp it would have been the same. The law of hospitality in the desert obliges strangers to be received and lodged and fed at any hour of the day or night. It is not necessary to announce oneself, as I did, or to ask who the host is. The guest is a guest, no matter what his name or standing, and it is the duty of the host to care for him and protect him as long as he is in the camp, as if he were a member of the family. During the whole time I was in the Sahara, I never carried a pistol or felt the need of one.

But this time I did not care who our host was. I was ravenous and wanted food as quickly as possible. But I had forgotten the ethics of nomad welcome. We were honored guests, and a feast must be prepared. A lamb must be killed and roasted, and the whole meal cooked for us. I groaned inwardly and remembered a frightful solecism of Gertrude Bell when she was new to the desert.

She had arrived at a camp just as we had. After sitting around for over an hour drinking coffee, she had imagined that it was too late to dine. She was disappointed, but very tired, so she had slipped into the tent and gone to sleep. No one liked to wake her when the banquet was served, but it had taken her months to live down what appeared to the Arabs to be deliberate rudeness.

So I just sat back with my back against the tent pole and tried to still the gnawing at my stomach with coffee. I was not sleepy. I was alert. I felt as if something unexpected was going to happen. Not anything personal. Something in the nature of an earthquake. Something to do with the desert.

In spite of its ancient lava peaks in the Ahaggar, I do not think that the Sahara is subject to earthquakes, yet its moods are no less unpredictable than a country of active volcanoes. The extremes of heat and cold. The wind that whispers and sings and then screams. The majestic silences. The roar of the sandstorms. The clear, golden sunrises, the sand-shrouded orange sunsets. The plain: one week parched and cracking from heat; the next a rain-drenched morass, green and dappled with meadow flowers, blue and mauve and pink. The dancing mirages. All those things give it the personality of something alive, something charming and wanton; again I say, something like a woman. The Sahara is itself a creature. One does not demand or expect anything of the people who live in its wilderness. They do not count. They do not really belong. The Arabs themselves call the Sahara the Garden of Allah, where God, in the cool of the evening, can walk without being jostled by the mortals He created. I had begun to think as the Arabs about the desert. I discounted the human element. So, when she appeared out of the ghostly moonlight and crouched beside the old nomad, I was caught off guard.

It is hard to tell an Arab's age, but this girl was probably in her middle twenties. Although dressed as a nomad, she was different. Her clothes were newer, cleaner. Her hair, though plaited, did not look as if it had been dressed five years ago and left to accumulate the dust of the Sahara. It was glossily black and tied with a fresh ribbon. Her face was not made up, but neither was it weather-beaten. It was as fresh and white as a dewy gardenia. The nose was Semitic, but not too much so. The lips were full and red. In the moonlight I could not see if they were touched up. She had very big and very black eyes. They were not brown or dark brown with black pupils. They were black, jet black. I had never seen eyes like that before.

For a few minutes the girl sat close to the old man, staring at me. It was not a rude stare. It was, rather, a careful examination of something unusual and unexpected, something she wanted to make sure about. And I stared back equally interested. When the staring was finished, she smiled. It was a friendly smile and charming. Turning to the nomad, she asked:

"Who is that?"

The old man glanced quickly at me and down at the girl.

"He is our guest," he said, "a friend of the caid Madani."

"He is not a nomad," said the girl. "He is not even an Arab."

Madani laughed. "Of course he's a nomad *and* an Arab. A good Moslem, too."

122

The girl shook her head. "He may be a good Moslem, In sha Allah, but he's not an Arab."

"And how do *you* know?" Madani teased.

The girl shrugged her pretty shoulders. "By his nose. He has not the nose of our people, neither has he the teeth. The only thing which *might* be Arab are his hands. They are small and nicely shaped."

Madani chuckled. I began feeling self-conscious at this analysis. The arrival of dinner changed the subject. But even while I ate, the girl continued to stare. Sometimes she smiled. It was a disturbing smile. It was so young, so fresh, and, at the same time, was that of a mature woman, a woman who knew a great deal about life; above all, a woman who knew her own mind. For though every passion and primitive instinct of her sex was written on the girl's beautiful face as she watched me from the other side of the fire, one had the impression that her head controlled her emotions.

She disappeared as suddenly as she had come. Neither Madani or our host took any notice. They were discussing the eternal pasture question and were so engrossed that I could not ask them the things which burned at the end of my tongue. I had to wait till Madani and I were alone. Then I said:

"Who was that girl?"

Madani shrugged his shoulders. "Her name is Belara," he replied.

"Is she the daughter or the sister"; I hesitated, "or the wife of our host?"

Madani shook his head. "No," he answered, "she is no relation."

"But she has a husband in the camp? A family?"

Madani shook his head again. "No," he replied, "she has no husband and no family."

I stared at him. Surely he was not going to pull some Antinea yarn on me. Quickly I said:

"But she must have a father somewhere around?" And I added, as Madani did not reply at once, "She *is* an Arab, I presume? She *is* a nomad?"

"Yes, yes," said Madani, "she's an Arab and a nomad, but I don't know who her father is!" And the way he said it sounded like: I've a perfectly good idea who her father is, but I'm not going to tell you. It's none of your damned business."

So I tried another approach:

"What is she doing in this camp?" I inquired.

"She is pasturing her sheep," replied Madani. "She owns flocks. What else would she be doing in the southern Sahara?"

With that, he closed up and rolled over on his carpet. I had broken all the rules of Arab good manners with my questioning. But I could not help it. That girl had intrigued me, and Madani's evasiveness had added to my curiosity. So I lay on my back trying to figure it out for myself, hoping that sleep would bring the solution. But sleep would not come, and my restlessness increased. It was hot, too, and the ground felt hard; so did my pillow. Finally I got up and slipped out of the tent.

The moon was high up in the sky, and the desert was a lake of luminous glass. Except for the black tents, everything was like polished silver. The Sahara wind was singing a serenade.

I sat down beside the tent, dizzy with the loveliness of this gleaming night. In a few moments a figure came cautiously across the space between the tents. In the moonlight I could see the white skin and the black eyes of Belara. She seated herself beside me and put something into my hands.

"I've baked you a date and almond cake," she said. "It's very good. Taste it."

I took a cautious bite. However nasty it might be, I was not going to tell her that I did not like the cake she had baked specially for me. But it was not nasty. It was very good. I said so. I said so enthusiastically, comparing it to the usual, nauseating Arab sweets.

"That is because of the dates," declared Belara proudly. "The nomads think only of dates as something to eat when there is nothing else. But dates have a wonderful taste, good dates. I love good dates. I eat them all the time."

"And you drop the stones by the roadside."

Belara looked up quickly. "Yes. Why not? Is it wrong?"

"No, but it explains something."

"Explains what? Don't talk in riddles. I don't like riddles unless they are good. Do you know any good ones?"

I laughed, "Your way of talking is much more like an Occidental than an Arab nomad," I said. "I wouldn't be surprised if you spoke English or French."

"French, yes, but not English," she replied instantly in French.

"And as my French is much better than your Arabic, I shall talk to you in French."

"But where on earth did you learn French?" I exclaimed. There were very few nomads, except the important chiefs, who had a word of French, and certainly none of the women.

Belara laughed in that enchanting way of desert people.

"I'll tell you one of these days."

"One of these days?"

Belara nodded. "Yes, I'm coming with you. From now on, you won't be alone."

"But!" I began.

Belara put her hand over my mouth. "No buts," she said. "I have waited a long time for someone like you. Perhaps for you. Now I've found you, I'm not going to let you go. —How many sheep have you?"

"About a thousand."

"Wonderful. I have the same number. That will make two thousand. Our partnership will be half and half. In every way it will be half and half."

"But," I said desperately, thinking of Madani's reactions to such an idea, and of those of the pious Ali; "but how can you, a Chamba, join up with the Larbas? Desert tribes don't mix just like that."

Belara nestled against me. "Don't let *that* worry you," she said, "I belong to the Larba people. I'm only here because of the drought up north. As far as that is concerned, I'm as good a Larba as you are." She laughed. Her head rested against my shoulder. For a while she said nothing. Then she knelt before me and looked into my eyes. "We will be very happy," she whispered. She kissed me quickly and disappeared into the moonlight.

I spent the rest of the night outside the tent. When Madani came out for the prayer, he found me asleep on the ground. As soon as we had finished praying, I told him bluntly what Belara had proposed. He considered me for a moment and then said:

"I think it's a very good idea. Living alone as you do is not good for any man."

"But Madani," I protested, "I don't want a wife. I don't want to be married."

"Who talked of marriage?" he inquired. "I do not suppose that Belara would marry you anyway."

"But—" I began again.

Madani halted me. "Don't become Occidental and complicated," he said. "Here you have a beautiful girl, clever, wealthy, charming, offering herself to you, and you begin to fuss. You ought to think yourself lucky. Besides, what can you do about it? As it was written, it was written. If Allah has so destined, so will it be."

He turned away and mounted his horse which a shepherd held. I mounted mine. Together we rode into a stream of sparkling gold as the sun sent its first rays joyfully over the Sahara.

CHAPTER XIV

FORTY-EIGHT HOURS PASSED without any sign of Belara. I was beginning to think that I had dreamed the whole thing, when she appeared. I saw her first. That is, I saw a gaily decked bassour swaying on a camel which padded slowly toward our camp. A camelherd brought the camel to a halt and made it kneel. Belara stepped out of the bassour.

"Ouf!" she said, "I hate traveling on camels. I prefer walking. I usually do." She looked up at me smiling. "Aren't you glad to see me? I'm sorry I didn't come sooner, but I had to round up my flocks, and some of the Larba sheep got mixed up with some of the Chamba sheep. But I'm here. Where's our tent?"

I had seriously made up my mind to tell Belara that this idea of hers which sounded fine in moonlight just would not work in the sober sunshine. But she was so charming, so childish, so obviously sincere that I did not have the heart to. I had also a fairly good notion that what *I* said or wanted would not make much difference. I had fallen in with a young lady who was accustomed to having her own way, and with Madani agreeing with her plan, I probably did not stand a chance. So I led her to the tent, which she looked over critically. But all she said was:

"I have better and thicker carpets. Yours will do to rest against the ground. And we'll throw out those grain-stuffed pillows. How can you sleep with your head on such things?"

"There wasn't anything else."

"There's wool, isn't there?" she exclaimed. "There's enough wool around to stuff a thousand pillows. My! but you're as dumb as a nomad." She looked up at me and smiled. "Now, don't look so glum," she went on, "we're going to be very happy, you see if we aren't. Now I must go and see about my tents and my people." With a nod, she was gone.

I looked after her puzzled.—"We're going to be very happy."—
Maybe we were? Maybe I *was* lucky. Maybe I was being exactly
what I had been trying to escape from—a stuffed shirt, a somber
Briton, logical even in his love-making. I must snap myself out of
this way of thinking. If I was to have a companion, I could not
have chosen a prettier one or a gayer. Whatever else she did, she
would certainly liven things up in the camp. Madani seemed to
approve. If the saintly Ali did too, who was I to make objections?

For the moment, however, we were on the move, and there was
no time for more than packing and unpacking. There was hardly
a moment even for "getting acquainted." Rain had fallen heavily
in the North, and Madani was anxious to get back. So was Belara,
and for a different reason. She wanted to have her hair done and
go to the Turkish bath. She confided this to me alone. "No one else
would understand," she whispered. "These nomad girls replait
their hair once a year, and they never bathe from the day they are
born until they die."

That way of looking at things pleased me, but made me wonder
how my Arabs would accept Belara. I need not have worried. Before
she had been in the camp a day, she had made friends with the
other women and knew the names of their children. She had
told Ali to take charge of her sheep as well as mine. She had eaten
the first meal in our circle. Her position in the camp had been
settled without a word being said.

During the trek north she did the same share of work as myself
and Madani. Her only luxury was her private bassour when she
was tired of walking.

The change when we reached the oasis pastures was unbelievable.
Where we had left a yellow, scorched, grassless land strewn with
dead or dying animals, we found a green country, bright with desert
flowers. Every ewe had a lamb at foot, and the camels' udders were
bursting with milk. Rain was still falling, and the river bed around
the oasis was a turbid, raging torrent. There were reports of camps
and flocks being swept away by the floods. To get inside the oasis,
we had to ride for two miles through six inches or so of muddy
water. More than ever, I realized how little I knew about the Sahara.

Madani was exultant. He laughed and giggled and rubbed his
hands. "Gold from the skies!" he kept on exclaiming. "Liquid gold

from the skies. This will repair all the damage of the sirocco. Hamdullah!—Hamdullah!"

The oasis, too, had changed. From the apprehensive city of anxious tradesmen whose livelihood depended on the nomads' prosperity, it had become a bustling business center. The coming of the flocks, drawn from all parts of the desert by the news of the rain, was trebling business. The coffeehouses and shops were jammed. The streets were filled with happy, smiling Arabs splashing through the mud. The only gloomy faces were those of a group of tourists. Outside Atalla's shop they stood in shiny raincoats with water dripping from their umbrellas which they had just bought. In unison they denounced North Africa and the Arabs and the desert and the fool tourist agency which had sent them on this trip. Why hadn't they stayed at home? One traveler in particular, a bony, masculine woman with a voice like a corkscrew, was getting so indignant that I could not help staring at her. Suddenly she turned on me:

"And you, you lousy Arab!" she shouted. "What are *you* gaping at? Get out of my sight before I push you.—Shoo!"

The sudden attack caught me unawares. I forgot my robes and my turban and what I looked like after months on the desert. Without introduction I said:

"Listen, lady, if anyone's going to do any pushing around here, it isn't you. Get the hell out of here yourself. Scram! The whole bunch of you!"

Incredulity, amazement, consternation came and went on the faces of those tourists. Their mouths opened and shut. They looked at me and at each other. Then they went down the arcaded street as if a prairie fire pursued them. Atalla, who was standing at the entrance of his shop and had seen but not understood, laughed.

"Very good, very good!" he said in his only English. "I sold them all the umbrellas I ordered from Algiers when the rain began. Now I hope they go back to their homes." He smiled and patted my arm. "I hear you brought Belara back with you?"

Before I could ask him how this news had traveled ahead of me, he had darted back into his shop, which was full of shepherds buying trinkets for their wives. It occurred to me that I ought to get Belara something. But what? She was not just another nomad girl dazzled by a colored scarf or a bottle of cheap perfume. So I left it. Afterwards I was sorry, for when I returned to the camp without a gift, she was disappointed. I explained the reason. Belara smiled.

"Don't you know, blue-eyed Roumi," she said, "that when a woman loves, it does not matter what her man brings her? The value of the present has no meaning. It is the thought, the gesture."

She laughed, and I knew that she had forgotten about it. Belara had a pleasing faculty for not letting things upset her for more than a few moments. She was as changeable and unpredictable as the Sahara. One never knew what her next mood would be. This is a trait of most females, but in Belara it was more pronounced than in many because of the mixture in her of East and West. In some ways she was fanatically Arab; in other ways she was liberal and Occidental.

In mind, in heart, in all her fundamentals, she was Arab. She had a solid admiration for her people and all they stood for. Unlike most nomads, she knew their history since the invention of Islam and for the thousands of years before. She was proud of the culture they had brought into the world. She was resentful that they had lost their commanding position in global affairs. She wanted to see that position re-established. She wanted the French put out of North Africa and Syria. She thought that the other Arabs could get along just as well without the British.

"Though, of course, you do not agree, arrogant Roumi," she exclaimed. "You think that England should have all the best parts of the world, with the leftovers for France or America. Even the desert you grudge the Arabs."

I assured her to the contrary.

"Empires have always been the causes of wars," I said. "From the times of the Assyrians, through the Greek and Roman and Arab and British eras, imperialism has done no good. Even today we have learned no lesson. We are rushing toward another fight with no more scruples than Alexander or Caesar or Sidi Okba. As long as we have empires, I don't care whose, as long as strong nations impose themselves on weak, it will be the same story."

"Then you would let the Arabs have their own rulers and their own countries?"

"I certainly would—the Arabs, the Tahitians, and the people of

130

India and the Dutch Indies. I see no reason why we, or anyone else, should force ourselves on folks who don't want us."

"Especially as you only do it to get what you can out of it."

And so we would go on planning and discussing, and discussing and planning a world where people would be free and happy and have their own flags and their own ways of living, whether they were black, white, or yellow.

"For," said Belara, "*you* wouldn't like it if a mob of Arabs landed in England and tried to make you into Moslems and stopped your drinking, and had couscous served in all your restaurants."

The idea made me laugh. I suddenly had a delicious mind's-eye glimpse of my club in London invaded by a host of robed, turbaned Alis, and the consternation of the Blimps. I heard them spitting into their moustaches—"Damned natives, don't know what the world's coming to!"—and writing letters to the *Times* about it. I thought it might be rather a good thing to let these "empire builders" see colonization from the other angle.

The only problem Belara and I could not solve was who should rule the Arabs. She was a conservative and not in favor of Occidentalizing her people. She did not want one of the Young Turks as co-ordinator of Arab destinies. She said that the West had proved nothing by its civilization or "progress." It might be a good thought to go back to the old ideals.

"I've not known many Occidentals," she added, "and none who knew anything about the Arabs. When I've suggested that we, with the Jews and the Greeks and some of the Chinese, were civilized peoples before the Christians had been heard of, no one seemed to believe it. But you know that it was the Arabs who kept Greek culture alive, kept all culture alive while Europe was wallowing in the Dark Ages."

"Yes, I do, and if the others don't, it's the fault of our teaching. It's the idea of educating everyone superficially with a kind of Europe's-the-source-of-everything-good propaganda." I told her of the little Arab boy I had heard proclaiming his ancestors were the Gauls.

Belara snorted: "That's it! The French want to make us like themselves. They force everyone to go to their horrible schools. In the North a lot of Arab children are growing up without any Arabic. They teach them only French history. They never tell them about the Arab empire or Arab literature. What's worse, they don't give us this education because they want us to benefit, they do it so they can stay here and fill their pockets with what should be ours. They don't even let us vote!"

"I thought they did."

"Only if we become French citizens, which means giving up all kinds of Moslem principles. It becomes a question of deciding whether we want to vote and forget Islam or keep our religion and not vote. No one hesitates."

But, with what was almost fanaticism about the rights of Arabs, she was Occidental in her views concerning their own way of living. She had moments of being revolutionary. She believed that women should have an official say in the running of a community. She thought they ought to be allowed to choose their husbands and pray openly in the mosque. The reserved gallery for female worshipers, she disapproved of. When I pointed out that in some Catholic churches this system of segregating the sexes was practiced, she was not impressed. A woman, she insisted, had as much right to proclaim her faith in public as a man.

Nevertheless, she did not want the harem and the veil completely abolished. She wanted the system modified. When she went to the oasis, she did so completely shrouded; but among men whom she considered to be of her own standing, like the Bash Agha and Daylis and Atalla, she had no hesitation in uncovering her face. For anyone so lovely it would have been a shame to do otherwise!

It was through Belara that I learned all I did about Arab women and harems. She had a house in the oasis, and to it she would ask friends and have me there. No explanation was given, but there was a tacit understanding that no one should be told. Over cups of tea and coffee she would get the women to discuss their family problems as if I were not present. If some of the conceited husbands I knew who peacocked about the streets had realized what their women thought of them, it might have deflated them. Or perhaps they did know. Perhaps they behaved like that before us because they could not do so at home?

Those clandestine "teas" at Belara's convinced me more than ever that eighty per cent of men can be taken in by women, and one per cent of women can be taken in by men. I mean, of course, after the parties concerned have known each other a while.

"Why do women over twenty pay any attention to men's courting?" I asked Belara. I could put that question because I had never courted her. "Do they really believe all they're told?"

"They would like to." And as I smiled questioningly, Belara continued. "Almost every woman would like to find a sincere man. Love, of course, plays a big part; but, with sufficient love, sincerity and reliability will outbalance money and looks ninety times out of a hundred."

"You think that happy marriages depend on the men?"

"Yes, generally. A normal woman who is cared for, treated as a friend, and properly made love to, is not going to complicate her existence by running around looking for something outside."

I was happy with Belara. There was never a dull moment. She was a girl of so many moods. Again I say, she was like the Sahara. I never knew how she would wake up in the morning or what she would be thinking about when she went to bed at night. One evening, after a day of continued change of tempo, I said to her when the others had left us:

"Your way of loving is the most restless, changeable thing I have ever known. Sometimes it flows like a mountain torrent in flood, sometimes it dries up like a desert watercourse."

Belara was sitting on the floor of the tent weaving a carpet. Without looking up, she said:

"That is how love is."

"That is how love is." —But it took an Arab to make me realize that truth. Belara made me realize a good many things. She taught me a good many things. Yet, from an Occidental point of view, she had no education. She knew her own classics and about what was going on in the world, but of reading and writing French she only had the elementary rudiments. I used to give up part of every evening to writing lessons. She had no idea of spelling and was too impatient to bother over such "silly details." So I invented a phonetic French orthography which she picked up quickly. The vocabulary and grammar presented no difficulties; she knew the French spoken language almost perfectly. I never found out how or where she had been taught. I never found out, either, who her parents were or why she had this independent fortune. Of her origins she would never say a word, in spite of her assurance the first night we met. That she was pure Arab, there was no doubt;

but whether Larba or Chamba or Ziban, I could never discover. Sometimes I thought that she came from much further away. She had the easy gait of the nomads, she had their laughter, she lived as one of them; but there were moments when she showed a dignity, a sense of things which did not belong to any Sahara camp. I never learned anything definite about this girl of mine with the great dark eyes, and I do not suppose I ever will. I am not sure that I ever wanted to. I was content with her, and who she was did not matter. When we separated, I felt as though I had lost something very precious.

Our parting was as unexpected and as sudden as our meeting. One evening she came to me in the tent and, kneeling before me, said:

"Queequee—" She always called me that. I do not know why or what it meant. But to her, I was Queequee. "Queequee, I come to you now as the friend you have shown yourself. I come for forgiveness and understanding. Queequee, I have to leave you."

"Leave me?" I asked anxiously. "You're going away? Not for long, I hope?"

Belara bowed her head and whispered: "Yes, Queequee, for long. For ever."

I did not know what to say. Unpredictable as Belara was, I was not prepared for this without warning. I wondered if something in my instinctive Occidental way of behaving had upset her. As if sensing these thoughts, she said:

"This has nothing to do with you, dear. I am the only one involved."

"But where are you going? You couldn't live away from the desert."

"I'm going to be married."

"To be married?"

Belara nodded "Yes," and added under her breath, "to Sidi el Hadj Abdallah, the Marabout of Teniet el Had."

"The Marabout of Teniet el Had?" I repeated unbelievingly. "But he's an old man! You must be crazy, Belara! You can't like an old fellow of seventy. He can't mean anything to you?"

"He doesn't," she said. "Marrying him is like becoming a nun. That is as it should be. Queequee, I've been thinking about this for a long time. I can't go on living in this irresponsible way. I'm not an Ouled Naïl, I'm not an Occidental. I belong to Islam, and Islam calls for more than just doing what one feels inclined to. Until I saw you, I just lived, putting off the time when I must marry and go into seclusion. But when I saw you, things seemed different. I cared and it was fun, and then I cared more and it was still more fun, and then, one day, I realized that all this fun led to nothing.—Yes, dear, to nothing." Belara paused and looked at me steadily. "One day you will go back to your own people, you must, it is right that you should. But I couldn't go with you, you know that, any more than you could stay here always. So I have made up my mind. I go to the Marabout, who has been asking for me for a long while, long before you came along. He is a good man and needs my flocks and my houses and my money for Islam, and I shall be a nun. It is better so." She came closer to me. "Our love has been great and beautiful, let it end without regrets. It is better so.—Now take me in your arms and let's forget about it. Let's have no weeping, no goodbyes. I will go when I go, soon or late; but whenever it is, remember, Queequee, that I will always love you . . ."

And one morning she was gone. No one told me, I did not have to ask. I just knew it was all over. With that admirable tact for which the Arabs have no equal, the matter was not mentioned. We carried on with our work as usual and only talked of things connected therewith. Once only was it referred to. Out of one of his silences, Madani remarked:

"Women are strange creatures. When they love, their emotions surpass anything a man can feel. They become sublime."

It was his only comment, and I said nothing.

I never saw Belara again, but I heard from her.

A short while before she had made up her mind to leave the Sahara, I had given her a fountain pen and a bottle of green ink. She loved all that was green, and my gift had made her take more pains with her writing lessons. Six or seven months after her disappearance I received a note. It was scrawled in green ink over a page out of a copybook. The envelope was addressed in such a way that only a mind reader can have understood for whom it was intended. I do not know how the letter got out of the Marabout's zaouia to the post, but it was delivered.

The text was an incoherent mess: thoughts set down as they came into Belara's head.—She seemed to be leading a cloistered existence from every angle and to be resigned to it; not necessarily happy as a nun who has followed a call, but resigned. One passage in the letter read: "I have everything I need and I do as I please in the zaouia. But there are moments when I become impatient with the restraint, when I feel suffocated and I long for the open plain and the desert and the wind in the Sahara—oh, how I long for it!" And at the end of the letter, she wrote, "I knew many men, but you were the first I loved and you were the last. I am like a virgin who gave herself many times but only her real self once, and then died. It is well so."

For some years this one-sided correspondence continued. In different parts of the world I received the ill-addressed envelope with the green scrawl inside. The theme and tone of the letter were always the same. I wish she had written in classical Arabic. Some of the thoughts were sheer poetry.

Knowing nothing of Belara's background, I shall never understand why she did what she did. As far as I can see, it served no good purpose. She was not a person for nunneries and cloisters. She belonged so much to the Sahara. She *was* the Sahara; the wind in the Sahara, restless, never the same for two hours running, trying one's temper to the limit of endurance and then breaking down all resentment with her smile. . . . I wonder what would have happened to Belara if she had lived in London or Paris or New York. She would probably have been spoiled. Perhaps not. She was one of the most sincere, ingenuous women I ever knew. Her name meant Crystal.

CHAPTER XV

WHEN THE TIME CAME ROUND for the summer migration to the hills, I did not move with the others. I wanted to see the Sahara in its hot weather dress. I wanted to be alone for a while.

The sun heat in the Sahara has no equal. In Java and other tropical countries the temperature is uncomfortable. People stay at home during the middle of the day, but it is not dangerous to be out of doors. In the Sahara during June two minutes in the open without something on one's head puts one out, probably for good.

From the moment the fiery rim of the sun appears over the horizon until its blazing disappearance at sunset, it is like living in a furnace. Even the desert wind dwindles to a weak breeze. Neither is there much respite after dark. The night is so short that the earth has little time to cool before it is daylight once more. No one moves while the sun is up, man or beast. All trekking and pasturing is done under cover of darkness. I do not know what happens to wild animal life. It is never seen. So ceaselessly dry and fiery is the atmosphere that one even begins to wonder if forests and seas and meadows were not something in a dream.

To get away from the desert during the hot months is more exhilarating than champagne. As soon as one reaches the highlands north of the Sahara and begins to see trees and green grass, life stirs in one. It is like coming out of ether. During the early days after escaping from the heat, one cannot tire of the freshness of everything around. A lake does not seem true. One stares at a stream as one might at a picture, wondering what one would do if one had that water to dispose of in the desert. Until a summer has been spent in the Sahara, the luxury of living in a temperate climate is not appreciated. One understands why the Arabs, before the days of Islam, regarded the sun as an angry deity to be placated.

137

Madani must have gauged how long I could stand the heat, for just as I was considering making a dash for the coast, I had word from him. The sun was setting in a breathless atmosphere of purples and golds when a tribal retainer in his blue burnous stood at the entrance to my tent. In his hand he held a letter.

I opened the envelope and found a page torn from the dirty notebook. It was a royal command to come and stay at the Bash Agha's farm in the Atlas. There was no suggestion that I might refuse, or start when convenient. The note concluded with: "You will take the bus to Djelfa on Thursday night (this was Thursday evening), and, on Friday morning, the train from Djelfa to Boghari, where a car will fetch you, In sha Allah."

"In sha Allah." That was the most important part of the letter! But in my haste to escape from the heat, I passed it over. Only taking time to tell a shepherd that I was off, I mounted my horse and rode into the oasis.

I made the bus around midnight. I made the train around six A.M. I made Boghari around midday. But I made no Madani car!

Boghari is one of those miserable half French, half Arab hamlets in the Atlas foothills whose only excuse for existence is the railway. And this is not a very good excuse. Only two trains a day come there, one going from Algiers to Djelfa, the other from Djelfa to Algiers. The railway has only one track, and only at Boghari can the trains pass. So they both arrive at the same time. The Algiers train picks up alfa, the Djelfa train sometimes delivers a passenger or a letter. The activity in Boghari station lasts for less than one hour in the twenty-four.

However, there was nothing I could do but wait and hope that the car would come soon, "In sha Allah." It was terribly hot, but it was possible to sit under a roof instead of under a tent, which made a change. After two or three hours of silent contemplation (I had no newspapers or books and no possibility of getting any) I became bored and then hungry. An Arab boy was also sitting in the station, probably waiting for the train next day, so I asked him if he had seen a car belonging to the bash agha Jelloul or any other member of that illustrious family. The boy replied that he had not, but he remembered having heard that the bash agha Jelloul had driven through Boghari sometime in May. It was now

July. He was not positive about this, but he seemed to have overheard his cousin telling his sister of some such event. Or perhaps he was thinking of the year before. He was not sure.

I expressed my thanks for the information and asked if he was sure of remaining where he was for the next few hours. —Yes of that he was certain. —I thanked him again and begged him to bring word to me at the caravanserai if a car appeared outside the Boghari station. The boy promised, and I set out in search of something to eat.

There was a French inn in Boghari, but I preferred the honest dirt of the caravanserai to the grimy sheets and the bedbugs of the *auberge*.

The theory that all hotel bedrooms are alike, and all one has to do is to close the shutters, draw the curtains, and turn on the light to imagine one's self in Brussels or Bordeaux or Barcelona, had never convinced me. Even Michael Arlen, in town clothes writing in his hotel room in Algiers with the sun blazing outside and a fire blazing inside, did not persuade me that he had created an atmosphere for a story about London in a fog. Those things did not work on me. I was too sensitive to smells. So I turned my back on the Hotel de France and went to my caravanserai.

Caravanserais used to be the refuges where the caravans took shelter from bandits after dark. Today there are no bandits, but the caravanserais are still used by travelers who park their cars and their camels and their horses and sheep in the courtyard for the night. The courtyard is about 150 feet by 300 feet and is surrounded by stables and dormitories and cafés. It is entered by a wide gateway which is closed at sunset. In the early days of the French occupation fierce fights raged around caravanserais, with the diligences just making the sanctuary, pursued by sharpshooting Arabs. It was much like the Wild West days of America and at about a contemporary period.

I breezed into the caravanserai's café-restaurant with a comprehensive "Salaam aleikum!" (Peace to all!), and asked for food and coffee. I did not order it. I did not speak with the arrogance of the white man and say, "I want!"; I said, "I would like." And having used the polite Arab formula, I was given a golden pile of couscous and some marga and some goat stew.

While I ate, two Arabs who apparently knew me by sight,

139

came to my table and began inquiring as to the state of my health. I reassured them and begged them, in turn, to convince me that they were not ailing. When we were all satisfied about this, the object of the visit was revealed. How were the pastures in the Sahara? My answer must have been disappointing, for in less than five minutes the two men had excused themselves and returned to their own group. I could not hear what they were saying, but the wagging of heads and the shrugging of shoulders suggested that the information was negative.

The fact is that I did not know anything about pastures. The only reason I kept sheep at all was in order to live this roaming life of the nomads. I knew that Madani and Ali had been born with more instincts about sheep raising than I would learn if I spent all my life on the Sahara. So I left everything to them and did not usually expose my ignorance by allowing myself to be cornered with conundrums about pastures or the like.

Feeling better after my dinner, I returned to the station. Here the boy told me that there had been no sign of a car. With the sun now setting, it did not look as if there would be any sign that evening. I confirmed my suspicion that the boy was waiting for the noon train next day and asked him to warn me if any of the Bash Agha's people put in an appearance. Then I went back to the caravanserai and fell asleep on some bales of alfa.

Boghari is fairly high and the night was comparatively cool, so I did not wake until someone came to move the alfa to the station. I had some more coffee and some more couscous (the goat stew was finished), but I did no praying. I felt I might blaspheme and call maledictions down on Madani and all his tribe!

The whole of Saturday passed without any change in the situation. By nightfall I was irritated. I imagined myself being asked for a week end at home and having no one meet me for days. It would be annoying there, but I would at least have a drugstore and a newsstand to relieve the monotony. Here there was nothing but couscous and coffee. My irritation increased. I made up my mind that if no car turned up before the train next day, I would go to Algiers. I would let Madani and his family go hang!

My thoughts must have been carried on air eddies, for at sunrise on the following morning Madani's car drove into the caravanserai with the Bash Agha's Numidian chauffeur at the wheel. He

waved me good day, refused an offer of coffee, and said he must
get back to the farm as he was in a hurry. I could think of no
sufficiently sarcastic comment, so I joined the black man on the
front seat and we started to climb into the wooded hills above
Boghari.

The greenery and the smell of vegetation and the fresh mountain
air calmed me, and when, three hours later, we arrived at the
farm, I had little resentment left.

No one was at home, so the chauffeur led me into a patio over
which grew a vine heavy with grapes. It did not seem possible.
He opened a door which gave onto the patio and ushered me into
a room in the middle of which was a huge brass bed. That seemed
even less possible. However, I was going to take advantage of this
dream, if it was a dream, quickly, and in five minutes I was
between the sheets. Before I had had the time to appreciate them,
I was asleep.

When I awoke, it was afternoon. Madani was sitting beside me
on a wooden chair writing in his dirty notebook. He greeted me
in the traditional manner. But the bed was making me feel Occidental, so I made him no satisfactory report on my health. Instead
I asked what had happened to the car. He looked puzzled, so I
added:

"Supposing I invited you to stay and told you I'd send to fetch
you on Friday and the car did not turn up till Sunday, wouldn't
you ask questions? Wouldn't you want to know what had
happened?"

"No," he answered, and smiled as if that settled the matter.
Then as an afterthought he added: "You're here, aren't you?"

"Yes, I'm here," I replied, "obviously I'm here, but I could have
been here two days ago instead of wasting my time in Boghari."

Madani looked at me thoughtfully and inquired: "What would
you have been doing if you had not been in Boghari?"

I shrugged my shoulders and fell into the trap: "I don't know.
Nothing much."

"Well, what are you fussing about? You can do 'nothing much'
just as well in Boghari as in the Sahara or as here. Come, dinner
is ready."

He gave me a friendly pat and went out.

In the patio, I found the Bash Agha and the agha Daylis and

Marhoun, and various other members of the clan whom I had met at the wedding. They all embraced me and cross-examined me about my health. It took nearly two courses for everyone to be satisfied that we could look forward to a period without illness. But no one asked me why I was three days late in arriving or what sort of journey I had had. They probably imagined that I had ridden all the way from the Sahara.

I was glad to find that my hosts kept nomad hours. I had not slept properly for so long, and this bed was like hashish after the sun-baked earth of the desert.

In the middle of the night, there was an earthquake. It did not last long, but for a few moments the farm quivered. The household rose in commotion. Children screamed, servants shouted, dogs barked. The Bash Agha rushed into my room fully dressed, proving that, even when away from the camp, these men never took off their clothes. Seeing me still between the sheets seemed to surprise him.

"My friend," he exclaimed, "you lie calmly in bed while the earth shakes and trembles?"

I laughed. "Your bed's too comfortable," I said. "Besides, according to you, if I'm fated to die in an earthquake I shall die in an earthquake wherever I am!"

The Bash Agha's eyes twinkled. With a meaning glance, he silenced me and went out of the room closing the door quietly. Two minutes later I heard him berating the others for daring to question their destiny. Next morning no one mentioned the earthquake.

Soon after sunrise we motored into the mountains to visit some of Jelloul's cattle which were grazing in the cedar forests. Where the road came to an end, we exchanged the car for horses and rode along shady tracks that wound through sweet-smelling glades. After riding for years over stony, glary plains, the feeling of the turf beneath the horse's hoofs and the trees above my head was as dreamlike as the bed. The exercise and the clean air also made me hungry, and I prayed that someone had had the sense to bring a sandwich or two. Nothing could have surprised me more than to find, on getting back to the place where we had left the car, obvious signs of a full-course dinner. That is the Arab way. In the matter of meals there are no half measures. One either spends the whole day without a bite or else sits down to a feast in the most out-of-the-way place.

This meal was excellent, too excellent, and we all fell asleep afterwards. That is, we deliberately lay down and shut our eyes and did not open them again till late afternoon.

As I came to, I could not imagine where I was. The golden sunlight glinting through the blue branches of the cedars. The smell of grass and flowers and cattle. The soft, cool air. None of them seemed real. I felt as if I had been transported back to a period long before I had thought of going to live in the Sahara. For a while I lay still, letting memories flow slowly back. Then I stretched and, in so doing, put my fist in Marhoun's eye. Marhoun looked at me questioningly and laughed. The others stirred. In a few minutes we had all piled into the car and were bumping back to the farm, where we all went to sleep again.

Before sunrise next morning we were on our way to a village thirty kilometers distant where the weekly market was being held. The road was thronged with men on horseback and on foot, with sheep and goats and donkeys. We were greeted on our arrival by a retinue of local chiefs and members of the Bash Agha's family. For half an hour there was a dignified exchange of salutations, of hand kissings and forehead kissings and shoulder kissings. It was a ceremonious scene of ancient ritual detached completely from an age of railways and radios.

The selling and buying of sheep at an Arab market takes a long time. Most of the transactions are left to the head shepherds. The chiefs stalk around for a while feeling sheeps' backs and examining wool, but they only really come to the market to meet their friends and to gossip.

Having nothing to gossip about and having, as usual, not been offered or given any breakfast before I started, I persuaded Marhoun's younger brother, Sheik Ali, to come with me to the local inn for a bite.

We sat down in the café and the waiter was just bringing us our breakfast when, without a word, Ali jumped up and went into the street. Rather taken aback by the suddenness of his move, I followed. Still without speaking, he went into another inn, sat at a table, and gave the identical order he had given in the other place. Suspecting that he had sensed something "unclean" in the first restaurant, and not wishing to appear an ignorant infidel, I asked no questions. This time the breakfast was brought and placed before us. But before I had time to pour the coffee, up sprang Ali again and made for the street. Afraid that I might be in some way be responsible for these delirious movements, I went after him and caught up with him just as he was going back into the original café. This time I asked the reason.

"Didn't you see?" was all he said.

I shook my head. "Didn't I see what?"

"My great-uncle, the agha Yahia!"

It sounded like a Shakespearean ejaculation, but all I said was: "Well, what about your great-uncle, the agha Yahia?"

"He came into the first café we were in."

"So what? Don't you like your great-uncle, the agha Yahia?"

"Of course I like my great-uncle, the agha Yahia," he replied, "but I cannot remain seated when he is in the room. I cannot remain seated when my father or my uncles are in the room."

I nodded. "Yes, of course, but what happened in the second café?"

"My great-uncle, the agha Yahia, came there, too."

"I see," I said, "and I suppose we shall go on chasing around the village until we find a place where your great-uncle, the agha Yahia, does not come."

Sheik Ali shrugged his shoulders.

"But I am hungry," I protested, "and I want my breakfast."

"So do I," agreed Sheik Ali, "but what can we do?"

I thought for a moment, then I said, "I don't know what *you* can do, but I know what *I* can do, and I'm going to do it right now!"

With that I returned to the second café and, taking my coffee and bread, seated myself at the table of Sheik Ali's great-uncle, the agha Yahia. He was a kindly old gentleman and seemed glad of my company. I explained what had brought me to sit with him. He smiled politely, but he made no suggestion that his nephew join us. As far as he was concerned, Sheik Ali might wait all day for his coffee.

The Arabs respect age. Age and dignity are the only things they pay any attention to in judging a man. Military or tribal ranks mean nothing to them unless they are accompanied by personal

144

qualities which are found equally among the rich and the poor, the highborn and the lowborn. The Arabs are natural socialists.

The bash agha is the paramount chief, the caid is the head of the tribe, but their authority does not depend on their titles. The poorest nomad has as much right of access to the bash agha as his son or his grandson. But neither the poorest nomad nor the son or the grandson may be seated in his presence or smoke in his presence or talk lightly on a serious matter in his presence. Neither will a tribesman go to his caid for help or advice if he does not command respect. He will go to the oldest nomad. Most caids and sheiks do command respect, otherwise they would not be holding these positions.

Although it is usual for a son to one day take his father's place, it is not the rule. The bash agha's son has a better chance of becoming bash agha than anyone else, but if he does not show the makings of a good ruler by his own personality, he will be passed over. The father will be the first to recognize that his son must not inherit the scarlet cloak, and will designate someone else.

Neither does the red and gold impress anyone but tourists. Except among the chiefs of the Zibans, whose headquarters are at Biskra, the tourist center of southern Algeria, Arabs do not go in much for dressing up. A foreigner has no idea of who an Arab may be by his clothes. Marhoun was a dandy; so were many of his unimportant friends who spent a lot of time in Algiers, while Madani usually looked like a shepherd who could not afford a new outfit. Yet when Madani appeared at a tribal council, everyone knew that his place was to preside.

It was the same with me. No one cared whether I was rich or poor. They respected me because I had more dignity than the average Occidental. I did not fly into rages or order people about or hurry or want things which the desert did not supply. I behaved as they thought a man of family should. They did not know what an effort this was sometimes. If they had, they might have respected me more!

The Arab is a democrat, almost a communist. He does not know the meanings of these words, but he believes in what they stand for. He does not feel that because he was born poor he need necessarily die poor—In sha Allah. There is no class or caste rule to prevent him from having as good an opportunity as his neighbor.

If, on the other hand, misfortune pursues him, he knows that the more fortunate will look after him. It is the sacred duty of the well-off to care for the badly-off. I have seen Madani, carrying a loaf of foreign bread which he had bought for his home, meet a beggar and without hesitation give him the loaf and return to the bakery for another loaf for himself. There is no people which practices what Jesus taught as our attitude toward the other fellow as the Arabs do, provided the other fellow is a Moslem. Even to Christians and Jews charity in the southern oases is liberal.

We spent most of the day at that market. Madani sold a lot of sheep and bought a lot. The rest of the family appeared to be doing the same. The transactions seemed rather futile. They were like those carried out on the stock exchange, but in a more picturesque atmosphere and with less noise.

On the way back to the farm we called on several local chiefs and landowners. At each home we were saturated with mint tea and fed nauseous cakes until I felt sick. At one of the houses the Bash Agha met an aged cadi who wanted to play chess. So they sat down and had their game while the rest of us stood and waited, regardless of the fact that it was long past our dinnertime. However, I made no comments. I was afraid that if I did, Madani would ask me what else I could be doing!

CHAPTER XVI

WHAT IMPRESSED ME MOST about this visit to the Bash Agha's farm in the Atlas Mountains was the way everything was accomplished without fuss.

It all looked vague, and there appeared to be little attention paid to time. The sending of the car forty-eight hours late to Boghari seemed muddleheaded and annoying for me, but it did not really matter. When something important had to be done, it was done. It was well done, too, and with no discussion.

I felt I was among people who had developed the art of being efficient without bureaucracy and without worry. I had the sensation that these were men with well-balanced minds who were capable of running their own affairs.

The Bash Agha had a few official retainers supplied to him by the French government. He had also a taleb who wrote his letters. But he had nothing resembling an office.

The Kadi had a court where he tried cases without aid of counsel or jury. The accused or the litigants who appeared before him were judged according to law or tradition, but chiefly by common sense and a knowledge of the circumstances and the people concerned.

The caids handled their tribal problems as might fathers the quarrels of their children. The complicated question of census and tax levying was made uncomplicated by dealing with it in a straightforward way, without forms to fill up.

Everything that looked like red tape was barred.

But when it came to referring matters to the French, even in the simplified military offices of the Sahara, one was lost in a maze of litigation and documents and functionaries whose lives were guided by government decrees.

Few Arabs who could avoid it had their differences settled by the French, and it was not surprising. Even to one like myself, accustomed to the bureaucracy of the army, the system of administrating North Africa was a revelation of complication. To an Arab it was incredible nonsense.

Algeria is not considered as a colony but as part of France. It is divided into departments with elected French representatives who sit in the upper and lower houses of parliament in Paris. It is, nevertheless, under the jurisdiction of a governor-general who is appointed by the Ministry of *Home* Affairs for periods of six months, renewable or revokable without notice. In other words, the governorship is a political appointment, and the governor is not chosen necessarily for his ability to deal with Orientals. Even if he has ability, he can do little on his own initiative without running up against the members of parliament, who fear centralized power and the cutting of red tape.

Under the governor are *préfets, sous-préfets, juges de paix,* and *commissaires de police,* like Cyprien Couteau, just as in France; and they are responsible to the government in France. In places, however, where there are more Arabs than French citizens, the local government is in the hands of an official called an administrator. The administrator wears an elaborate uniform but is a civilian, and he combines *all* the duties of all the civil authorities of a one-hundred-per-cent French community. This functionary is responsible to the governor-general.

South of a line drawn east and west through Djelfa, however, these *préfets* and administrators have no jurisdiction. These Southern Territories are under the military. The officers have nothing to do with the government in France and are responsible to a more or less permanent official in Algiers called the secretary-general. He, in turn, is partially responsible to the governor. That is, being himself permanent, he can establish his own policies without having to await the consent of the ever-changing appointee of the premier in power.

It is the most muddle-headed organization imaginable, even more complicated than the outline given here.

For example, in our oasis, where everything was ordered by Arab or military law, there were a number of French officials. There was Cyprien Couteau; there was a *juge de paix;* there was a *notaire.* The only civilian Occidentals whom they could have tried or put in prison or drawn up deeds for, except themselves, were Monsieur Paoli, the Superior of the White Fathers, some White Sisters, and myself. I believe there was also a schoolmaster, but I never saw him.

The Arabs naturally sensed this disorder and kept clear of it. They did not need prisons for their wrongdoers or Code Napoléons for their lawsuits or title deeds to the Sahara. If the Bash Agha or the Caid or the Kadi could not settle their troubles, they did it among themselves, quickly and primitively.

One of the reasons the French impose their schools in every Arab center, even in the far South, is, as Belara said, to make the people French-minded. They want to get them so entangled in their way of thinking and administrating that Arab tradition will be forgotten.

An Arab well saturated in the greatness of France in the past, and hearing no mention of the greatness of the Arab in the past, cannot help getting an idea that the French are a paramount people. The schoolmasters minimized the role of Britain in world affairs and referred to America vaguely as a country of cowboys, redskins, and film stars. This is no exaggeration. I have spoken to some of these mediocrities who were appointed to train the minds of the young Arabs and found that they had no idea of what the United States represented. That she had her own writers and poets and composers and painters was news to them. However, whether they knew or not, their instructions were to build up France and get the Arab to believe that if he became French-minded, everything else would be easy. This was the idea in making the taking of French nationality possible only to Arabs who abandoned many of their Koranic rights. The French knew the strength of Islam and wanted to undermine it.

The French treatment of the Arab was a mixture of condescension and liberality. An Arab could stay in the same hotel as a Frenchman. If he fancied the Ritz and could afford it, the Ritz was open to him. If he visited Algiers or Paris and found himself at a dance, no one would think it peculiar if he danced with a French girl. If he held a commission in the French army, he was by right a member of the officers' club and any other club catering to members of the same class. He was not treated like Indians in India, where even a maharajah could not set foot in the Bombay Yacht Club, to which any British bank teller or second lieutenant could belong. He was not excluded from foreign clubs as the Chinese were in Shanghai and Tientsin. He was conscripted into the French army and fought France's enemies wherever they happened to be. He paid taxes. Both in Algeria and in France he was treated almost as if he were a Frenchman.—Almost.

He could not vote and he could not sit in parliament or have any say in the government of the country to which he paid taxes and for which he fought, unless he naturalized himself French. But, as explained, this was made almost impossible by terms he could not meet without offending his faith.* He had a certain say in the administration of Algeria, but not enough to count. The French colonists, with whom he was obliged to do business, treated him with ignorant condescension. They spoke to him in the second person, which would be all right in Arabic and among Arabs but is a sign of familiarity or superiority in French. He was expected to entertain lavishly when officials visited his territory, but he rarely had his hospitality returned, and received no compensation outside an occasional decoration. There were many other small indignities put over on the Arabs by the French; but taking everything together, it amounted to this:

The big chiefs, who had motorcars and fine clothes and had little direct contact with business, were made to feel equal to the French—up to a certain point. The less important chiefs and the other Arabs were made to feel inferior. This did not take in anyone, big or small; and if the bash aghas accepted this flattery and bestowals of the Legion of Honor, it was because that was the easiest thing to do. Nor did this prevent them all from wanting independence from the French, and their own form of government.

How this independence is to be achieved is another matter.

The trouble is that the Arabs are not, strictly speaking, one people any more than the inhabitants of the United States are. But whereas the Italians and the Germans and the Irish and the Russians and the English who constitute the American race all live in one large area with defined boundaries, the Arabs do not.

The Arab peoples are scattered all the way from the Atlantic coast of Morocco to the Arabian coast on the Persian Gulf. An

---

* It is said that General de Gaulle is making concessions to the Arabs of North Africa and has modified the clauses governing naturalization. This is still only a gesture and a long way from the autonomy which the Arabs want.

area of about 3,300,000 square miles and a population of over 50,000,00. They are under a number of different governments and in varying stages of autonomy and subjection. They have not even a common language; for although classic Arabic is understood by a few educated men in each of the Arab states, the tongues of each group of inhabitants differ. Many words are the same, but the nomad of the Sahara and the shopman in Cairo and the boatman in Baghdad will be no more intelligible to each other than an Italian and a Frenchman and a Spaniard of the same class. The only thing which all Arabs have in common is religion. And this common trait is so great that it almost makes up for the other handicaps. Islam is infinitely more binding than Christianity and can knit together peoples living at the opposite ends of the earth under totally different conditions.

But even if there were no geographical or language obstacles in the program of Arab independence, there would still remain the so far unsolved question: Which Arab shall rule the Arab empire?

Whereas the bash agha of the Larbas would never admit the sovereignty of the bash agha of the Zibans, so much less would the emir of Transjordania accept to be under the ruler of Saudi Arabia. Neither would any of these swear allegiance to the king of Egypt or the king of Irak. And if one of these men were so pre-eminently superior that he would *have* to be recognized as paramount chief, what would be the attitude of his subjects? How would a Baghdadi feel about the sultan of Morocco, or a Moroccan Riff about a Syrian leader? Where would his seat of government be? Algiers? Cairo? Baghdad? Mecca? Riyadh? Who would compose the cabinet? What kind of government would it be? If parliamentary, how would the voting be carried out? How would the nomad vote be recorded?

The autonomy of the Arabs is as desirable as that of all Asiatic peoples, but it is the most difficult to work out.

Even the problem as it confronted the people among whom I lived was obscure. If, for example, a young man like Marhoun developed into a leader and an administrator; if the other nomad tribes accepted him by virtue of his personality as their chief; if the Arabs of the Atlas and the coast towns felt he was the right man to govern them; if all these improbable contingencies took place—what would be the attitude of the Moslems of Morocco and Tunisia? There is no doubt about the answer. They would object.

As far as I could see then, and as far as I can see now, there is only one solution: to form a number of autonomous states like Irak and Syria and Egypt and Morocco and Algeria, with local rulers. Let all these states have the same flag and possibly an interchange of members from their respective governments. Let them accustom themselves to thinking of themselves as autonomous, but all fundamentally Arab. From that let them evolve into something of the nature of the United States with a federal government and an elected president or emir with his capital in Medina. It is the burial place of Mohammed and by that virtue could be regarded as the natural place for an Islamic ruler to reside. It would seem much more normal for a Moslem to look for guidance from there than from Fez or Beyrouth. But wherever the capital and whoever the ruler, this problem must be tackled now.

If it is not, if the same mistakes are made as with the Sir Henry MacMahon agreement and the Lawrence pledges and the French treaties after the last war, there will be trouble. From the Arabs' point of view this may be a good thing, as it will unite them to obtain autonomous recognition. But it will not be so good for Occidentals.

This tie of Islam will be put to the test and will undoubtedly not be found weak or wanting. The Arabs will be backed by the Moslems all over the world, and before Europe knows what is happening, she will be fighting most of Asia. And if Europe starts fighting most of Asia, America will probably have to fight what's left over.

Already the British government's allusion to the Atlantic Charter's not applying to Asia, and France's breach of faith in Syria are having serious repercussions. The Arab autonomists are making full use of these statements of policy.

"Look at Syria," they say. "When the French were down and out and needed friends, they promised the Syrians independence. The day they were on their feet again and had arms and soldiers, however, they went back on their word. This is not propaganda. It is fact. If you don't believe it, read for yourself in the American or British press. When you have read, think a moment." They say: "Listen to the Cairo declaration. The Asiatic territories which

For over thirty months I had done absolutely nothing for which I could show anything except an increase in my flocks. And this had had little to do with me. Did this matter? What better thing could I have done? Was this all I had been destined for? Was "escape" really my goal? Had my elaborate education and careful upbringing been given me so that I might become a nomad of the Sahara? Why not? I was happy, wasn't I? But so were the Arabs, who knew no better. Was that to suffice? I was still young. Were the remaining years of my existence to be immersed in the inertia of fatalism? Would I live and die a bedouin of the desert? ... And, as I thought of these things, sleep gave up sulking and came to me eagerly as a woman whose lover will not be tricked into wooing her.

I did not wake until my horse stirred with the dawn. The Sahara was taking shape again. The rim of the world, dove grey, slowly whitened. Irridescent now, the night whispered away to the west. As I sat up and ate the rest of my dates, the blush of morning crept into the sky. Across my mind flashed a line from the ancient Greek ... "Dawn, hater of lovers."—I do not suppose I had thought of those words since I left Eton.—Eton!—My thoughts began once more to turn over the problem of the night before. Quickly I called my horse and saddled it.

The sun was shooting its first shafts of golden light across the desert as I caught sight of the bassours swaying on the backs of the camels as my caravan slowly plodded its way south.

I rode up to Madani who led the caravan huddled on his snow-white stallion. I saluted him with the stately morning greeting of the desert people. He unhuddled himself and breathed in the fresh autumn air. But he did not say anything. He did not ask me where I had been. He was not interested. If I liked to spend the night on the desert without food, it was nobody's business but mine. But I was in a talkative mood and, rather incoherently, I let flow the thoughts which were troubling me.

Madani made no immediate comment. For over an hour he rode on as if he had not heard. Then he said:

"'You are probably right. You have lived with us as one of us. You have prayed with us and eaten with us as one of us. You have shared the good with the bad. To the shepherds you are as much a nomad of the Sahara as I am. But although I love you as my brother, I know better. Inside of you is the Occidental, and the Occidental is stirring." He paused, and his blue eyes were filled with concern. "But I do not wish to see you leave us, and I cannot advise you. I am too young, and this matters touches me closely. Soon we shall come to the parting of the caravan tracks. One track leads to the south, the other to the east. I will take the track to the south. You will take the track to the east. In three hours you will come to the oasis. There you will find the Bash Agha, In sha Allah. Go and see him. He will tell you what to do."

When we came to the parting of the caravan tracks, Madani nodded toward the east, and with a quiet "Beselaama"—"Peace go with you"—he rode on.

Once more I was alone in the blinking, glittering desert. The sun was hot, now, and playing its picture-making games. Great lakes sprang up before me and shimmered away as I came near. Fantastic animals on flamingo's legs appeared in the middle distance and, as I approached, flew into the air like prehistoric dragons. The air was as heavy as the silence. But I rode on in the midst of this vast solitude less lonely than in many gay crowds in London and Paris.

After three hours exactly, I came within sight of the oasis. At first I thought that the tens of thousands of palm trees bowing to the lilt of the wind might be mirages. But I glanced at my watch and marveled once more at the accuracy with which Arabs timed distances instead of making guesses at mileages.

I went straight to the Bash Agha's house and found him sitting on a carpet playing patience. He welcomed me with a jovial mixture of ritual and banter. He refused to hear a word of my mission until we had lunched. This we did amply on the floor. The Bash Agha was thinking of other things, and I was too hungry to talk, so we said nothing until the grateful "Hamdullah" warned the servants to pass the ablution water and serve coffee. The old man's water pipe was set before him and lit. With a smile which encouraged confidences, he leaned back against his cushions.

I tried to order my speech better than in the morning, but it was still confused. However, Jelloul seemed to follow and nodded his head as I made each point. Once or twice I thought he had gone to sleep. But when I had finished, he wasted no time and, less sentimentally, said much the same as Madani. He concluded his remarks with:

156

"I do not think, though, that you can make a change suddenly. You have become used to desert life, to roaming, to having the sunrise and sunset your masters. If you went to live in America or Europe tomorrow, you would go crazy. Besides, we do not want you to go. If you will take the advice of an old man who knows the world of the Roumi as well as the world of the Moslem, I suggest you become one of the oasis dwellers. We will find you a house here, and you can gather your things about you—those books"—his grey eyes twinkled—"which Occidentals read so eagerly and then throw away. If you want, you can have your friends visit you, but don't give up your camp or your flocks. You can spend three, four, six months in the desert, whenever you feel inclined; the rest of the time in your oasis home. In this way you can regain touch with what is now making you restless and, In sha Allah, retain your Arab friends."

The old man took several pulls at his pipe, which he had almost allowed to go out while talking. Then he looked up with a questioning smile. I smiled back and nodded. The interview was over. I walked into the street an oasis citizen.

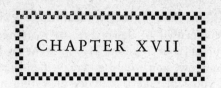

CHAPTER XVII

THE HOUSE WHICH THE Bash Agha found for me in the oasis looked like a cake. It was square and white and had a kind of crenelated green fringe around the edge of its flat roof. But it was not the white walls and green fringe which produced the cakelike effect and made it different from other houses. It was something so unexpected in any normal dwelling that it escaped one's notice. I used to make bets with non-Arabs that they could not tell me at a glance in what way my house was unlike any in Europe. Only the most observant noticed that it had no windows!

It had a green front door. It had a green stable door. It had a door leading into the garden, but its four outer walls were blanks. Unless one went inside the house, there was nothing to indicate that there was anything behind the walls. It might have been an unfinished Hollywood set. But it was not unfinished, and the nonpiercing of windows was not an oversight. It was intentional.

An Arab who can afford to have a house can afford to have wives. Wives must not be seen by passers-by or be tempted to look at passers-by. Hence no windows on the outside of the house. This does not mean that I, or any former inmates of this building, lived in stifling obscurity. There were plenty of windows, but they were on the inside!

Like most Arab houses, the cake house was built around a pillared courtyard open to the sky. Onto this courtyard opened four living rooms and a kitchen. That is, they became so after I took possession. Before my day they had been used for the weaving of carpets and the stabling of goats.

A brick stairway led up to an open gallery on the second floor where there were four bedrooms and a kind of huge lumber room.

All these rooms, as well as those below, had windows looking onto the courtyard. From the gallery the flat roof could be reached.

On the same level as the first floor was another courtyard with storage places for wood and a kind of primitive laundry. This led into a third courtyard where there was stabling for two horses.

On the other side of the house was a miniature garden which, with that incredible fertility of desert soil when watered, supported, in addition to the inevitable date palms, six other kinds of fruit-bearing trees. One winter I grew tulips under branches heavy with oranges and lemons.

Except for the floors, which were clay-tiled, the house was made of mud covered with plaster and whitewashed. It was over a hundred years old, and unless there was a cloudburst, the proprietor expected it to stand up for several more centuries. The rent I paid for this mansion was the equivalent of four dollars and fifty cents a month.

But if I had a house and a garden and fruit trees at a ridiculous rent, I had no furniture and no obvious means of getting any.

If I had been willing to go on living like a nomad, taking my meals on the floor, eating with my fingers, sleeping on a carpet, the furnishing would have been simple. But I did not intend continuing in this way. In the first place, I was tired of it. In the second, the Arabs would not have expected it. To live as they did in the camp, where there was no means of living in any other way, was all right; as was also the wearing of Arab clothes suited to desert requirements. But in a house, the natural home for an Occidental, I must be Occidental. When I got tired of chairs and plates and neckties, I could always go back to camp.

To solve the furnishing problem, I had to become inventive. I had to develop instincts of Mr. Robinson without any of the natural resources which the South Sea Islands furnished the Swiss family.

Between the oasis and the city of Algiers six hundred miles to the north, there was not a store where I could buy a stick of Occidental furniture. There were carpets, and cushions, and appliances for making couscous, as many as I wanted, but no beds or tables or cups or saucers. The only person who had anything like what I needed was Atalla Bouameur. He had some hideous Damascene chairs and stools made of stained wood inlaid with mother-of-pearl. These were better than nothing, so I bought some and added some carpets and cushions and couscous platters. Pots and pans I also found, but not a knife or a fork or a spoon.

At the suggestion of Mohammed ben Tahar I borrowed some of these from Monsieur Paoli while, from the same source, Blanchet produced a lot of empty wine cases. These we nailed together and painted to serve as dressing tables and washstands. The two boys were as energetic as they were inventive, and worked devotedly. Blanchet like a faithful dog who does not know why he likes his master, but just likes him. Mohammed because he saw this an opportunity to rescue me from the "savages" who lived in the desert, and hoped to have someone with whom to exchange his philosophies.

With their help I got hold of some servants. I had suggested that Mohammed and Blanchet join my household permanently. But they had declined. Blanchet stated frankly that he hated regular work. As long as he could earn enough by odd jobs, he would make no change. Mohammed, without actually saying so, made it clear that he belonged to the intelligentsia and would only accept clerical or, preferably, literary employment. However, the staff which was produced, though less picturesque, was probably more efficient.

The cook's name was Ali. It sounds confusing to have had so many around with the same name, but Ali alone or Mohammed alone conveyed nothing. An Arab's full name had to be accompanied by that of his father: Daylis ben Jelloul, Marhoun ben Daylis, and so on. I do not remember what the name of the father of Ali was, but he had sired a first-class cook. He had worked in French inns in North Africa, and with the aid of a cookery book which Mohammed ben Tahar translated for him, he turned out Occidental meals which would have been good anywhere.

The butler, Ahmed, was sixteen. He was a serious boy and quickly learned to be a good valet and waiter.

The "housemaid" was Ahmed's brother. His name was Sliman and his age fourteen. Sliman worked in fits and starts and, occasionally, had to be spanked. But he bore no ill will and accepted life with a laugh.

Moussa was the groom. He was a gloomy man, but a horse lover as well as a horse master. From the way he rode, he must have had nomad blood.

The combined wages for all four servants amounted to the equivalent of twelve dollars a month. I also dressed them. Not because I had to but so that they would look nice. That, even, did not run me into more than fifty dollars a year.

The only female member of the staff, and she was hardly a member, was the "laundry maid." She was a scraggy, ageless Jewess called Liza. There are no words in the English language to describe her, but when I think of anything repulsively hideous, I say, "As ugly as Liza."

But though waited on and cooked for and laundered, I was still without proper furniture. Madani finally took the problem in hand.

First of all, he had mattresses made and stuffed with wool from my sheep. Then he wrote to a cousin in Algiers and had him send some box-spring mattresses which could take the place of beds. With these came an assortment of crockery and silver and linen. The carpets and the curtains I had got in the oasis. A month after my taking possession of the cake house, it looked and felt comfortable. Three months later no one would have imagined that it had ever been the home of goats. The only thing which no one could help me over was a bath.

Except in the hotel, there was not a house in the oasis which had water laid on or any form of modern plumbing. Arabs do not bathe except at the hammam, and the water for drinking and cooking is carried into their homes in buckets. But the hammam takes a long time, as well as being exhausting if made use of daily. Besides, it was a bore to walk to town every time I wanted a wash. I had a few old-fashioned basins and pitchers. These were better than nothing, but not enough. Once more I had to think: What would Mr. Robinson have done under similar circumstances?—He would have *made* a bath, of course.

Unfortunately I was not domestic or mechanical-minded, but I had studied history. I began, therefore, to consider bathing throughout the ages.

Before we had plumbing and taps and water heaters, how did people take baths? There was, of course, the Roman system, but that was much the same as the oasis hammam. That did not help. I must try again.

How had my grandparents washed their bodies when they were

161

young? How had Queen Victoria and Napoleon? How had it been done before that? Something clicked in my head. —Had not Charlotte Corday assassinated Jean Paul Marat while he was sitting in his bath? To sit in a bath long enough to allow a young lady to plunge a knife into one, it must have been a comfortable and warm bath. It must also have been in the bather's home. If J. P. Marat, in the latter half of the eighteenth century, could have hot baths in his house without any central heating or modern plumbing, why could not R. V. C. Bodley in the first half of the twentieth century and under the same sanitary conditions as at the time of the Terror?

I ordered a bath from Algiers. An ordinary white metal bath which should normally have stood in a tiled bathroom with taps and waste pipes and other gadgets. I had it placed in the lumber room on the second floor, against the outer wall of the house. In this wall I knocked a hole where the waste pipe should have been. In the hole I placed a kind of wooden spout which, when I took the plug out of the bath, sent the water cascading into the alley below. I instructed Ahmed to build a fire every evening in the second courtyard, and on it to heat buckets of water. These Sliman carried upstairs to the bath. It took three hot and two cold to fill it. In this way I could enjoy the luxury of a warm bath in my own house, and without fear of being murdered. But though there was no Mademoiselle Corday to molest me, the bath led me into other trouble.

The soapy water, as I have explained, shot straight out of the bath into the alley or street which skirted one side of my house. The surface of the street was, like everything else in the oasis, made of mud. Mud is firm to walk on as long as it is dry. It is not firm to walk on when it is wet. As, however, it is never really wet in this part of the world, the mud street goes on unchallenged. My mud street, or rather the water of my bath mingled with the mud street, might have continued also to go on unchallenged, if it had not been that this particular street led to the cemetery.

An Arab funeral is not anything like the same rite in America or Europe. The corpse, wrapped in a shroud, is placed on a kind of stretcher and carried to the grave on the shoulders of chanting men. Crowds of people follow in the procession. Some of these are friends and relatives of the corpse; many just happen to feel in the mood for a funeral. But regardless of the degree of kinship or acquaintanceship, every ablebodied man must, for a few yards, take a hand at bearing the "stretcher."

Where the alley passed beneath my bathroom was the last lap before reaching the cemetery. It was, therefore, the spot where an almost free fight began for the privilege of giving the corpse a helping hand to its final resting place. The chanting, too, became louder and fiercer, and groups of men who had nothing else to do swelled the procession. One can, thus, imagine the confusion when, on the morning after my fourth or fifth bath, a man in one of these funeral processions who was just relieving one of the corpse bearers, slipped in the slime. With his feet going away from under him like greased lightning, he let go of the stretcher, and the corpse was precipitated into the mud.

The rest of the parade, singing fanatically and unaware of what had happened in front, pressed on and piled up on the stretcher carriers, who were feverishly trying to recover the corpse. In less than a minute, that dignified chanting procession had become a heap of bellowing creatures slithering about like players at a football match on a wet Saturday afternoon.

I was quite ignorant of what had taken place, and at first no one attributed the funeral mishap to anything having to do with me. But when the same thing occurred a second time at precisely the same spot, and then a third time, the wise began to smell coincidence. —Why was this part of the funeral route always wet and muddy? An investigation followed, and my bath had to be moved to the opposite end of the lumber room where the water could leak into the garden.

The only other attempt I made to disturb the traditions of the oasis was also a cause of my losing face. It was much later on in my stay in the Sahara and had to do with making ice.

To nomads living in a tent in the desert the drinking of water is a luxury in itself, and no one worries whether it is cold or not. But in an oasis where water is plentiful, one becomes particular.

Monsieur Paoli used to have ice sent down to him from Algiers. By the time it reached him, fifty per cent had melted, so he had none to spare for me. One day I saw an advertisement for a contrivance with which ice could be made *by hand*. "By hand" was of paramount importance, as in the oasis there was no electric or oil power. All lighting was by candles or petroleum lamps, and machines could only be worked by manual labor. Since the wording of the advertisement was so reassuring, I sent for the ice-making device and the book of directions.

Arabs are not exactly inquisitive, but they know everything that is going on in the communities in which they live. From the moment Boukamel, the Mzabite owner of the Djelfa bus line, had glanced at the invoice announcing the ice machine, the news became common property.

Accompanying the two men who delivered the packing case at my door were Blanchet and Mohammed ben Tahar. They were quickly followed by Atalla and a little later by Daylis and Sheik Ali. The men who had brought the case felt themselves too much involved in this ice-making project to leave, so they stayed on and helped Ahmed and Sliman get the thing out of its box. Moussa and Ali the cook had been joined by Faradji ben Chayeb, the owner of my house. Everyone was poised, ready to witness the first miracle of ice making in the Sahara.

When the contrivance was cleared of its wrappings, I read the instructions. They covered two sheets of paper but said little else than to fill the container with clean water and turn the handle. The chemicals would do the rest.

With the instructions carried out, I set to work to show off my magic; but although I turned that handle until my arm ached, although Daylis turned the handle and Sheik Ali turned the handle, the water remained at precisely the same temperature. Neither did the turning of the handle by my four servants and then by Mohammed and Blanchet and Atalla have any effect. Nor did some powerful work by the men who had brought the packing case, and by my landlord, do anything but make the water slightly warmer. There was more energy put into changing that water into ice than by the Negroes in their savage dancing in Chellala. The experiment lasted almost as long. Many hours after I had gone to bed, I could hear the whirring of that handle as other inhabitants of the oasis came to see if they could not perform the miracle of turning water into ice. But it was all to no avail. The water remained tepid.

The day following the experiment, I ran into Monsieur Paoli, who said: "I hear that you have been trying to make ice out of Sahara water?"

164

I said, "Yes," casually. I was feeling a trifle touchy.

Monsieur Paoli laughed. "Do you suppose I would import hundreds of kilos of ice from Algiers, half of which melts on the way, if I could make ice out of Sahara water?"

"Why can't you make ice out of Sahara water?" I inquired. I was eager for a little face saving.

"Because it is full of all kinds of salts," answered Monsieur Paoli. "Did you not notice its effect on you when you first came to live here?"

I nodded. I certainly had noticed. Although excellent to drink, the water in these parts had the properties of strong Enos. I wonder what would happen if one put fruit salts in a frigidaire.

But although I could not make ice, I still wanted cold water. Jean Paul Marat had given me a bath; someone else might help me to find a cool drink. Letting my mind wander in the same way as before, I had a solution in forty-eight hours.

In years, I had to go back further than the French Revolution. In mileage, not so far. I remembered the Mzabites. I remembered the skins of icy water which hung in the gates of their holy city. That water was fresh on the hottest day. It had probably been like that for a thousand years. Within a week, I had a skin hanging in the draft between my two courtyards. Twelve hours later I had an icy drink. I do not know what the scientific explanation is, but I was always able to serve colder water than Monsieur Paoli with all his imported ice.

I was now living luxuriously. Baths, beds, plates, knives, forks, laundering, several meals a day; strong, black, bitter Indian tea, and groundless coffee. My physical needs were looked after. If I lacked anything, it was from the mental angle. Although I now read two-days-old Algiers papers, I still had no books. But like the rest, the books materialized without even as much effort as for the bathing and drinking.

A knock at my door one afternoon admitted a round, red-cheeked, sandy-moustached, dumpy Frenchman. He wore an inappropriate blue business suit, laced-up black boots, grey cotton gloves, and a starched shirt and collar. In his hand he carried a straw hat; under his arm was a bulging brief case. He introduced himself as Auguste Veau.

I invited Monsieur Veau into the living room, ordered wine, and inquired to what I owed the pleasure of his visit?

"Monsieur," said the little man meaningly, "I am a man of letters. A commercial man of letters, or, if you prefer it, a commercial traveler. I travel in encyclopedias. Monsieur, may I have the honor to furnish you with an encyclopedia?"

He opened the brief case and drew out one of those dummy bindings with specimen pages. After a sip of the wine which Ahmed had served, he went on: "I do not have to tell a European of the stimulation which the possession of an encyclopedia can give." He paused and, as I made no comment, added: "I feel sure, Monsieur, that you will have no hesitation in letting me put your name down for a complete edition of this up-to-date encyclopedia?" Monsieur Veau paused hopefully and drank more wine.

Maintaining the salesman's pedantic manner, I replied: "Monsieur, while I appreciate all you have said about the stimulative effects of an encyclopedia, I am afraid that such a work can be of little use to one such as I whose home is in a Sahara oasis."

Monsieur Veau put down his empty glass and looked at me as might a schoolmaster contemplating a pupil with arrested development. For a moment he said nothing. Then, taking the dummy encyclopedia, wetted his thumb and began to turn the pages.

"Of little use," he muttered; "how strangely at fault you are, Monsieur. How unenlightened, how blinded by this dark continent!" He cleared his throat and, tapping one of the pages of the encyclopedia, said, "Now, here is a complete treatise on the making of glass. Would you not, Monsieur, like to know how to make glass?"

I shook my head. "No, Monsieur," I replied, "I do not wish to know how to make glass."

Monsieur Veau, who had been studying the sample page, suddenly looked up and said almost menacingly: "Do you know what glass is made of, Monsieur?"

"No, Monsieur," I answered, "I do not know what glass is made of."

Monsieur Veau leaned forward and said almost in a whisper: "Monsieur, it is made of sand!" And as I showed no emotion, he added, "Think, Monsieur, of all the glass which you could make in the Sahara!"

166

Seeing that I still remained impassive, Monsieur Veau quickly turned over some more pages of his encyclopedia. Once again he looked up radiant.

"Ah, Monsieur, this will surely interest you. The curing of eels. I am sure that a man of your education would wish to know how to cure eels."

Again I shook my head. "Monsieur Veau," I replied, "There are no eels in the Sahara. If there were, I would want to eat them, not cure them."

Monsieur Veau hardly heard me. He was skimming through the leaves of his book. Every now and then he looked up with a tentative suggestion.—"Embroidery? No."—"Stained glass windows? No."—"Medieval armor? No." Finally he raised his head triumphantly. "This time, Monsieur, I have found a topic which I am *positive* will appeal to you. Bookbinding!"

To Monsieur Veau's relief, I showed some reaction.

"Monsieur," I said, "I do not want to know anything about the binding of books, but I would enjoy having the books inside the bindings. If you can sell me books which I can read, I am your client."

Monsieur Veau finished another goblet of wine. He put away the dummy encyclopedia and took from the brief case a catalogue of books. Before the bottle was finished, I had agreed to buy on the installment system the complete works of Dumas, Gide, Hugo, Hermant, and the Tharaud brothers. I had also subscribed to an atlas.

It is a pity that Monsieur Veau was not a writer himself. He would have had a wonderful tale to tell. Every year he set out from Paris with his catalogues and samples to tour the Sahara. In the same blue suit and the faded straw hat, he visited the remotest oases. Sometimes he was away for ten months, calling at these strange and often savage places with no more concern than if his circuit had been the Rhone Valley. When I asked him who bought his encyclopedias, he told me, "Chiefly Arabs." They could not read what was written on the pages, but they liked having the red-and-gold-bound volumes which gave them a reputation for learning. It was Monsieur Veau and his travels which first gave me the idea to write books myself. But not yet. To attain such a state of mind would take time. For the moment, I was barely out of the nomad chrysalis. I was still trying to accustom myself to this new way of living.

This was no pose. I was discovering that it was much simpler to return to the primitive than to the modern. As I dressed each morning, I realized how completely I had lost my Occidental habits. My stomach, no longer accustomed to breakfasts and mid-day meals, did not call me instinctively to table. My day was regulated by the sun and not by clocks. I did not know what to do with myself when I was not on horseback. After dinner I wanted to go to bed. Once in bed, I could not sleep. At first I could not make out why. I would drop off almost as soon as my head touched the pillow, but I would be wide awake in an hour and tossing around most of the night. It was not because of the bed or the covers or the lack of air. I had few blankets, and the courtyard in the middle of the house made it the draftiest place imaginable. It was not indigestion or nerves. It was something quite unexpected. If I had not mentioned my insomnia to Daylis, I might never have found out the cause.

He said: "Your head's cold. When I go to a hotel in Algiers or Paris, I undress and get into bed like a Roumi, but unless I have something on my head, I can't sleep."

I realized that he was right. After years of sleeping in a turban, my head could not accustom itself to the night air, which was getting sharp as the winter drew on. Henceforth I wore a fez in bed and had no more sleepless nights. Today, even, on the rare occasions when I cannot drop off at once, I put on a hat. Nine times out of ten it works faster than any sedative.

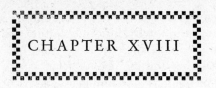

CHAPTER XVIII

Although I had a house, I had not, strictly speaking, become an oasis citizen. Not like Atalla Bouameur or Mohammed ben Tahar. I had a kind of dual personality.

One day I would be strolling on the arcaded street looking like any tourist. The next, I would be riding across the Sahara, indistinguishable from an Arab. While my physical self sometimes craved beds and baths and black tea, my heart belonged to the desert. After a period of doing things at specific hours for no possible reason except habit, my mind revolted, and I would be off. If the camp was near, I rode there on the horse which I had bought for my amusement around the oasis. If the camp was far, I took the bus and had one of my shepherds wait for me by the roadside with my grey stallion. Sometimes I remained with my nomads for a week; often I did not return for months. When I got back, I found everything going at home as if I had only been out for the afternoon. Sliman filled the bath. Ali cooked the dinner. Ahmed took my burnouses to brush and hang up. The next day I was on the arcaded street looking as if I had just arrived from Algiers.

For the first time since my birth, I was doing what I wanted. I was leading the life that suited me. I was content. I had found a home and a family. The desert was my father. The oasis was my mother. My parents differed in appearance and ways of thinking, but they could not be separated one from the other.

The oasis dwellers are just as much part of the Sahara as the nomads. In fact, unless one has lived both the oasis life and the desert life, one cannot claim to know the Sahara. It is the oasis people who do the thinking, who are the constructors. It is they and their fellow city dwellers who have guided the political destinies of the Arabs, in spite of being in a minority. The nomad has been the fighter, the soldier, the pioneer who has carried Islam to the ends of the world more by love of adventure and fanaticism than by a wish to inspire with his Arab culture. The nomads and the sedentary Arabs are as different as possible, but they make up one entity like a father and mother.

The oasis way of living is quite unlike the desert way. It is unlike living anywhere else. It is rather like being on an island among people whose every thought is centered on that island. The oasis folk are more stay-at-home than the inhabitants of any American provincial town. They never leave the perimeter of the oasis. Some, like Atalla, made occasional trips to Algiers, but the majority remained where they were. Quite a few I knew had never set foot in the desert and had no idea what the country was like ten miles to the south. They had nothing remotely in common with the nomads.

The nomad is a traveler, a warrior, a hunter. He is a man of gunpowder, of the sword, of the tent. The vast expanses of the desert, with their dangers and privations, are essential to him. It is in that setting that he shows his qualities of patience, of abstinence, of courage and duty. His instinct is to move. If he loses his camel or his horse and is, in consequence, immobilized and becomes sedentary, he is humiliated and quickly degenerates. He does not despise the oasis dweller, neither does he fight him, but he considers him a subordinate and does not wish to be like him. The oasis people form a commercial and rural democracy of pedestrians in contrast to the nomad horsemen, the gentlemen of the sword, the least of whom has the dignity and courtesy of an aristocrat.

To the desert Arab, luxury is unknown. On the Sahara he must always be on the alert. He can only relax when he comes into the oasis. It is to him what a port of call was to a sailor a hundred years ago.

With the invention of frigidaires and air conditioning and radios, a sailor has practically all the comforts afloat which he has on shore. A nomad on the sea of the desert has not. He is as much cut off from life's primary needs as Vasco da Gama's men when they rounded the Cape. He is often longer away from "land" than were the Portuguese sailors of the sixteenth century. He is just as limited in his use of fresh water. Until one has made one's home in the desert, it is hard to appreciate the luxury of plenty of water.

An oasis exists because of water. A fault in the rocks has sent one of the prehistoric subterranean rivers to the surface. Within this perimeter of surface moisture anything will grow, from a strawberry to a date, from a rose to a bougainvillia. A few yards outside the perimeter, nothing will grow unless there is rain. The water has disappeared again into the bowels of the earth. But though the water in an oasis is sufficiently plentiful to make a nomad feel he is in Paradise, it is not plentiful enough to be wasted. So its use is regulated. One of the most important functionaries of these desert communities is the water controller. His responsibilities are greater than those of any bank president.

The oasis is divided into seven areas, one for each day of the week, and each area has one water day. The water is captured at a point where it gushes from the ground and is sent swirling along stone channels called seguias, which border the gardens. Leading from the channels into the gardens are padlocked sluice gates. The keys of these sluice gates are held by the water controller.

At the hour appointed for a garden to be watered, the controller dams the seguia and opens the sluice. He lets the water run into the garden for an allotted number of minutes according to its size. My garden had eleven minutes every week, and during that time I could do as I pleased with the water, or as Ali ordained. Once my eleven minutes were up, the controller closed the sluice and flooded the next garden. Nothing that I could say or offer would induce him to give me a second more of water. His integrity was incorruptible.

This running water which never dries whether there be drought or floods is, like all nature's miracles, taken as a matter of course. I never met an Arab who wondered why the water was there or where it came from. I did not think about it much myself until, one day, Blanchet appeared at my door with a bucket of fish, some of which were still alive. I asked him where he had caught them. He grinned. "In the seguia." I gave him a few francs and asked Ali if the fish were good to eat. He said they were, so I had them for dinner. They would not have passed for trout, but neither did they have that muddy taste of certain river fish.

Some time later I was talking to a geologist and told him about the Sahara fish. He was interested but not surprised. He had never eaten any, but he knew all about them. He said that the same fish were found in the Niger and in the Nile; also in the Congo, the Sea of Galilee and Lake Chad.

"Which means," he added, "that, in comparatively recent times, fish were able to make their way by an all fresh-water route from the Sahara to Central Africa, Egypt and Palestine."

I asked if these rivers still flowed underground and joined up with these ancient watercourses. He said, "Probably, but not toward the east." A huge upheaval in the Quarternary era had "beheaded" the rivers flowing in that direction, but it had been fairly well proved that the Sahara rivers found an outlet to the south. As if to confirm this, I read not long ago that in a water hole below the surface of the desert near the Touggourt oasis a live crocodile had been found. The nearest point from this place to the natural home of a crocodile would be the Niger, a thousand miles away!

Compared to that of a nomad, the day of an oasis dweller is monotonous. He has none of the trials of looking for pastures, none of the moving, none of the riding after game. Even in the matter of weather he is not much troubled. Rain is welcome in the oasis and the sirocco is disliked, but its effect is chiefly the indirect repercussion on the nomad's spending power. Locusts are really the only things which damage and disorganize the oasis people.

An attack by locusts is nearly as awe-inspiring as the sirocco. No one knows exactly where they come from, and they appear as unexpectedly as the hot wind.

My first locust experience was in the spring, when everything in the oasis was fresh and green. I was sitting in the garden when Ali came out and looked up at the sky. He shook his head and said: "Grasshoppers!" Then he went back into the house.

It seemed a silly sort of remark for one's cook to make without context, but I looked up at the sky myself. It was filled with black specks. The kind of specks one sees when the liver is out of order. Before I had time to give the idea much thought, however, the sun disappeared in shadow. A huge cloud was sweeping over the sky. The oasis was shrouded in a kind of eclipse twilight. With the darkness, everything came to life with a clatter.

From out of the houses rushed people with pots and pans, beating them frenziedly until the alleys and gardens echoed to a hideous hullabaloo. As the uncanny darkness increased, so did the noise. Then, suddenly, it began to rain creatures from the sky. It was another of those baffling Sahara experiences. With these myriads of locusts dripping into my garden, I felt as helpless as during the sirocco. Not so the servants. With brooms and sticks Ali and Ahmed and Moussa and Sliman flung themselves against the invaders. They might just as well have defied a thunderstorm. For every locust they killed, a hundred others took its place. Within two hours of the appearance of the plague there was not a leaf or blade of grass in the oasis. There was also a great number of dead locusts. For the next week we had locusts in every shape and form for breakfast, lunch, and dinner. They were excellent. If they had not been so expensive to feed, I would have started a locust restaurant. Cooked, they look and taste like succulent prawns. I envy St. John the Baptist his diet of locusts and honey.

Apart from the locust scourges the oasis peoples' lives were humdrum. They all got up early and prayed. Then they went to work. Some of them were shopkeepers, some were gardeners. Some had both shops and gardens. The shopkeepers sold groceries and hardware and haberdashery. The gardeners grew fruits and vegetables, a little wheat, and a great many dates. Owing to the country's height above sea level and its liability to frost, our dates were not of the top grade, but they were good enough.

There are as many varieties of dates in the world as there are apples and pears. They grow in desert soils from southern California to the Tigris and Euphrates. The owners of the Muscat-type date palms make incomes which would be worth-while anywhere. Ours were coarse dates and not fine enough for exporting. Those that were not eaten in the oasis were pressed and sold by the cubic foot to the nomads. These "bricks" kept indefinitely and furnished food for men and camels.

But although our fifty thousand palm trees did not make fortunes for their owners, as in the Ziban tribal areas, they were an important source of oasis revenue and were carefully looked after.

The date palm does not bear fruit until it is eight years old, and is not mature until it is thirty. After that it will go on giving dates till it is a hundred; sometimes longer, if well cared for. The care is essential, especially in the matter of its sex life. Most plants make love with the assistance of insects or birds, sometimes with just wind, which seems unsatisfactory but produces results. The palm cannot even do that and has to be fertilized with human

173

hands. Walking in the oasis during February or March, one is often startled by the sound of chanting in the skies. It is the palm fertilizer, way up on the top of the female palm inserting male pollen into a cleft in her head. While deputizing for the male tree, he sings encouraging hymns.

The date palm is said to be the Tree of Life which grew in the Garden of Eden. It is the most likely of any legend. The date is probably the only food which men and animals and birds can all live on and thrive. Not the date we used to eat in London and New York around Christmastime. That date is picked before it is ripe and has lost its moisture and most of its food values before reaching us. The fresh ripe date, filled with desert sunshine, is energy-giving, nourishing, and thirst-quenching. A lump of crushed dates cut from the brick is a meal in itself. The date palm, when it is past bearing, supplies beams for the roofs of houses, branches for thatching, and bark for burning. If we go a bit farther and consider others of the large palm family—the sago palm, the oil palm, the betel nut palm, and many more—a man living on an estate entirely planted in palms would want for nothing.

The Arabs add that the vine is the Tree of Knowledge. When man first made wine and got drunk, he neglected to look after the Garden, which soon became desert and he had to go elsewhere to live.

The oasis people have no grapes with which to make wine, but they have that terrific liquor made from the sap of the date palm, called lagmi. Lagmi, drunk fresh, is cool and has rather a sickly taste not unlike overripe dates. In that form it is harmless. Allowed, however, to ferment, it becomes as potent as ten-day-old corn whisky. Not many of my fellow oasis dwellers bothered about lagmi or any other liquor. They were good Moslems and hard workers. Besides, they were gay naturally and did not have to drink to laugh.

Besides the obvious occupational differences between the oasis people and the nomads, two essentially city traits struck me when I first began living in a house. Prayers were almost always said en masse in the mosque when the muezzin called from the minaret. Dinner was not immediately followed by bed. It was the same contrast as between the old-fashioned farmer and the townsman.

Family prayers and early bed. Church or chapel, evening at the club or theatre.

The Arabs did not gather together and go to church in their best clothes, but they always said some of their prayers at the mosque and, on Friday, listened to the Imam's sermon.

At night, when the meal was over, they did not roll onto their rugs and go to sleep. They went out. Some of them to the café and cards and chess. Some of them to visit. Some of them to the Ouled Nails to look at the girls and listen to the music.

Although Mohammed (the Prophet, not Tahar) disapproved of music, the Arabs, other than members of puritanical sects like the Mzabites, love it and give up much of their spare time to it. There are many kinds, but they fit into three main categories.

The dance music and the military music are furnished by a short trumpet with a bell-shaped mouth and stops like those on a flute. It is called a raita. The raita player blows through a reed mouthpiece and produces a sound not unlike the skirl of the bagpipes, only much shriller. The ear-piercing squeals of the raita are accompanied by a tamtam or a debourca, one or both. The tamtam is an oversized tambourine. The debourca is made of pottery and looks like a flower vase with a skin stretched over the mouth. The combination of these instruments is ear-shattering and should be listened to at a distance or in the open air.

The other wind instrument is the flute. It can be long or short, and is made out of a hollow reed with eight stops. There is no mouthpiece, and the sound is produced by blowing across the end of the instrument. I never discovered how this was done, but the music from a nomad flute had a mellow sweetness which was as much part of the desert as the wind. Sometimes the flutist is accompanied by a tamtam or a singer, sometimes by both; but however one heard the nomad flute, its melancholy music was as drugging as the Sahara moonlight.

Most Arabs can sing, and some of their finest music is their religious chants. These were forbidden in the mosque but could be heard in private homes or outside the tombs of marabouts. There was no accompaniment except from the tamtam, which added an inspiring rhythm not unlike that of the Negro spirituals.

From an Occidental's point of view the Arab music with stringed instruments is the most entertaining. They consist of mandolins, guitars, and a kind of primitive violin which is held upright on the knee and played as might be a double bass. This was the kind of music which I encouraged. The raita I left to the Ouled Nails, the reed flute I enjoyed in the camp, the chants I handed to the marabouts. The mandolins and guitars I made a fuss over.

Among other unexpected things which the Sahara surprised me with was a string orchestra which played for the sake of playing and gave concerts for the joy of giving them. The members of this orchestra all lived in the oasis.

The leader was Mecheri, Daylis' tailor who had made my first pair of Arab pantaloons. He was tall and pale and emaciated, and wore a small black moustache under an aristocratic nose. He bore a strong resemblance to Alphonso XIII. If I could have traced back Mecheri's ancestry, I am certain I would have discovered a Spanish hidalgo in Seville or Granada sometime in the fifteenth or sixteenth century. Mecheri's playing, too, had the rhythm of Spain. When he twanged his guitar, the Arab tailor vanished, the oasis vanished, the cake house was transformed. It was the Alhambra, the Alcazar, Andalusia when Arab culture had made Spain great.

The mandolinist was Amida, who kept the haberdashery store opposite the Turkish bath. He was round and chubby. He ate a great deal, he slept a great deal, but he forgot food and bed for the sake of music. He had not the artistry or the talent of Mecheri, but he played and sang with the enthusiasm of one who played and sang because he loved it.

The name of the third member of the orchestra was Ahmed. I do not know what his father's name was but he was nothing like Ahmed the "butler." As a matter of fact, he was never referred to except as *the* Khodja. This was his title as a sort of chief clerk in a government office in the oasis. He was a typical Arab of no particular family standing. Well-built, bearded, stupid, and good-natured. He did not play any particular instrument, but he could be relied on to keep time with the tamtam. He also sang in tune. The reason he belonged to the minstrel troupe, really, was that he liked going out. His job did not earn him much, and his home life was dull. The other musicians alternately teased him and used him as a beast of burden to carry their instruments. The Khodja did not mind. As long as he could tag along with the band, he was happy.

Draoui, who was the real moving spirit of the orchestra, was a hunchback. His poor little frame was twisted and shriveled, but like many men whose bodies are deformed, he had a brilliant mind. Draoui was one of the few Arabs I knew with whom I could hold a sustained discussion on practically any subject. I do not think that he had ever traveled further than Algiers, but he could talk on politics and literature and foreign philosophies as clearly as many well-educated Occidentals. He was also an expert with the debourca.

This flower-vase tambourine has several tones, which are varied not only by the drumming with the fingers but by the pressure of the hand or the arm on its earthenware sides. Draoui used to put as much expression into his debourca as Mecheri into his guitar.

Atalla was the fifth and unofficial member of the quintet. All the musicians were his friends, and when he had time, he went around with them. He was more of a guest artist than a regular performer.

Some of the gayest evenings of my life belong to those spent with my quintet. Sometimes we had dinner. Sometimes we started after dinner. Sometimes we sat and talked, but the party was chiefly given up to music. The tunes ranged from Arab classics to Hispano-Mauresque or definitely Spanish, with occasional Occidental pieces adapted to Arab tempo. There were a few original compositions by Mecheri which made me wish one of us knew how to score music or record notes. But whatever was played, it was never tiresome and often kept us up all night. These men performed as much for their enjoyment as mine. The only conditions they insisted on were, not to perform for people they did not know and never for Arab chiefs.

"Fate," said Mecheri, "has made of us oasis tradesmen, of which we are not ashamed. Our professions are what they are, and we do not wish to be considered anything which we are not. We are, nevertheless, not musicians hirable to amuse the socially high placed of the oasis community, people in whose presence it is not considered right for us to sit except when playing. We are musicians by inclination. When we cross the threshold of your house, we cease to be tailors and drapers, we even cease to be Khodjas. We are gentlemen of leisure, playing for our own pleasure and the pleasure of our friends."

And as Mecheri delivered himself, the Court of the Lions seemed to materialize around him and the scents of the Generalife Gardens fill my pillared courtyard.

Even when the Bash Agha tried to make me use my influence to get Mecheri to come and play for him, he decoratively refused.

"Tell Sidi el Hadj Jelloul ben Lahkdar," he said, "that I will make him the finest clothes south of Algiers, for which I ask no compensation but the honor of making them. Tell him that I will be his tailor, In sha Allah, until death parts us, but that our respective positions make it impossible for me to sit beside him and sing to him as I do to you."

In the summer we used to go to friends' gardens in the oasis and lie under the orange trees and listen to music till it was light. Once we transported ourselves and our instruments to the home of a marabout who liked having a good time and discarded all saintly camouflage when Mecheri and his companions were around.

The Marabout lived at a place called Kourdane, which I did not know except by name. It was about twenty miles from the oasis and was visited three times a week by one of the less modern buses of Boukamel's fleet. There was practically no road, and it took two hours of shaking and bumping to get to our destination. But the orchestra did not care. It was going on a vacation, and every member sang ceaselessly all the way there.

From the time I came to live with the Arabs, they were always springing unpremeditated surprises on me. I was always braced for the unexpected. Lately the shocks had been less frequent, and I was beginning to think that the Sahara had nothing new to teach me. This trip proved that the Sahara always has something new.

Kourdane, which I had supposed was an oasis or a village, turned out to be nothing less than a palace or castle. It had the varied architecture of Windsor, the grace of Chenonceaux, the majesty of Versailles. The effect of this noble building rising out of the desert was more fantastic than any mirage. Until the bus stopped before an Italian landscaped garden, flagged with white marble and interspersed with flower beds and fountains and tall cypresses, I thought it was a mirage. I glanced questioningly at my friends, but neither they nor the inmates of the bus seemed to be in the least impressed. The Khodja was being loaded with musical instruments, while Draoui already led the way to a great horseshoe stone stairway with wrought iron ballustrades which I seemed to remember having seen at Fontainebleau.

At the top of the stairs stood the Marabout. He also was a surprise, as he was quite black. Not a coarse negroid type, but finely sculptured from jet or ebony. Save for a scarlet fez, his clothing was snow-white. His only ornament was a large turquoise set in an old silver ring which Atalla and the musicians kissed. He welcomed me with a smile and told me in cultured French that he had heard of my renown, and led the way into the living room. It was vast and in proportion with the rest of this fantastic place. The furnishing was Occidental, but with genuine Oriental antiques, the first of the kind I had seen since I came to the Sahara. As I let myself down onto a Moorish throne, I looked across at Atalla. Patting the chair which he was occupying, he winked.

We drank a little tea, while the Marabout inquired politely after our healths, but without the anxiety of our friends in the oasis. Then he excused himself and handed us over to a kind of steward, who took us to our quarters. These opened onto a long gallery which overlooked another decorative garden, landscaped in French style. Again I noticed the taste and richness of the furnishings of the rooms; the four-post beds with their brocaded curtains, and the carpets into which my feet sank. Then I saw that my room was not a room but a suite. I thought one of the others would be sharing quarters with me, but the steward shook his head. Every guest had a bedroom, sitting room, and dining room. In the days of the Marabout's father and grandfather, meals were served separately and privately to each visitor.

My mind went back to the story of Antinea and the Atlantide.— I was once more in that mist. I was as baffled as when I had first come to the Sahara. What was this place filled with antiques standing in the middle of European gardens, and all about them the infinite desolation of the desert? I turned to the steward, but he had silently disappeared. A feeling of being more alone than ever crept over me. During my other dilemmas in this baffling country, I had always had the practical, staunch Madani around; but now, with the exception of Atalla, I was with men who belonged to a dream world. I was just wondering where I could find Atalla when he walked into my apartment. With his hands in his coat pockets, he quietly appraised the furniture and the draperies and said:

"What waste!"

I suddenly felt my feet making contact with earth again.

"Atalla," I exclaimed, "what *is* all this?"

Atalla seated himself on a Scheherazadean divan and began to talk. What he told me was as extravagant as the rest.

The grandfather of the present marabout had taken part in a rebellion against the French round about the time of the Franco-Prussian war. The revolt had been subdued and the marabout exiled to France. Here he had met and fallen in love with a French *gendarme's* daughter called Aurélie Picard. Although the marabout was black, he was intelligent and handsome, and Aurélie had married him. Soon after, he was pardoned and returned with his wife to Kourdane. Aurélie was a clever woman and ambitious. Her husband was enormously wealthy and had no idea of how to manage his fortune. The *gendarme's* daughter took this in hand and began by building this palace and creating the gardens which she felt would be worthy of the holy man's position. She had architects and landscapers come from France, and spent millions of francs in having what she wanted, done in the way she wanted it. When all was finished to her satisfaction, she took over the business side of her man's life. Maraboutism was put on an orderly footing. The parasites were sent away. The needy from all over the country were cared for according to their rightful merits. Rank made no impression on her. It was said that when bash agha or beggar came asking for shelter, he was given a suite and waited on without distinction.

Aurélie became a Moslem by conviction, but she refused to veil herself or live in a harem. Such was her personality that not only did she overcome the strong prejudices on this matter, but she inspired so much respect that when her husband died, she took his place. For some years afterwards she remained Maraboute of Kourdane, administering the place devoutly and imperially. Today the name of the *gendarme's* daughter is more venerated than that of the marabout.

I inquired where all the millions came from.

"Marabouts of Kourdane are the heads of the Moslem order of the Tijanis," replied Atalla. "The Tijanis have branches all over the world, and their headquarters are at Ain Mahdi a few miles from here. Ain Mahdi has been a holy city since the eleventh century. There is a Tijani seminary there to which tribute is sent from Arabia, India, Malaya; wherever there are Tijanis."

"The marabout who met us is the grandson of Aurélie Picard?" I suggested.

"Yes. His father was not so dark, but he married a Negress, and the black strain has taken the upper hand."

"Has he inherited any of his grandmother's qualities?"

Atalla shook his head. "No. He's kept a certain outward dignity when he meets strangers, but he's really very ordinary. He doesn't look after the place, he drinks among his own gang and spends a lot of money on the girls.—You'll see tonight."

Which I did, and it was all in keeping with the setting. Not as Aurélie Picard had intended it, but in the spirit of the first owners of the furnishings, now long dead and buried in Fez and Tlemcen, and perhaps in Granada.

Dinner was served at seven in an immense banqueting hall. The places were laid Occidental fashion at a long polished table which was probably loot from some Spanish monastery. The mechoui and all the other dishes were Arab, but they were served Occidentally on dishes and plates. The dishes and plates were made of gold. Everything was made of gold. The knives, the forks, the spoons, the goblets. From beakers of wrought gold, champagne, cooled exactly right and of a first-class vintage, was poured into the goblets. I saw that Atalla was not refusing it; neither was the Khodja. The others I could not see, as there were about fifty men sitting at the polished table, and the flickering candles in their golden candlesticks did not give much light. Neither could I see our host. When I remarked on this to Atalla, he replied that he was not there. This was one of the few remaining traditions of Aurélie Picard. She had felt that it made a holy man much more important and mysterious if no one saw him going through the mortal processes of eating and drinking. In this particular case the tradition stopped there, for when we moved to the living room for our coffee, our marabout joined us. For a while he graciously kept up his part. He made appropriate remarks to me. He had Mecheri play obvious Arab music. He called on Atalla to sing and Draoui to give a solo on the debourca. It was all much more formal than in my house.

I do not remember what actually changed the atmosphere, or whether anything in particular did. It was as if someone had heaved a huge sigh and cried, "For the love of Allah, let's have some fun!"

In a moment the Marabout and his retainers had shed their stately holiness. A couple of Ouled Nail girls who had been sitting discreetly in a corner began to dance. A few more appeared at the doorway and were pushed forward by a lot more behind. Mecheri picked up the mood, and the classic melodies became a wonderful mixture of *danse du ventre* and fandango. Another orchestra materialized as if a djinn had brought it. In less than half an hour all relationship with the semi-Occidental world of the oasis, less than twenty miles away, had been severed.

Numidians, with faces like polished ebony, circulated among the guests carrying golden platters of sweetmeats and golden trays on which were golden goblets of champagne and golden cups of coffee. From three-tiered candelabras hundreds of wax candles enhanced the golden effect. Their soft light fell on the men and the women who reclined casually on the damask-covered divans. The air was filled with incense and music. The conversation and laughter rose and fell. There was abandon, but it was not jarring and it was full of color. There was movement, but it was rhythmical and graceful.

I have seen many performances of Rimsky-Korsakoff's ballet *Scheherazade,* but the most elaborate of these productions has been like a weak water color in comparison to the performance that night in the sumptuous setting which the daughter of a French *gendarme* had created in the Sahara Desert.

CHAPTER XIX

THE FAST OF RAMADAN followed soon after the visit to the Marabout at Kourdane. It was to be my first among the oasis people. I had observed the fast with the nomads in the desert and had not found it a hardship. As we ate only once a day anyway, a little longer without food did not make much difference. In an oasis, with all this business of punctuality and routine and several meals, it would probably be irksome.

Because the Moslem year has thirteen lunar months, the seasons when the religious feasts fall vary. Each year they are one month later. A Ramadan fast in December, when the days are short, is not trying. A Ramadan fast in June or July is. This fast was falling in April.

Ramadan starts the day after the mufti or the kadi has seen the new moon with the naked eye. In the event of a cloudy evening it starts on the report of a reliable person who has seen the moon somewhere else. In remote oases the mosque officials are allowed to judge for themselves. However, on principle, Ramadan begins on the same day all over the country. It ends as soon as the next new moon is visible. Sometimes, owing to bad weather, a community may fast overtime.

From the moment that it has been decreed that Ramadan has begun, all believers must observe the fast for at least twenty-eight consecutive days. During this period they must not eat or drink (not even medicine) or smoke from before dawn until after sunset. If, for some reason such as a long journey or sickness, the fast is broken, an extra day or days of fasting must be carried out at the end of the month.

The opening of Ramadan is signaled by the firing of a gun. Until the fast is over, the gun is fired nightly as the authorization to eat. The order to fire this gun is given by the Imam when he can no longer distinguish a black hair from a white hair held at arm's length.

From that moment any amount can be eaten and drunk and smoked until before dawn. The procedure is usually to have a meal at the firing of the gun and another around midnight. Between meals there are visits to friends and to cafés. But there is no music and no passing the time with Ouled Nails. One of the penitences of Ramadan is abstaining from sexual intercourse. A conscientious Moslem will even forgo thoughts on sex. One Arab I knew used to do numbers of extra days of fasting because he had thought about women when he should have had his mind on the mortifying of his body.

At first sight this fasting by day and eating by night does not seem a great ordeal, and it is not one in the desert. Out there, there *is* no water or food to be had once one has left camp, and few nomads smoke. Fasting is more a rule than an exception. In the oasis it is an irritation, an irksome and annoying duty. From the time one gets up and cannot drink a glass of water, even put water in one's mouth to wash one's teeth, or have breakfast or suck an orange off a tree or go into a café or light a cigarette, and so on through the day, one is balked at every turn until it gets on one's nerves. Some Arabs, who are used to smoking a lot and spending much time in the café, get so jumpy that one cannot go near them. When Ramadan falls in the height of summer, with long periods of blazing sunlight, thirst adds itself to the trial.

For men who have no work to do, it is admissible to stay home and wait for the sunset gun. For the working man, there is no such solution. Fasting or full, he must carry on as usual. But, for some psychological reason, no one seems to be able to relax. Jelloul and Yahia and Daylis, who could have stayed in bed all day, paced the streets like caged tigers.

Even I, who had books to read and thoughts to keep me occupied, could not rest. I could not accustom myself to this empty day without meals. I could not reverse things like a night watchman. I had to be about and see how the others were feeling. I did only one fast in the oasis. After that, I went to the camp before Ramadan and stayed there until it was over.

When, at last, the new moon proclaiming the end of the fast is seen, the oasis goes crazy. No one thinks much about bed, and at daylight the streets are filled with men and boys in new clothes. However poor, every Arab must honor the Feast of Ramadan (Aid el Serir) in something new. I had no new clothes, so I walked about the oasis in a dinner suit which the Arabs had never seen.

The grand prayer takes place in the open with every male inhabitant, from the Bash Agha to Blanchet, taking part. I did not. In my dinner coat and boiled shirt, I would have spoiled the picture. But I watched the amazing spectacle of hundreds of robed figures bowing and bending and prostrating themselves on the edge of the infinite desert. I had again that sensation of being baffled, of being overwhelmed by something too big for me to grasp. The golden rays of the sun clothing these rows of praying men in divine light gave an impression of strength. If the Arabs did not have temporal power, they made up for it by spiritual force. In that nerve-wearing fast followed by this unanimous glorifying of Allah I felt something in Islam which believers in other faiths lacked.

After the prayer everyone returned to the street, where, on this one annual occasion, the Ouled Nail ladies were allowed to walk around unguarded. In bright dresses, with colored scarves on their heads, unveiled and glittering with bracelets and anklets, they strolled hand in hand. The men took little notice of them and concentrated on embracing their brothers and uncles and cousins, and finding out how they felt after the fast.

A huge midday meal finished the celebration, those who could not afford a feast being looked after by those who could. Although the Aid el Serir lasted officially for three days, that lunch was the climax to the month's fast. The raitas squealed, the tamtams banged, the cafés and the Ouled Nails made up for lost time, but the oasis quickly returned to normal until another Ramadan moon.

There are many other Moslem feasts, but the only one which caused any stir compared to the Aid el Serir was the Aid el Kebir, which took place two months later.

On this day everyone who could afford it was expected to kill a full-grown sheep and eat it with his family. Those who had not the means were cared for in the usual Moslem way by the wealthy, who killed sheep on their behalf.

The belief is that when the souls of the dead departed go to enter Paradise, they will have to follow a narrow path as thin as a razor. The souls whose mortal selves have killed many sheep will be greatly assisted in this perilous crossing by the slaughtered creatures, reincarnated. It is an odd thought and confirms my views on the stupidity of sheep. If it were goats who were called upon to do this, they would certainly pitch the souls who had cut their throats into the flames of Gehenna.

I killed quite a number of sheep in honor of the Aid el Kebir and kept the families of my servants as well as those of Blanchet and Mohammed ben Tahar in mutton for days.

I hope that when the time comes a suitable escort of sheep will be waiting for me at the entrance of Paradise. I hope that my two boys will be there, with Mecheri and Draoui and the rest of the orchestra. I could not do without them beside the sweet waters surrounded by those perpetual virgins whom we are to wed spiritually. I will need something more tangible. I have an idea that they might like me to be there too.

It was through the orchestra that I was initiated into the smoking of keef. I had mentioned to Draoui one evening that I had been disappointed at finding none of the legendary hashish on which I had been led to believe many Arabs lived. Draoui was amused. He said that he had never had an opportunity to sample hashish in its traditional form, but he knew a certain amount about keef.

"What is keef?" I inquired

"The dried flower of the hemp. It is the basis of hashish; or, if you like, hashish is keef disguised in a sweet with a bit of opium added."

"How d'you take it?" I asked. "Like snuff?" A dried flower somehow did not sound like a dream-making aphrodisiac.

"You smoke it," said Draoui. "If you won't tell, I'll take you to a keef den. But you mustn't say anything. Keef smoking is against the law, and the Bash Agha is always trying to close down on the smokers."

I promised to keep my mouth shut.

One evening Draoui called for me. He was accompanied by Mecheri. We walked in silence to a part of the town I rarely went to, not far from the Ouled Nail quarter. In a narrow alley we stopped before a house which, save for a yellow light in an upper-story window, was in complete darkness. The only sound was the tinkle of a mandolin. Draoui tapped gently on the door. The mandolin stopped, and we heard someone coming cautiously down the stairs. A few whispered words were exchanged, bolts were drawn back, and a heavy wooden door was opened. We all stepped into a small lobby dimly lit by a flickering night light. The man barred and locked the door again and led the way up rickety stairs. At the top of the stairs was a long, bare room without furniture. An acetylene lamp sent a ghastly white light over fifteen to twenty men who crouched on the floor. Some of these I recognized as well-to-do tradesmen of the oasis, but the majority were poor folk almost in rags. But whether they wore cloth burnouses or tattered gandouras, they all had the same drawn, haggard look, and their eyes glittered feverishly.

At the far end of the room the Arab who had let us in attended to a charcoal fire on which he brewed coffee and tea. A Negro handed round cups and glasses and mugs of water which he drew from a sheepskin hanging from one of the rafters. In the middle of the room squatted the mandolinist, playing dreamily with a faraway look in his shining eyes. There was hardly any stir at our entrance. A few men looked up and as quickly went back to their smoking of small metal pipes with bowls not much bigger than acorns. The air was thick and heavy with a sweet, rather sickly odor, not unlike new-mown hay.

As no one seemed to be interested whether I was there or not, I seated myself in a corner with Mecheri and Draoui. The Negro gave us each a pipe and a paper sack. I watched Draoui fill his pipe with a grey-green tobacco-like fiber from the sack, light it, and inhale deeply. Mecheri did the same. As neither of them passed out or had convulsions, I did likewise. The taste of the smoldering hemp was not unpleasant; neither was it pleasant. It was rather like the smell. New-mown hay. The effect was certainly not mind-shattering. I had no feelings of exhilaration or of brightening eyes. Though, for that matter, no one showed any emotion. Except for the mandolinist—and he played like an automaton—everyone might have been dead. I glanced at Mecheri and Draoui and was surprised to see that, while their bodies were relaxed, their eyes had developed that peculiar glitter. Perhaps I *was* glittering? I had no means of finding out, so I gave myself over to smoking, hoping that something would happen.

I forget how long I remained in the keef den or how many pipes I filled and lit, but at no time had I any sensation that I was doing anything wrong. I felt less guilty than when my brother and I had our first smoke of chopped-up cigarette butts in a discarded pipe of my father's. However, when I got back to my house and into bed, I could not sleep. I just could not sleep. A change of hats had no effect. Walking round the courtyard had no effect. A meal of bread and cheese had no effect. Lying on my back and shutting my eyes had no effect. I could not sleep. I was wide awake and felt in no need of rest. So, after a while, I gave up trying. I got up and dressed. Then I did a lot of energetic tidying of my room. I chopped wood. I hoed the garden. When it was daylight, I groomed my horse and went for a ride. On my return I ate a large breakfast, but still I did not feel sleepy. I did not feel sleepy all day. It was not until past midnight, twenty-four hours after my first whiff of keef, that I had any sensation of drowsiness.

That is the effect of keef. It is like a terrific tonic, such as benzedrine. The habitual keef smoker hardly ever sleeps and rarely eats. He is always easy to detect. His eyes are bright, his face is pale and drawn. His limbs are thin and his movements restless. But he is not dazed like a man under the influence of a drug. On the contrary, his reasoning is clear and his mind lucid. When, eventually, the physical strain gets too great, he falls into a coma. Sooner or later, he never wakes from this coma. The artificially stimulated heart and the undernourished body give out. But keef is cheap and gives a lot of pleasure to its poor addicts while they last.

As I had no ambition to stay awake for a week and no one to whom I could give the benefit of my lucidity, I did not take to keef. I only smoked it once again. I tried it out to see how it would affect writing. The result was strange.

I smoked keef on and off for two days before going to my desk. I made no plans what to write. I just sat down one evening after the servants had gone to bed and wrote. By morning I had covered over fifty pages with clear pencil script. I did not know what I had written, and I waited to read the manuscript until I had slept and felt normal.

My keef story was a fantastic, and yet sober, account of a man's emotions after death. It described in detail all he felt while dying, all he saw after the doctor had pronounced life extinct. It told of the conversations of his friends and relatives around the death-bed, and described the funeral. The piece did not lead anywhere. It had no plot or construction, but there was a wealth of un-believable detail. To any but myself it would have only seemed a pointless story. To me it was fascinating in that I had no idea of what I had been writing and no recollection of how or why the ideas formed themselves in my head. Many of them I never thought of or knew about. I felt no tiredness, physical or mental, after doing the work. I stopped because I had nothing more to say. I have no doubt that if I had gone on, I could have covered a hundred pages or more with writing that night. I did not experiment again because being a writer was not then my goal. Perhaps, when the war is over, I will return to the Sahara and buy a pound of keef and see if I cannot have it produce me a book. If one's mind made any sense under the influence of the sweet weed, one could write three books in a month.

I mentioned this keef question from an entirely impersonal angle, to our local doctor. He was the mottled-faced major of the French army medical corps who preferred Dijon to the Sahara. He lived chiefly on anisette, which he drank under the arcades outside Monsieur Paoli's hotel. His reaction to my query was the usual one of the French toward anything the "natives" did. He con-demned keef smoking as a weakness of savages who knew no better. I tried to reason with him and make him see that keef was no worse than anisette, and better suited to the Arab. But he would not understand.

Nevertheless, what I said was true. The Arab or the Chinese or the Malay, with a glass of something, becomes brutish. But with opium or keef, to which they are accustomed, they remain out-wardly normal. The reformers who would abolish opium smoking and the like in the Orient do not think. They do not realize the harm they can do by substituting liquor for a drug to which the Asiatic is accustomed. They do not consider what would happen supposing a band of Orientals appeared in London or New York and said that henceforth no one must touch highballs or martinis. Opium, yes! Keef, yes! Hashish, yes!—but not alcohol. This is not far-fetched. It is what the Occidental preacher and his kind take upon themselves in the Orient.

My Arabs knew practically nothing about England or America

except through the missionaries. Few of these had gained any foot-hold in the Moslem world. Their rare converts were down-and-out Arabs who by professing what the Christians taught, could get themselves food and clothes. But the well-to-do Arabs resented the missionaries who tried to interfere with their lives.

"Who are they," they exclaimed indignantly, "to take this holier-than-thou attitude? We know all about the Christian beliefs. We know all about the Jewish beliefs. Neither of them suit us. We prefer our own."

Our doctor was not a missionary, but he was a reformer. He soaked anisette and hoped the keef smokers would do likewise. I do not know what his medical qualifications were, but I am glad I did not fall ill in the oasis. The only time I saw this *"médecin major"* at work was on a dental case!

I had had to go to the hospital for some iodine or the like. There was no one in the dispensary, but hearing a commotion in one of the wards, I went there. The door was open and gave me a clear view of the "operation" in progress. Seated in a kind of garden chair with arms was a soldier. Holding on to the chair were two Arabs. Holding on to the soldiers were two other soldiers. Standing in front of the soldier was the red-faced doctor in his shirt-sleeves. Grasped firmly in both hands were a pair of forceps which gripped one of the soldier's teeth. When I arrived, a terrific tug of war was going on between the four men who held the soldier and the chair, and the doctor who held the tooth. I do not know who won. It gave me a pain to watch.

The Arabs do not go in much for medicine. They are too well. Madani occasionally took drafts from a bottle which his cousin had sent him from Algiers as a Ramadan gift. He said it was for his digestion. I am sure that neither Madani nor any other nomad had ever the smallest symptom of indigestion; but when Madani had an idea, it saved time to leave him with it. He once let me take a sip from the bottle. The mixture tasted strongly of peppermint. I suggested that one thing his system did not need was mint. But he did not reply. He had faith in that bottle from Algiers. That was the basis of most cures in the Sahara—faith healing.

Headaches and the like were taken care of by amulets and words written by marabouts on pieces of linen and sewn into the clothing. Ali, the cook, once looked after an infected finger I had with poultices of garlic and other herbs which some witch had prepared. I eventually had to go to Algiers for treatment, but the unsterilized pudding applied nightly to a festering wound had soothed me and not given me blood poisoning. Perhaps she was a good witch.

The hakim, or toubib—the Arab doctor—existed, but he never put in appearance among us. He was not necessary. He was no more necessary than the other functionaries which the Occidental way of living has created. The more I lived with these people, the more convinced I became that the neurotics, the crazy, the drunks were the deliberate product of the brand of civilization in which I had been brought up. The people of the desert did not rush to specialists for check-ups or operations. They never became insane. They had long ago discovered what a mess drinking made of men.

As long as I was living in the desert, I never had a worry, I never had a cold. Already when I came to the oasis, I had unnecessary things to think about. Money to pay servants, clothes to suit the occasion, hours at which to eat. By the time I had reached Algiers, the complications had quadrupled. People began to intrude themselves on me, the noise of the streets kept me awake, I was jostled from morning till night. It was not until I had revisited the fringes of my world that I realized how far from it I had strayed, how little I had missed it.

And that is a true and honest statement. During the whole time I lived in the Sahara Desert, I never missed anything I had left at home. Since I have lived elsewhere, I have constantly missed the Sahara Desert. I have constantly missed its deep silences, its singing wind, its admirable people, its security from all the troubles of our Western culture. Until I go back there, I shall go on missing it.

CHAPTER XX

IN EVERY SAHARA OASIS, there were many Jews. In ours there were over thirty. I did not get to know them until comparatively late in my stay in the Sahara. I had had dealings with them at the markets and had sold them sheep, but I had never had the same intimate relationship as with the Arabs. This was not from any anti-Jewish feelings on the part of the Arabs. It just so happened that my life did not, for a while, take me to the Jews.

There was no Arab anti-Judaism or, as I have heard it said, Arab anti-Semitism!—Semite anti-Semites?—One might just as well speak of American anti-Americans.

The Israelites, Hebrews, or Jews, as they are differently called, belong, with the Arabs, to the great Semitic branch of the human race said to be descended from Shem, the eldest son of Noah. Whether the designation Jew denotes a faith or a nationality, has never been proved to me. In my opinion, "Jew" should be used to refer to religion, and Israelite or Hebrew for nationality.

To illustrate: If I feel so inclined, I can become a Jew. I can receive instruction in the tenets of the religion and practice the Jewish faith as I did the Moslem. However, nothing can make me into an Israelite or a Hebrew, any more than my years of living in the Sahara made me into an Arab. Jews who are baptized into the Christian church become Christians, but not Britons or Frenchmen or Americans. However authentic their passports, however fiercely they profess the beliefs of Protestants or Catholics, they continue to be Asiatics. They continue to be Asiatics as I continued to be European in spite of my prayers five times a day. So I say that a Jew is a Jew, and a Moslem is a Moslem, and a Christian is a Christian, regardless of nationality. That is the way the Arabs of the Sahara looked on the matter. However, as it is customary to refer to the Hebrews as Jews, I shall do so.

It is obvious to anyone who reads this book that I do not use the adjectives Semite or Asiatic disparagingly. I have no feeling about "color," and if I had, it would not apply to Semites: they belong to the white Caucasian race. It used to irritate me when insular Britons criticized me for "going native and living with colored people." In the first place, my Arabs were no more colored than I was. Madani and Daylis and Jelloul had fair hair and light eyes. But if they had been black or brown, it would not have affected me. Neither had I gone native any more than had the Asiatics who came to Europe and wore Occidental clothes and lived in Occidental hotels. The word native is as much applicable to an inhabitant of the United States or Great Britain as to a South Sea Islander or an Eskimo. But whereas Polynesians are colored, neither the Arabs nor the Jews with whom I lived are. They are Semites, white Caucasians. They are the same people. They sprang from identical stocks.

Until the appearance of Moses, the Jews were just another tribe or group of tribes living on the borders of the Arabian peninsular. Until shortly before the beginning of the Christian era they were nomads. Israelite nomads. The reason these Israelites got themselves mixed up with the building of the pyramids was that old question of sheep and pastures which formed the basis of most of our Sahara conversations. The Land of Goshen was a fertile grazing area in northern Egypt. There the Israelite nomads followed their flocks. When, after their escape from Pharaoh under the guidance of Moses, they wandered about the country round Mount Sinai, it was for the same reason that Madani and I wandered about the Sahara—to feed their sheep. Jesus spoke of himself often as a shepherd caring for his sheep because, even at that time, it was a simile which every Jew would understand.

Abraham was a nomad. His family and descendants were nomads. If Abraham or any of his contemporaries were resurrected today, they would be the only people who would find their country much as they had left it. The tents, the pastures, the shepherds, the shepherd's clothes, the breed of sheep are as they are described in the book of Genesis.

The early books of the Old Testament are stories of nomadic life. When Madani sat by the campfire and told of the manna episode and of Moses finding the water and of Joshua, and I added a yarn about shepherds who watched their flocks by night, everyone understood. To our nomads the summaries of the chapters of the book of Exodus might have been contemporary headlines of Sahara news.

Jews are always thought of as shopkeepers, as theatrical producers, as moneylenders. They are Magnins or Goldbergs or Shylocks. Their ancient and dignified background has been forgotten. Until I went to live in the Sahara, I too imagined Jews in this way. And if I did, it was a good deal the Jews' own fault. Those whom I rubbed shoulders with, those whom most people rubbed shoulders with, had subordinated their majestic past to something less worth while.

The real Jews, the great Jews, the men deserving of consideration and respect, are those who have not let the modern way of living interfere with their traditions. They are no longer nomads and have become sedentary people, but they have maintained all their ancient ideals. Of such a kind were the Jews of our oasis.

From the Arabs they were almost indistinguishable. To a tourist, a Hebrew in his robes or an Arab in his were the same. The features, the build, the calm were similar. There was a slight difference in the intonation of the Arabic. The Jew's gait was less easy than the Arab's, inclined to shuffling, and more rapid. The clothes had a difference, too, which I could not describe unless I had an Arab and a Jew before me. It was like Madani with his footprint of an unmarried girl in the desert. He knew it was an unmarried girl. I knew a Jew when I saw one. The transient Occidental did not.

Some of the oasis Jews wore European clothes in the street, but in the house they always went back to their robes. Robes suit Jews. Business suits do not. The majority have bodies the wrong shapes for tailored jackets. Their legs were not made for trousers. Their pointed heads are suited to turbans or skullcaps, not to Stetsons. A turban never fitted my Aryan head properly.

The Jews in the oasis, then, were sedentary people like Amida and Mecheri and Draoui. They had gardens and shops, but they were chiefly merchants. They imported grain, they exported sheep. They were our main contact with the outer world.

The Jews of the oases depended on the nomads of the desert for a livelihood. The nomads depended on the Jews. Without the nomads, the Jews would have had no sheep to buy; without the Jews, the nomads would have had no one to sell their sheep to. Or if they had found Arab dealers, it would have been an uncertain and vague undertaking.

The sheep business in North Africa was important. Something like five million sheep left the Sahara every year for distribution to Algeria and France. The Jews handled the whole thing admirably. During the time I was living in the Sahara, I never heard Madani or Daylis or Jelloul or Ali (the head shepherd) complain of a deal made with Jews. They observed the current market prices, they knew what they wanted, they paid cash. When we came to the market with our lambs, we knew that the Jewish merchants would be there to take our goods, pay us for them, and absolve us from all further worry. How the sheep got to Algiers or France was the buyer's business.

In every way the Jews and the Arabs got on admirably. The Arabs were in far greater harmony with the Jews than they were with the French. Even over the Crémieux decree, which gave the Jews of North Africa unconditional French nationality and did not concede this right to the Arabs, there was little friction. The Arabs understood the French motives for this discrimination. They respected the Jews, and the Jews repected them, and they remained on the best of terms. It was not unusual to meet prominent Jews dining with the Bash Agha; and, while Jelloul did not go out much himself, I often went to Jewish homes with Daylis or Madani. The Jews were far less restricted socially among the Arabs than they are among the people of the United States.

The only places where there were sometimes clashes between Jews and Arabs were in Algiers and Oran and Constantine. Here, periodically there were mild pogroms, with Arabs burning Jewish shops. I have an idea, though, that these incidents were brought about by Occidental politics. I have the same idea that the strife between Arabs and Jews in Palestine has the same origins.

Hostility between the Jew and the Arab is not a matter of course. There have been Jewish persecutions by Arabs, but so have there been by Englishmen and Spaniards and Germans. The Jews, being successful in most things they undertake, breed jealousy; the jealousy breeds reprisals. That is all. In the Sahara, where the

Jews and the Arabs worked hand in hand, there was no cause for reprisal, so there was no trouble.

If unprovoked by outside influence, there is no reason why the Jews should not work as peacefully with the Arabs in Arabia and Palestine as in the Sahara. There is nothing logical to prevent a settlement of the Occidental-created controversy, if the Jews really *want* to go back to Palestine, which I doubt. I had an excellent illustration of this lukewarmness to a Jewish home for the Jews while I was living in the oasis.

It was before Hitlerism and mass execution of Jews. It was even before the days of acute refugee problems. It was the time when Zionism was beginning to be a popular topic to discuss without anyone's knowing what it meant.

The late Lord Melchett, at that time Sir Alfred Mond, came to see me. I do not recollect what his official designation was, but he was a member of the British government in office at the time. I had known Mond since the days when he used to visit my father, and had a great affection for him.

He was interested in Zionism and Palestine, and may have been one of the instigators of the Balfour Declaration. I do not remember, and it has no bearing on the story. What does matter is that Mond saw his native land from the point of view of a wealthy man who has idealized from afar something which he has at heart, but which he knows will never affect his way of living. One day he asked me to put him in touch with some of the prominent North African Jews, so I arranged an elaborate lunch in the cake house at which every guest was Hebrew. During the meal and afterwards Mond held forth on the future of the Jewish people and the rebirth of Zion. The minister under the British crown had disappeared. The Oxford graduate had been transfigured. Here was one of the major prophets pleading the Israelite cause with the sincerity of Moses before Pharaoh. He was superb. I felt sorry that he was not robed like most of the other guests. He concluded his exposition with:

"I hope, my friends and fellow believers, that I may count on you to come and help us straighten out our affairs in Palestine, form a vanguard for the settlers who will soon be reviving our ancient name."

Up to this point every sentence in Mond's speech had been

listened to with eager interest; but at this personal exhortation a kind of shudder rippled over the audience. Mond sensed something was amiss, and repeated what he had just said rather differently. There was still no response, no suspicion of a response, not even a murmur of insincere approval as after a bad lecture. Mond's listeners had nothing to say, or if they had, would not say it. It looked as if my Zionist party was going to end in fiasco. Then our biggest grain and sheep merchant in the oasis, whose fortune would probably have compared not unfavorably with Mond's, suddenly looked up and said:

"*Go* to Palestine?"

"Why, yes!" exclaimed Mond. "Have you not understood what I have been talking to you about? Have I not made myself clear? We want to remake Zion. We want to repopulate our native land. To do this, we need the right people. Of course I expect you to come to Palestine."

The old Jew took a deep breath. He glanced quickly from Mond to the other men who sat around tense and silent, and asked:

"Sire Mond, if we accompany you to Palestine, on what are we going to live?"

Mond hesitated for a second. Then he said: "On the Arabs."

The old Hebrew shook his head:

"Sire Mond," he declared, "the Arabs can help, but only when there are Gentiles involved. I speak, Sire Mond, from experience, as one who knows. A Jew cannot live where there are no Gentiles."

He nodded his head, and all the other Jews nodded theirs. Mond let his eyes rest on each of the eager upturned faces. His forehead was furrowed, his eyes were as bright as a keef smoker's. He lifted his head to the sky for guidance. When he spoke again, it was as a man to whom a revelation has been made. With simplicity, he said:

"I believe you are right. I had never thought of it that way."

The shoulders of my guests relaxed. They smiled. They sighed deeply. Their relief was great to find that in spite of the expensive English clothes and the ministerial rank and the title of British nobility, Sire Mond was before all a Jew who had no difficulty in seeing things as they did. There was a moment's silence. One of those dramatic silences which gives a fleeting glimpse of something outside the Occidental's scope of understanding. I felt during those few seconds as far removed from the men who sat in my courtyard as if oceans and continents had separated us. I knew that they had forgotten that I was there. They were thinking as they, the Jews, thought. Mond broke the silence with:

"I hope, nevertheless, that I may count on you all here today to help the cause in other ways?"

This time the assent was spontaneous and unanimous. ...

The old Hebrew who had spoken so straightforwardly to Sir Alfred Mond was Jacob Maklouf ben Lalou. In addition to being an importer of grain, an exporter of sheep, a banker, and the owner of a store in the oasis and in Algiers, he was also the mayor of our community. No one had any idea what his duties were as mayor, but every now and then he would be glimpsed wearing an old-fashioned Prince Albert and a straw hat, making for the military headquarters of the oasis, with a tricolor sash of office about his middle. He always looked ill at ease in those fancy clothes and returned as soon as possible to his robes. However, he liked Occidentals to call him *Monsieur le Maire,* and pretended that he had a great deal to say in the affairs governing our well-being.

Jacob ben Lalou and I quickly made friends. He was an intelligent, cultured, practical man who thought clearly. He took an interest in international politics and knew what was going on in the world, which was more than I did.

Although he was in favor of maintaining Jewish traditions and condemned young Jews who forgot the teachings of their faith, he did not believe in Zionism from the idealistic Palestine angle. He looked on the project to send Jews back to live in their one-time native land as futile and impractical. He said that the Jews had expatriated themselves voluntarily to go and live in Russia and France and America, and he saw no reason why they should not go on living in those countries. He said:

"My home is in North Africa. It has been the home of my family for over six hundred years. Why should I wish to uproot myself and go to a place where I have no interests? Do you suppose that your friend Sire Mond would give up his home in England, or the Jewish bankers in New York give up their homes, to spend the rest of their lives fishing in the Sea of Galilee? You bet they wouldn't, any more than I would. I am a Jew, Monsieur Bodley, I am proud to be a Jew. I pray that my children and my

198

children's children will continue to do honor to the Jewish faith, as my ancestors have through the ages, but I also hope that they will continue to do it here where they were brought up."

There was at that time, of course, none of today's acute crisis in the fortune of the Jews. Even with that crisis, I agree with ben Lalou. The solution to the Jewish problem is not Palestine. The Jew has ceased to be a nomad or even a country man. With few exceptions, he belongs to the big towns. He thrives under difficulty, in competition where quick thinking is essential. He does not belong to the open plain or the orchard. He is much better off in New York or London. As ben Lalou said, he migrated to Europe of his own accord. His home is in the countries he adopted. When the war is over, that is where he should go. He will be much happier in his grimy cities than grubbing about in the fresh air of Palestine. One of the objects in defeating Germany is to let people have their own opinions and worship as they please. With that achieved, it will be possible for the Jews to return to where they came from—those that are left.

Whenever I was tired of bash aghas and not in the mood for guitars, I would lunch or dine with Jacob ben Lalou. He had an expert cook, whose work was supervised by Madame Lalou. At least, that is what I was told. I only saw her in the distance and never spoke to her. Although there was no harem in the Lalou home, the women never appeared when strangers were there, and in the street they went veiled.

I cannot remember all the succulent meat and vegetable dishes which were served at the Lalou table, but they were different from the Arab and more varied. The Jewish desserts were far superior. Especially I think of a spiced pastry, light as lace and stuffed with jams and candied fruits.

Ben Lalou had a tribe of relatives who lived around him. In fact, every Jew within a hundred kilometers of the oasis was some sort of Lalou. Once I met them all. The occasion was the circumcision of my friend's great-grandson. An invitation card one associates with weddings bade me attend the ceremony of circumcision of—Abraham Maklouf ben Lalou, at 11:30 A.M. at the home of the Mayor.

Mayor ben Lalou owned several gardens in the oasis, but he did not live near any of them. He had an apartment above his store on the main street. It was almost as discordant in an oasis as the Marabout's palace in a desert.

The store was large and covered the whole of the first floor. In it could be bought anything from pots and pans to dates and wheat. It was looked after by the Mayor's brother, David ben Lalou.

David was painfully ugly and had cross-eyes. On every day except Saturday he wore a large and grimy white apron over some sort of business suit which, apparently, had no coat. I never saw David that he was not in his shirtsleeves. He completed the outfit with a celluloid collar, a made-up tie, and a cloth cap. David had little of his brother's worldly intelligence. His thoughts revolved around wheat and beans and dates. Even on Saturday, when he appeared washed and shaved in his robes, one felt that he regarded the commandment to respect the Sabbath as a divine error of judgment.

Above the store was Jacob's apartment. In its planning and furnishing, it might have been the home of a retired provincial official in France. The chairs and the tables and the carpets had obviously been ordered by sets from a catalogue. The wallpaper belonged to the unmodernized country hotel. The lamps had white glass shades. There was nothing African or Arab or Saharan or even Jewish about these stiff living rooms. The only part of the house which gave one a slight whiff of the patriarch was Jacob's bedroom. This, one day, he showed me as he might have a shrine. It was rather like a shrine.

In the middle of the room was one of those fine old four-poster beds curtained with rich brocades, such as I had seen at the Marabout's in Kourdane. Oriental carpets and religious prints covered the walls. On the floor were thick homemade rugs. A brass candlestick stood on a dresser which had no relation to the pitch pine furniture in the living rooms. The windows, which had obviously never been opened, were heavily shrouded. The little air in the bedroom was loaded with stale incense, and proved my contention that Jews do not belong to the great outdoors, but it was venerable and in keeping with six centuries of North African Lalous.

"There," said the Mayor, proudly and, at the same time reverently, "is my bed. In that bed, Monsieur Bodley, I have slept with my wife for nearly fifty years! In that bed have been begotten my sons and my daughters. In that bed they have been born. No other

man but I has slept in that bed and no other woman but my wife."
The old man touched the embroidered coverlet affectionately.
"Today, Monsieur Bodley," he went on, "the young people, male
and female, Jew and Gentile, run around disregarding their temple
and their God. They defile the marriage bed, they defile themselves,
their unrighteousness shames us. Behind my back they laugh at me,
Monsieur Bodley, because I am old-fashioned, because I have kept
my marriage vows. But I swear to you that there is no greater
felicity than the faithful love of a man for a woman. It has
something sublime which nothing in our worldly life can equal."

However, on this feast day, Jacob ben Lalou was not thundering
like a Hebrew prophet. He was bustling around as excited as if
this were the first circumcision in his family.

The living room was jammed tight with Lalous. Flashy young
Lalous from Algiers with sleek hair and diamond rings. Fat, prosperous Lalous from the dusty plains of the wheat country. Old, old
Lalous with skullcaps and long beards. But whether they were
in robes or business suits, there was an atmosphere of respect in
this gathering that belonged to the centuries which had made the
Lalou tribe. All these men (there was not a woman in sight)
behaved with dignity and courtesy. I could not believe that any of
them laughed at Jacob behind his back.

In the middle of the room was a high chair of carved wood
with a red plush seat. I had noticed it when I had been visiting
Jacob, but I did not know what it was. Now I learned that it was
the throne of circumcision. It belonged to the Jewish community
of the oasis but was kept in the security of ben Lalou's house, as a
holy relic might be. Soon it was occupied by the Rabbi in his
ceremonial robes.

When Jacob was sure that everyone was there, he instructed one
of the flashy young Lalous, the father of the child in whose honor
the party was being given, who thereupon left the room. In a few
moments he returned, carrying the smallest infant I have ever seen.
The poor mite was asleep and unprepared for what was in store
for it. With one hand the Rabbi received the baby; with the other
he accepted a glittering knife which Jacob handed him from a
plush-lined case. With the aid of the father, the child was made
ready. The Rabbi intoned prayers. The room became silent. It was
rather frightening. I had a feeling that this was to be a human

sacrifice. I wanted to warn the baby that its life was in danger, but before I could move, the knife flashed in the Rabbi's hand. I quickly shut my eyes, and as quickly reopened them as the religious hush was broken by a piercing squawk. The Rabbi was handing the knife back to Jacob. The father was carrying the bellowing infant out of the room. Everyone else had relaxed. Servants appeared with trays on which were tumblers and jugs of water and bottles of anisette. Brother David brought me a drink. He still had on his apron and his cap, but had hung a burnous about him which partially concealed his shirtsleeves.

For a while there was drinking and smoking and laughter, until the air was heavy with the fumes of anise and tobacco. Then Jacob said something which I did not catch and led the way toward the door through which the father had carried his circumcised child. To my surprise everyone began flocking into a bedroom, where, in a brass bed, lay the mother of the baby. She was a beautiful young Jewess, but so pale and so tired. It seemed a shame to intrude on her. However, when I held back, Jacob would have none of it. I was not one of the family, but I was a friend and a most honored guest. So I joined the procession and shook the frail hand of the girl, who looked up bewildered by this mob of men who thronged past her bed.

When this part of the ceremony was over, we moved into the dining room, where the older members of the clan and I ate the biggest lunch I had eaten in years. The younger relatives were accommodated in another room. There was not much talking and no speeches. We just fed ourselves until we could feed ourselves no more.

As soon as the party broke up, I took my horse and rode into the desert. I needed exercise to work off the lunch. I needed, even more, solitude in which to think.

That ceremony had added strands to the magic web which this country was weaving around me. I had had that sensation of being gently pulled back into the past the first day I had arrived in the oasis. Every week something drew me further back. I was no more the man who had stepped out of that bus three, four, I could not remember how many years ago, than I was the agha Daylis. I was no more the man who had attended the signing of the peace treaty at Versailles than I was Mohammed ben Tahar. —I was more

Mohammed ben Tahar. —If, in those far-off times, I had been taken to the circumcising of the great-grandson of Jacob ben Lalou, I would have felt out of place, ill at ease. I might have laughed at the whole thing; I might have regarded these anisette-smelling Jews as beneath me. I certainly would not have known what to say to them. But I had felt none of those things. I had enjoyed the ceremony and the lunch. I had made my hosts feel that I enjoyed them.

By admitting me into the mother's bedroom, they had wished to make me one of them; and, without words, I had shown my appreciation. I had shown that I sensed the underlying motive of the visit to the tired girl. For it had been more than a gesture of congratulation. It had been symbolic. The smoking, anisette-drinking men, the Rabbi with the knife, the father carrying the child represented the male strength. But that strength had once come from a woman, so we were shown her. We were shown her as a symbol of motherhood. Frail and pale, but as necessary to us as the tree to the fruit, as the soil to the tree.

As I rode over the rolling plain and thought of this, the more I realized what a big part these Oriental women played in the lives of their men. One never met Madame Lalou or Jelloul's lady or Madani's lady, but they were there, always there. Although I would never speak to any of them, although I would not mention them to their husbands, although their husbands would never admit such a thing, I knew, and they knew, that it was their women who prompted their decisions. I believe that the ladies Lalou and Jelloul had more say in the running of the oasis, and the control of the thousands of square miles of pasturage around, than any mayor's wife or governor's wife in the United States or the British Empire.

The sun was setting as I came back to the oasis. The palms swayed and rustled to the lilt of the Sahara wind. The rocks from which the mosque sprang, dazzling white, were radiant in the rosy light. High above me on the terrace of the minaret the muezzin appeared. Turning to the four corners of the world, his voice rose clear and musical above the singing of the breeze—

"La ilaha illa Allah! Mohammed rasul Allah!"

CHAPTER XXI

THE SUMMER IN THE OASIS was more trying than on the desert. On the desert, one made up one's mind to roast. The heat was unbelievable, but there was nothing one could do about it. In the oasis there were all kinds of imaginary respites from the blazing atmosphere which only emphasized the feeling of being grilled. There was shade, there were darkened rooms, there was water; but they only stressed the discomfort. Whatever one did, wherever one went, that fiery reverberation of the sun pursued one.

The night was no better than the day. The rocks, the mud walls of the gardens, the mud walls of the houses held the heat, and did not begin to lose it till dawn.

Every evening I had several buckets of water carried up to the flat roof of my house. Throwing off the few clothes I had on, I soaked a sheet in water and wrapped it dripping around me. Then I lay on the bricks. For a while I dozed and even slept, but woke in an hour with the sheet hot and bone dry. Quickly I took another sheet from a bucket and started again. The dawn and the scorching sun were almost a relief to this pretending to be cool.

Mecheri and Draoui and Mohammed ben Tahar did not seem to be inconvenienced by the temperature. They slept in their gardens and carried on in the daytime as they did in winter. But I could not go on, so I sent a wire to Madani. He had migrated north with the flocks in May and was pasturing around Chellala. He wired back at once that he would be glad to see me. I could live in the camp or stay at the inn.

I began by staying at the Chellala inn. I wanted to pick up some of my lost sleep before going back to tent life. The day after my arrival, the Bash Agha asked me to dine.

Jelloul seemed to have houses wherever he went, or else accommodating relatives who turned out when he appeared. I was never

204

sure about this. But whoever the owner was, the Bash Agha always behaved as if he were in his own home.

Arab meals are good and satisfying, but they are not imaginative. Within three or four variations, they are always the same. When, therefore, the soup was followed by a dish of fish, I forgot my Arab manners and showed surprise.

The Bash Agha was delighted.

"You didn't expect that, did you?" he exclaimed.

"I certainly didn't. How were they kept so fresh? It's a hot trip from Algiers."

"These aren't sea fish," said the Bash Agha; "they come from Taguine, less than twenty-five miles from here."

There are no rivers worthy of the name in Algeria, and certainly none as far south as this; neither were these subterranean oasis fish. But I could not argue with the Bash Agha, so I said:

"The fish are very good."

The Bash Agha suspected that I did not believe him, so he asked:

"Would you like to catch the fish yourself?"

I felt that I was on delicate ground. If I refused, the old man might be offended. If I accepted, I might be putting him on the spot. I compromised by saying that I had no rods or lines. Jelloul paid no attention and remarked:

"I am going to Taguine tomorrow morning. If you will come here at eight, I will take you out. You can lunch with me there, and fish."

Although I was on the eve of changing myself from a sedentary into a nomad, I was still living Occidental-fashion. I was undressing when I went to bed and giving myself the luxury of being called at a reasonable hour and not merely getting up when it was light. However, being a few hundred miles from the desert did not affect the habits of my friends. Somewhere around six, one of the Bash Agha's retainers walked into my room as if it were a tent and said that everyone was waiting for me.

I bounded from my bed and looked out of the window at the clock in the village square. It was a little after six. I pointed out the time to the man, adding that I had been told to be ready at eight. He showed no interest and repeated that everyone was waiting for me. I gathered that he expected me to come along in my pyjamas. The real nomad, who rarely undresses and washes only at the Turkish bath, does not understand that a man cannot wake up and go straight to his daily duties. I tried to explain my shaving and dressing problems, but the man was unimpressed and left repeating that the Bash Agha awaited me.

Half an hour later Madani came into my room unannounced. He did not go through the usual ritual of early morning salutations and abruptly informed me that the Bash Agha was waiting. I said:

"But he told me to be there at eight, and it's barely seven now." He said:

"But the Bash Agha is ready."

I said, "Well, he should have told me to come earlier."

Madani shrugged. "The Bash Agha is waiting. Perhaps you will hurry. I will sit downstairs."

I laughed and began to dress. Oasis life had made me forget nomad ways.

I found the Bash Agha sitting outside his "host's" house smoking a meerschaum pipe. Around him stood a number of Arab chiefs. The Bash Agha greeted me and made no reference to my being "late." He did not seem to be in any hurry, and waited till he had finished his pipe before joining the driver on the front seat of the waiting car. Madani motioned me to get in behind and got in after me. The agha Yahia got in after Madani. Marhoun got in after the agha Yahia. The Kadi got in after Marhoun. Sheik Ali said:

"I don't think I'll come. There isn't enough room."

Everyone protested, so he got in too. The agha Daylis stuck out his pointed beard and flatly refused to make a ninth.

The Bash Agha turned around and said: "Well, if we're all here, let's go."

At the entrance to the village Marhoun suddenly asked: "Have we enough gas to get there and back?"

"In sha Allah," replied the driver.

The Kadi, who has a sense of the practical and dislikes impromptu nights in the open, objected. "I think you had better make sure."

The driver made sure and found there was enough gas to go about one mile downhill. We therefore turned back. No one seemed to mind. None of my Arabs made any comment. They remained as placid as if getting this gas were nothing more than a childish whim of the Kadi. I felt certain that they were thinking, "If the car lacks fuel, it is the will of Allah."

I said to the Kadi, "Lucky you thought of that."

The Kadi smiled wisely and winked. I had a great affection for this Arab magistrate who had been my host for the Marhoun wedding. With his fair beard and white skin, his slightly red nose and his clear blue eyes, he made me think of Alfred de Musset. He did not fit into this background of nomad Arabs.

When we had filled up, we moved off again. For about ten kilometers a dilapidated road wound its way through rocky hills. Then the hills gave way to the alfa plains which run down to the Sahara. My companions chatted gaily about their sheep, their crops, their horses, their falcons—all those subjects dear to these nature's country gentlemen. Occasionally they poked fun at the Kadi, who is not a farmer or a sportsman.

As soon as we reached Taguine, the chiefs went off to attend to their affairs and I was dispatched to fish. My guide was an ex-soldier who proudly wore the Croix de Guerre on his tattered burnous. He carried a long pole to which was attached two yards of thin rope with a hook knotted at the end. He also had a box filled with maggots.

After trudging for about half an hour through fields of standing barley, we came to a broad ditch at the bottom of which trickled a little muddy water. In the muddy water a few tortoises paddled.

"The river," said the guide proudly.

I must have looked disappointed, for he added quickly, "The fish are further on."

We followed the ditch for half a mile until we came to a slimy pool. The Arab squatted beside it and, after baiting the hook, handed me the pole. I took it, feeling inclined to laugh. I was reminded of that stupid Christmas game when one fishes for useless presents out of a tub. However, I lowered the worm into the opaque water and waited. Two minutes had hardly passed when I had a bite. Memories of tumbling streams, of lines hissing out, of bent rods flashed before me. But they were only memories. I had struck so violently, and the rope at the end of my pole was so strong, that I had jerked the fish out of the pool and onto the bank.

At the best I had expected to see some sort of mud fish, but I found a kind of carp with fins like a perch's, weighing about two ounces. I felt ashamed of doubting the Bash Agha and continued fishing. We visited three or four pools, and in two hours I caught about a hundred of these fish. The majority were about the size of the first, but there were at least a dozen weighing half a pound. Finally tired of this crane-like occupation, I went back to the house where the car had dropped me.

I found my friends sitting on a fine Djebel Amour carpet looking hungrily out of the door at four Arabs who slowly turned a lamb on a spit before a brushwood fire. I slipped off my shoes and sat beside the Bash Agha. I told him about my fishing, but he only grunted. The other chiefs looked at him anxiously. I saw that the old man was in one of his tyrannical moods. I said no more. One of the cooks came in and asked if he should serve.

"Of course," said the Bash Agha; "but where is the caid Madani?"

"He is saying his prayers," ventured Sheik Ali.

The Bash Agha said, "Hamdullah." But his eyes expressed, "Why the deuce must this half-wit pray at lunchtime?"

I wanted to laugh, so I went to the door. From there I saw Madani, with his burnous spread out on the plain, bowing and prostrating himself, oblivious of the appetizing fumes of roasting lamb. When he had finished, he remained for a moment gazing in the direction of Mecca. Then he joined us.

A low table and tray were placed before the Bash Agha. He motioned me to sit beside him. He called the agha Yahia and another aged agha, who seemed to have grown out of the earth at the smell of food. The others squatted at a respectful distance and spoke in whispers.

The long Arab meal began. As the Bash Agha's party finished each dish, it was taken to the other group, which had been joined by the chauffeur and the fisherman. There was no conversation until a bowl of skimmed milk had been passed around. "Hamdullah," sighed the Bash Agha. "Hamdullah," I repeated with Yahia and the aged agha, and was echoed by the younger chiefs. The ablution bowl was handed to each one in turn, and coffee was served. The tension of before lunch had disappeared. The Bash Agha and the old agha lit their pipes. The others looked on enviously. They were just edging toward the door for a cigarette outside when the Bash Agha's voice halted them.

"I wish to play cards!" From the folds of his gandoura he produced a greasy pack.

"Go on, Madani," whispered Sheik Ali.

"No, it's not my turn," he protested.

"And it's not mine," said Marhoun.

"The Kadi must play," suggested Madani.

There was a murmur of approval. The Kadi shrugged resignedly and squatted opposite the Bash Agha. The fisherman brought in some stones and placed them beside the players for counters. That ancient Hispano-Mauresque game which came from Spain when the Christian kings retook Granada began. The Kadi held good cards and played them well. The Bash Agha turned cross again; then he got sleepy. His head nodded. Soon he was asleep. The Kadi winked at me and, gathering up his winnings, slipped out of the room. I, too, dozed. Arab meals in the middle of the day are hard to keep awake on.

I was roused by Madani. "We ought to be starting back," he said, "but the Bash Agha is still asleep."

"Well, wake him."

Madani shook his head. "I can't. None of us can. Only you are able."

"Oh, I'm too sleepy," I replied; "why don't you tell the Kadi?"

Madani thought this a fine idea and joined the others, who waited at the door. My message made them laugh, and they began to push the Kadi in the direction of the Bash Agha. The Kadi resisted, and, in the scuffle, the brass tray on which lunch had been served fell with a crash on the floor. Like children caught doing something wrong, the chiefs scuttled out onto the plain. The Bash Agha opened one eye and seemed about to sleep again. However, he was prevented by the arrival of the aged agha to say that there was a man with a petition.

The Bash Agha sat up, settled his turban, and looked imperially about him. The other chiefs stopped their giggling and formed a dignified circle. The chauffeur ventured back and started to mend a tire. The petitioner was brought in and, after kissing the old man's shoulder, went and sat at a distance. For a few minutes he asked everyone how they felt. The Bash Agha and the others knew that the man had not come in just to say hello, but they observed the ritual. A lull followed. Then the storm burst. In a torrent of words the story poured out.

The man talked so rapidly that I could not follow everything he said, but I gathered that his flock had been stolen by nomads of the Bash Agha's tribe who had come up from the south to pasture here. The nomads had now returned to their own territories.

The Bash Agha did not reply at once. When he did, there was another flow of words. The aged agha commented shortly. Then there was silence again while the case was being considered.

It was an extraordinary picture belonging to the days of Moses. The Bash Agha on his throne of cushions. The chiefs in their burnouses grouped on the blue and red carpet. The petitioner eagerly talking, but without movement or gesture, his eyes anxious as he prayed for justice.

When the Bash Agha had weighed the case, he turned to the Kadi and asked him something. The Kadi nodded. The Bash Agha then gave judgment. Addressing Madani, he said:

"This affects your tribe. You will send a horseman forthwith to Beriane. He will apprehend the robbers and have them drive the flocks back here. When this is done, you will bring the culprits before me."

"In sha Allah," said Madani.

Justice had been rendered, A man was to ride to a vague place in the desert over a hundred miles away and bring back the robbers and the stolen flock. That was all. It was another example of the simplicity of Arab lawgiving.

The Bash Agha got up. The complainant kissed his turban, and we all followed the old man out and piled into the car. In a few minutes it began to pour. Rain in southern Algeria is good for the farmer, but not so good for the traveler, especially if he is in a car. As we made for "home," the usually dry river beds were beginning to trickle, the track was becoming slippery, the wind growing stronger. Soon we punctured. Everyone got out of the car and looked at the flat tire, but no one said anything.

"Suppose we change the wheel?" I remarked casually.

The driver shook his head. "The spare wheel is punctured too.

We must put in another inner tube, but I don't think it will last long."

The inner tube was got out. A preliminary pump-up revealed that it held little air. Another was found which was in better condition. The chauffeur and Marhoun fixed the wheel in the driving rain. The Bash Agha smoked his pipe sitting on the running board. The caids chatted and made fun of the Kadi, who shivered in his townsman's burnous. There was no excitement or recrimination against the driver. The man had forgotten to mend the spare tire. It was the will of God, and nothing could be done about it.

We started again, and slithered along the track and through rivers which were becoming torrents. After a while another tire went. We stopped and all got out of the car again.

"No more inner tubes," said the chauffeur.

We all climbed in and drove on. In a few minutes the original tire went again. We all got out and all got back. Slowly we crawled along on the rims. My feet began to get cold and wet. I asked Madani what was happening, but he was telling his beads and made no reply. I moved my legs about and discovered that my feet were dangling in space. Looking down, I found that the bottom of the car had fallen out. I had a sudden vision of myself and the other chiefs jerked off our seats and running between the wheels of the car without being able to make the driver hear. However, this catastrophe did not take place, as the car stopped of its own accord.

"No more gas," said the chauffeur.

"No more gas?" queried the Bash Agha. It was the first time he had spoken since we left the lunch place.

The driver shook his head. I heard Madani murmuring, "Mektoub." Otherwise there was silence as we stood there in the cold rain looking at the car. Then, suddenly, the Bash Agha said, as if to the skies, "I pray Allah that it is raining like this in the Tell.[*] My brother's crops are in great need of water."

"In sha Allah," they all said.

It was magnificent. For a moment I forgot the discomfort of my soaked burnous; but in a minute the Occidental in me had taken charge again.

"That's fine," I said, "but what are you going to do?"

"I don't know," replied the Bash Agha. "We are on no caravan

[*] A district of the Atlas Mountains.

track, and few people come this way. What do you suggest, my friend?"

"There's only one thing to do," I replied; "walk back before it gets dark."

"But the rain and the mud and the wind?" protested the Kadi.

"Staying here won't keep you out of the rain," I said.

He's right," agreed Marhoun. "We can leave the driver with the car, and we'll be home before six."

"Come on," said Sheik Ali. "I know a short cut across the hills."

The Kadi began murmuring again, but seeing that the seventy-year-old Bash Agha was ready to go, he shrugged his shoulders and fell into line. In single file, we started across the rain-swept plain. Soon we came to a goat track and began climbing into the hills. As we got higher, the mist closed down and wrapped itself damply about us. I no longer saw Madani, and the Bash Agha was only a dim form before me. The Kadi I did not have to see. His wail of maledictions against automobiles and excursions and idiots who lived in outlandish places never ceased.

After an hour we reached the crest of the hills and started down on the opposite side. The mist began to clear. Soon the rain stopped. In a few minutes the sun burst through the clouds and lit up the great plains of the Sersou with the blue Atlas Mountains in the distance. Everyone except the Kadi cheered up.

"You'll be in dry clothes soon, Kadi," I said encouragingly.

"Yes, and I'll take good care not to leave my home again," he muttered as he shook pebbles from his slippers.

My laugh was interrupted by Marhoun, who began to sing one of those melodious songs of the South. Madani picked it up and sent it back, trembling and melancholy. Marhoun returned with the refrain—

"My love is fierce as fire, and it consumes my heart."

I repeated the line to myself, realizing how little I knew about these people; how improbable it was that I should ever know any more.

CHAPTER XXII

ALGIERS SEEN FROM THE SEA is better than Algiers seen from the land. The ugly French buildings which dominate the quay are offset by the dazzling white of the kasbah, piling itself into a huge white pyramid behind. This had never struck me so much as on this sunny morning from the deck of the French mailboat which carried me over a gentle Mediterranean swell toward Marseille. Beside me, in a sky blue burnous, a silk gandoura, and white embroidered pantaloons, sat the agha Daylis. Through the camel-hair strands of his turban were threaded the golden cords of chiefdom.

It does not take long to become primitive. Although it was not more than four years since I had crossed the Mediterranean, this ship with its attentive stewards and white bathrooms was as strange to me as it might have been to Mohammed ben Tahar. I could not believe that I was going to Europe. If anyone had told me a month before that I would be doing this, I would have laughed. The whole idea had been begotten, conceived, and born on the spur of the moment.

Daylis had asked me as a favor to come with him to France as his guest. He had had some lucky deals that season and, after settling his accounts and putting aside a reserve, had a hundred thousand francs which he wanted to spend on a holiday.

"I'm sick of the Sahara," he had said. "I'm sick of North Africa. I'm sick of my relatives. I want to see new places and new faces. It's a bore to take a trip alone. I don't know many people in Europe, and none well enough to propose myself to as a guest. I hate the official entertainment the government feels obliged to dole out to Arab chiefs in Paris. If you'll come with me, you'll be doing me a big kindness."

Daylis' plea had been so impulsive and so sincere that I had been equally impulsive and said yes. Hence the sunny deck and the party clothes.

"No," remarked Daylis, as if following a train of thought, "it isn't much fun for an Arab in Europe alone. We entertain these friends of French officials who flock to the Sahara in winter. We give them mechouis to eat and horses to ride and Ouled Nails to play with. As long as they are with us, they are all over us; but the day *we* turn up in France, it's 'Oh, hello, fancy seeing you here. Drop in and see us sometime.'—and they are gone without giving an address. Sometimes I swear I'll never entertain another Roumi."

"Why do you?"

Daylis shrugged. "Oh, I suppose it's inborn, inbred hospitality. The old Arab idea that no traveler, rich or poor, can be turned away from a nomad's tent. We don't expect anything back, either; but somehow, with our own people, it always does come back. Not with the foreigner though!" He gave a snort. "At times, they make me mad!" He stared at the sea for a moment. Then he said, "I went to England, once, you know."

I jerked upright in my chair. "You did?" This was the first time Daylis had let this out. It was another of my Sahara surprises, so unexpected and yet so typically Arab. "When did you? Why?"

Daylis chuckled. "Some English people were sent me by the Governor or the Secretary-General, I forget which. I gave them a fine time. Banquets every day, gazelle hunts, falcon hunts, everything the Sahara can offer. When they left, they made me promise to come and see them in England. They also gave me their address. So, one summer, I went."

"Did you tell them you were coming?"

"No, I just arrived."

"Where?"

"In London."

"In that outfit?" The idea of Daylis stepping out of Victoria station in that azure cloak fascinated me.

Daylis nodded. "Yes, and believe me it caused a stir. I had half the children of London running after me."

"And what did your friends do?"

"They asked me to lunch."

"Is that all?"

214

"Yes."

"Didn't they show you the sights, the country? Didn't they introduce you to anyone?"

Daylis shook his head. "No. They were going away for the holidays, to Scotland or somewhere. I forgot the place. They said they hoped they'd see me when they got back in the autumn."

"So what did you do?"

"I took the next train back to France. At least I could make myself understood there."

Daylis stopped talking and watched the restless Mediterranean. I said nothing. There was nothing to say. Daylis' experience was typical. The white man and the "native." Fine to dine with and hunt with and stay with in his own country, but at home just a "native"!—"What on earth are we going to do with him? Oh, have him to lunch, and tell him we are going away."

This attitude was not entirely due to bad manners or arrogance. There was ignorance, too. Such men had been brought up to consider everything foreign as inferior. They had never taken the trouble to find out anything about the Arabs or the Indians or anyone else. It did not occur to them that many of these aliens were well educated, and as capable of intelligent conversation as themselves; some, more so. It never occurred to them that a man like Daylis was just as civilized as they were and had as much inherent refinement. They regarded him as a savage. I had heard their comments in the oasis, and it made me angry. But I had said nothing. What would have been the good? They would have looked at me as had the "peacemakers" in Paris at Ted Lawrence. I was another of those freaks like Sir Richard Burton and Lady Hester Stanhope. Like them I had wandered off the tracks.

Daylis took his eyes off the dancing waves. "Is it true," he asked, "that the British and the Dutch treat the people in their colonies better than do the French?"

I did not reply at once. I had to think this out. Daylis had the kind of mind which required a logical reply. Also I was not sure of the answer. Eventually I compromised. I said:

"I don't think that any strong nation which has taken possession of the country of a weaker nation thinks very much about the people. It may as an afterthought, but it is of secondary importance."

Daylis nodded. "Yes," he said, "but why should this be?"

"Because big nations take small nations for what they can get out of them. You never see big nations interfering with little nations which have nothing to give." Daylis nodded again. "Your Sahara is a good case in point. The French leave you alone, let you run the desert more or less as you like, because, if they occupied it themselves, they couldn't get anything out of it. Only your nomads can raise sheep there, and your raising of sheep gives France all she wants. But supposing the country became fertile or oil was struck, you wouldn't be left in peace for five minutes. You'd be put out and kept out. What's more, the other big nations would come along and try to grab a share. But you wouldn't get any. In all questions of empire building, the native people are considered last."

"Yes," repeated Daylis. "In all questions of empire building, the native people are considered last." He shook his head. Then he said: "There is very little sincerity in the world."

"Yes," I agreed, "though since I've lived in the Sahara I've found sincerity on every side."

Daylis said: "The nomad is genuine and frank. He does not know how to be anything but what he is. He does not know how to lie. He minds his business; but if you ask him his opinion of yourself, he will tell you. He is unspoiled."

I said: "He is like the Sahara."

"Yes," agreed Daylis, "he is like the Sahara."

Again he was quiet and stared at the sea. Then, turning to me with twinkling eyes, he exclaimed: "But what are we doing, discussing nomads and the Sahara? We're on a vacation! As long as those hundred thousand francs last, we can forget deserts and sheep and empires and all the rest. We'll leave those worries to Madani. For the next few weeks we're going to enjoy ourselves!"

I wish I had kept a diary of that holiday I spent with the agha Daylis in France. He had made up his mind to enjoy himself in the way that a nomad thinks he will take advantage of Paradise. From the moment we landed, we lived as an Arab chief would have during Islam's golden age. We had rooms at the best hotels, which we never seemed to use except for breakfast. We dined at the best restaurants. We lived on champagne and the finest food which

Daylis' money could buy. The only thing barred in our diet was mutton. Daylis gave me no explanation about the drinking. He ordered champagne at the first meal and continued to order it at every subsequent meal. He evidently meant to forget everything at home and expected me to conform. I did.

The whole episode was a riot. There was not a dull morning, afternoon, or evening.

We spent the first two weeks in Paris occupying a royal suite at the Grand Hotel. Daylis opened the proceedings by giving a few lunches for French officials who might be tiresome if they heard he was in Paris having a spree on the quiet. As soon as this formal entertaining was over, the little man rubbed his hands and said:

"Now! Now we have fun. You look after the entertainment. I look after the rest!"

We began with friends of mine who were intrigued to meet an Arab chief and find out what sort of people I had gone to live with. Daylis gave them quite the wrong impression. The sky-blue burnous and the silk gandoura and the champagne made them think that I had only changed the setting of my old way of doing things. I did not protest. They would not have understood. They had never believed that any man with their background could separate himself from the conventions of their upbringing. Now they were sure. They lived in a world of ingrained insincerity. Daylis, who was drinking a lot but knew how to hold his wine, missed nothing. One evening when we had returned to our suite from a late round of night-clubbing, during which one of the young women of our party had been taking a special interest in him, he said:

"I didn't know what to do. There she was, with her husband on the other side of the table, asking me if she couldn't come and see me here tomorrow afternoon." He shook his head. "If I were a French citizen, I'd be put in jail because I have three wives; but if I go to bed with this man's wife tomorrow, everyone will think it fine."

I do not know if Daylis had his affair. I kept away from our suite till dinner, and I did not ask him. Whether he did or not was not my business, but it annoyed me. I was all set for a good time; I was having a good time and enjoying it, but my mind had lost touch with love-making in society. I think that Daylis felt as

I did, because, without either of us saying a thing, we dropped social Paris as we had dropped official Paris. We went into the highways and byways, meaning the Grands Boulevards and the music hall lobbies. There were plenty of girls there, unattached and more amusing than my friends. They did not care where they went or whether the places were fashionable. All they wanted was to earn a few francs and be gay. When they discovered that there were plenty of francs and no obligations attached unless both parties felt like it, they went out of their way to have as much fun for as little as possible. One girl wept when Daylis insisted on ordering champagne when everyone had had enough.

Sometimes we let our ladies bring their boy friends. Some of these were tough guys, but seeing that we treated them on the level, they treated us in the same way. I learned more about Paris night life and had better food and finer wines in the most unexpected places, through the agency of my Arab chief, than in all the years I had lived in the city of my birth.

"It's quite simple," said Daylis. "Start off by making people feel that you are no better than they are. You probably aren't, anyway. Then, if you *are* better, it will come out of its own accord. I am the agha Daylis, so what? You are an English officer, so what? If that apache had had the same opportunities, he would probably have gone further than either of us."

Whenever I have remembered to follow Daylis' philosophy, I have enjoyed myself more than when I forgot.

From Paris we migrated to Deauville, from Deauville to Dieppe, from Dieppe to Etretat, from Etretat to Evian. Daylis, like all Arabs, loved anything to do with horses, and we had to go to all the race meetings. Finally, after six pleasure-hunting, wearing weeks, we reached Aix-les-Bains. Of the original hundred thousand francs, there remained our return tickets to Algiers and two thousand francs in cash. The following day we were to take the train to Marseille, and two days later we would be back in North Africa —In sha Allah. Unfortunately for my worn-out condition, Allah had destined otherwise.

After dinner, on what I believed to be our last night in France, Daylis asked me what I was going to do.

Without hesitation I said: "Bed." And made for my room.

Daylis said: "All right, but I'm going to the Villa des Fleurs for a final game." He had been gambling with amazing good luck in every casino he had been into. He winked and handed me a thousand-franc bill. "Here, take this," he added, "and keep it for emergencies. I don't suppose I'll lose the other, but one never knows. It is in the hand of Allah."

I put the bill under my pillow and was asleep almost before the light was out.

About three in the morning I was awakened by a rumpus at my door. As I turned on the light, Daylis came in with a strange woman on his arm. I felt grumpy, but I had to laugh. One could not help laughing with Daylis around.

Without introduction the girl said: "Your comrade is crazy." I nodded.

"Crazy?" roared Daylis. "I've just won thirty thousand francs. Is that crazy? Thirty thousand francs from one thousand! It's better than any ewe ever did in the Sahara."

"Yes," I said, "and you'll be able to convert that into lots and lots of ewes. Let me go to sleep."

Daylis let out another roar. "Convert my winnings into sheep? It's you who are crazy. We're going straight back to Paris to spend the money. And Rose is coming with us. Aren't you, Rose?"

"Your comrade is crazy," said Rose stolidly.

However, she was at the station next morning, and we all three traveled to Paris.

I have no idea who Rose was or how Daylis came by her. She was a nice-looking, respectable sort of girl, a Savoyarde peasant who had somehow strayed to the Villa des Fleurs in Aix-les-Bains. She had no sense of humor and took this jaunt to Paris in deadly earnest. When, after a week of wild riot and buying Rose clothes at the Bon Marché, Daylis gave her five thousand francs and said goodbye, she wept like a child who is losing its mother.

As soon as we boarded the train at the Gare de Lyon, Daylis went to bed. I did not see him again until he appeared on the platform of the Gare St. Charles in Marseille. He gave me a laughing good morning, but it was not the laugh of twenty-four hours ago.

As we drove to the docks, he looked up at the blue sky. He breathed in the air. He did not talk. He just breathed. I had a sensation that I was witnessing a kind of metamorphosis. He waited on deck with me until the ship headed for the open sea. Once more he breathed deeply, filling his lungs until his little body seemed to grow. He looked up at me with twinkling, smiling eyes.

"Africa!" he said, staring out across the glittering Mediterranean. With that he left me, and I did not see him again till dinner.

He was rested, but not talkative. He took no wine and ate sparingly. When we had finished, we went on deck and lay on two deck chairs. Above us the stars flashed whitely in the deep blue sky.

"Africa!" Why should that word have such a queer effect? "Europe," "America" had not the same sound—but "Africa"! It offered something which I would not find elsewhere. I saw the groove in which I had been struggling and realized how narrow it was. Going back to the fringes of my old life had proved to me that I was free from its restraint. Those people who had once been so much a part of my existence had not understood. They had looked at Daylis' burnous and tasted his champagne and had seen no further. They had not sensed the peace which throbbed inside of me. I could play around and drink and laugh and sit up all night, but I knew that at the end of it there would be release. There would be Africa. Even more intensely, there would be— "Sahara." —Someone seemed to have called?—I peered into the darkness, but there was nothing but the sea sparkling under the stars.... I let myself relax in my chair and realized that Daylis was talking.

"You cannot escape. You have to go back," he said. "When the Sahara has caught you, she never lets you go. You think you can leave and live in other surroundings, among other people, but it doesn't work. You have changed. You see men and women and things with different eyes. Whenever your mind relaxes, it comes back to the Sahara. Every little gully, every palm tree, every desert well, which you hardly noticed at the time, stands out as clearly and in more detail than the Arc de Triomphe. Everything calls to you, tugs at you, pushes you until you go back. You may run away often. You may run away for years, but in the end the Sahara gets you again. The Sahara weaves itself about you until you cannot move, until you do not want to."

Daylis stopped talking. Soon he was asleep. Soon I slept, too.

But those words had been engraved on my mind. I remember them as clearly now as on that autumn night in the middle of the Mediterranean. I remember every detail of that part of the Sahara where I lived. I can follow the bends of the road and the places where it dips. The number of troughs at the well where we watered after the sirocco are as clear in my mind as the buttons on my coat. The jagged hills, the eyes of Madani, the outline of the oasis are as vivid now as they were then. They will not have altered when I return.

Nothing changes in the Sahara.—Nothing!—Nothing can change it but another great cataclysm. Nations and dynasties and wars have come and gone, but the Sahara stays untouched. Its people stay untouched, and, In sha Allah, it will ever be thus.

Daylis did not speak again until we landed. Then he said: "I'm going to my father's house." —I wondered if there was any place where the Bash Agha did not have a house. He probably had one in Paris and Aix-les-Bains. "I am going to my father's house for a moment. If you will meet me at the station, we will travel down together."

He nodded and left me. He did not seem to consider it a possibility that I might wish to stay in Algiers. And he was right.

We arrived at the station simultaneously. Daylis was not yet in nomad dress, but the sky-blue burnous had been exchanged for a black one, and he had on his embroidered riding boots, instead of his white slippers, and dark pantaloons. He greeted me with a smile, and there was an undercurrent of excitement in his movements as he climbed into the train. Only once did he speak during the long journey south. He said:

"We had a fine time, didn't we?" I nodded. "I would like to thank you for your good company." He looked at me with twinkling eyes. I felt that he was picturing all we had done. Then he said, "We will have other good times, In sha Allah." For the rest of the journey he remained motionless, telling his beads.

News of our return had somehow preceded us. There was a crowd to meet the bus when it stopped outside Monsieur Paoli's hotel. In addition to Daylis' relatives and a sheik from Madani to say that he expected me at the camp, my four servants were there, with Blanchet and Mohammed ben Tahar, Mecheri, Draoui,

Atalla, Amida, and the Khodja. Each one had the broadest smile of welcome.

I thought of my first arrival in the oasis, when I knew no one. I remembered my loneliness and the hopeless feeling that if I went back to where I had come from I would be no less lonely. Today, all was changed. Instead of having left my home on the other side of the sea, I had come home to something which felt like home, to friends who were glad to see me, to the Sahara which called me. —As we walked up the street followed by our escort, men came out of shops and cafés and kissed Daylis' shoulder and shook my hand. Some of these I barely knew by sight, but all of them knew me and greeted me by name. When we reached the door of his father's house, Daylis said:

"We will ride out together tonight. My camp is not far from yours."

Once again he had not consulted me. He knew that I needed the Sahara as much as he. . . .

It was after midnight and the oasis was asleep when Daylis and I rode out onto the desert. Wrapped in our camel-hair burnouses, our turbans white in the mysterious light, we had rolled back into the past. We did not belong to today, we did not belong to yesterday, we belonged to always—to the always of the Sahara.

We felt the unseen arms stretching out toward us and the voice which called and the magic web which held us with a thousand perfumes. Delicately our horses placed their hoofs and played with their silver bits. Softly the wind sang through the scrub. Gently the desert air caressed us as, side by side, we rode untroubled into the majestic silence of the Sahara.

GLOSSARY

Agha	The second-ranking chief among Sahara Arabs.
Bash agha	The senior ranking Arab chief in the Sahara.
Bassour	A kind of palanquin placed on the back of camels for the transportation of women and children.
Burnous	A long cloak with a hood, made of camel hair or cloth or wool.
Bismillah	"In the name of Allah."
Beselaama	"Peace be with you." Usually used at the end of a talk or visit when saying goodbye.
Caid	The third-ranking chief among Sahara Arabs.
Caravanserai	An enclosed courtyard in which caravans take shelter at night.
Cavalier	French name given to an official Arab retainer attached to Arab chiefs and sometimes to government offices in the Sahara.
Couscous	Semolina. It is cooked over steam and is the staple dish of the Arab in the same way as rice is to other Asiatics.
Debourca	A kind of drum made out of pottery.
Djebel Amour	Mountain of Amour. A minor mountain system fringing the northern Sahara.
Gandoura	A white robe made of wool or silk.
Hadj	A pilgrim. Usually one who has been to Mecca.
Hamdullah	Praise God.
Hammam	Steam bath.
Imam	A mosque attendant. He is in charge of religious ceremonies and leads the prayer when said collectively.
Islam	Submission (to the will of God). The religion of the Moslems.

223

In sha Allah	If God wills it.
Kadi	The Arab judge, attorney, official receiver, registrar. He is connected with anything having to do with Moslem law, including marriages and divorces.
Kasbah	Fort. Today, the Arab section of a French city in North Africa.
Khodja	An Arab clerk in a French government office whose duties are to handle matters affecting Arabs. His chief work is to translate Arab and French documents.
Koran	The Bible of the Moslems.
Marabout	A holy man supposed to be descended from the Prophet.
Mechoui	Lamb roasted and served whole.
Mektoub	It is written (fated).
Moslem	Surrender to Allah. One who believes in the faith established by Mohammed.
Mufti	A Moslem official who is an authority on religion and law. The mufti sometimes explains the Koran in the mosque, and preaches.
Raita	A trumpet with a reed mouthpiece.
Salaam aleikum	Peace be to you all!
Shesh	The linen covering of the turban.
Sidi	Sir. His honor. An honorific title prefixed before the names of important or holy people.
Taleb	Teacher in the Arab schools. The taleb is also the official letter writer for the illiterate and sometimes a legal counselor.
Tamtam	A large tambourine.
Zaouia	A retreat for Moslem men and women, but chiefly women, in the homes of marabouts. Those going into retreat give the marabout all they possess and, in return, are looked after for the rest of their lives.